PELICAN BOOKS

ENGLISH FURNITURE STYLES

Ralph Fastnedge was born in London in April 1913, and was educated at University College School, at Oxford University, and the Courtauld Institute of Art, University of London. He served with R.A.F. Bomber Command during the war, flying, usually by daylight, over Germany and the occupied countries. He was awarded the D.F.C. in the summer of 1941, and subsequently served as a staff officer and as an instructor of aircrews. Later he was for two years Curator of the Holburne of Menstrie Museum of Art at Bath. He is now Curator of the Lady Lever Art Gallery, Port Sunlight.

ENGLISH FURNITURE STYLES

FROM 1500 TO 1830

Ralph Fastnedge

*

PENGUIN BOOKS

Penguin Books Ltd, Harmondsworth, Middlesex, England
Penguin Books Inc., 7110 Ambassador Road, Baltimore, Maryland 21207, U.S.A.
Penguin Books Australia Ltd, Ringwood, Victoria, Australia

First published 1955
Reprinted 1961, 1962, 1964, 1967, 1969, 1970

Made and printed in Great Britain
by The Whitefriars Press Ltd, London and Tonbridge
Set in Monotype Baskerville
Photogravure plates printed by
Clarke & Sherwell Ltd, Northampton

CONTENTS

FOREWORD

In preparing this book, I have had help of various kinds from colleagues, friends and acquaintances, whom I would like to thank. A list of their names, if complete, would be long, and inadequate as an expression of gratitude.

My debt to Mr Ralph Edwards, formerly Keeper of the Department of Woodwork, Victoria and Albert Museum, is great: the book was written at his instance, and he has given me valuable advice at all stages.

Mr J. Coburn Witherop is responsible for the many outline drawings which finely illustrate the text; and for these drawings I am especially grateful.

Finally, I am deeply indebted to my wife, Eveline, without whose collaboration the book would not have been written.

R. F.

LIST OF FIGURES

LIST OF PLATES

NOTE

Parts of the descriptions given in the captions to Plates 30 and 36 are now known to be inaccurate; but it has been decided not to alter these captions in the 1961 impression, as any alterations to the photogravure cylinders would add considerably to the price of the book.

The furniture shown in these plates is correctly described in the text and list of plates.

ACKNOWLEDGEMENTS

SPECIAL acknowledgement is made to the following for permission to quote extracts from published works:

To Longmans Green & Co. Ltd for material from *Passages from the Diaries of Mrs Philip Lybbe Powys*, edited by Emily J. Climenson, 1899.

To Longmans Green & Co. Ltd, and to the Verney family, for material from *Memoirs of the Verney Family*, by Frances Parthenope, Lady Verney, and Margaret H. Verney, 1892–4.

To Jonathan Cape Ltd for material from *Sophie in London, 1786*, translated from the German by Clare Williams, 1933.

To the Richards Press Ltd for material from *Dampier's Voyages*, edited by John Masefield, 1906.

To B. T. Batsford Ltd for material from *English Furniture, Tapestry and Needlework*, Lady Lever Art Gallery Collections, III, by P. Macquoid, 1928.

To G. Bell & Sons Ltd for material from the *Diary of Samuel Pepys*, edited by H. B. Wheatley, 1923.

To Sidgwick & Jackson Ltd for material from the *Purefoy Letters, 1735–53*, edited by G. Eland, 1931.

To the Oxford University Press, and to the Walpole Society, for material from *The Walpole Society, Vol. XVI* (*Horace Walpole's Journals of Visits to Country Seats, etc.*, edited by Paget Toynbee), 1927–8.

To the Cresset Press Ltd for material from *The Journeys of Celia Fiennes*, edited by Christopher Morris, 1947.

To Eyre & Spottiswoode Ltd, and to Henry Holt & Co., New York, for material from *The Torrington Diaries*, edited by C. Bruyn Andrews, 1934–8.

Other acknowledgements have been made in the footnotes. If acknowledgement has been overlooked, the publishers and author express their regrets and tender apologies, with an assurance of correction in any subsequent edition of this book.

*

Thanks are due to the following authorities and photographers for providing the photographs for the plates, to the owners of the objects illustrated, who are mentioned in the list of plates, and in particular the Director and Secretary, the Victoria and Albert Museum, the Curator and Trustees, the Lady Lever Collection, and the City Librarian, Liverpool (Pls. 40–6, 57, 59), who have all been most generous in allowing so much for reproduction: The British Museum Photographic Department (Pls. 1, 2); the Victoria and Albert Museum Photographic Department (Pls. 3, 4C, 7, 9A and B, 10A, B, and C, 12, 13, 16, 19, 22, 25B, 28A, 30, 47A and B, 53, 60A and B, 61); the London County Council and the Trustees of Sir John Soane's Museum (Pl. 48); the Art Institute of Chicago (Pls. 28B, 32); Leonard Card (Pls. 4A, 6, 8, 18, 21, 23, 26, 33, 36, 38); Edward Leigh (Pl. 15); Pickard of Leeds (Pl. 20); Stewart Bale (Pls. 27, 35); Cyril Howe (Pls. 25A, 34, 50B); Browns of Liverpool (Pls. 40–6, 57, 59, 63); T. C. Leaman (Pl. 62); L. H. Hilyard (Pls. 4B, 5); Strickland Studios (Pls. 17, 49A and B, 50A); John H. Freeman (Pls. 24, 64A and B); and Photopartners Ltd (Pls. 51, 52A and B, 54, 55A and B, 56, 58).

To unite elegance and utility, and blend the useful with the agreeable, has ever been considered a difficult, but an honourable task. How far we have succeeded in the following work it becomes us not to say, but rather to leave it, with all due deference, to the determination of the Public at large.

HEPPLEWHITE

Preface to *The Cabinet-Maker and Upholsterer's Guide*

CHAPTER ONE

THE PERIOD OF OAK

FROM THE EARLY SIXTEENTH CENTURY TO THE END OF THE COMMONWEALTH

PRECEDED BY BRIEF MENTION OF SUCH FURNITURE AS IS KNOWN TO HAVE EXISTED IN THE LATE MIDDLE AGES

IN the year 1472, Edward IV with his Queen, Elizabeth Woodville, and her ladies and gentlewomen entertained the Burgundian Ambassador, Louis of Bruges, Lord of Grautehuse, with some ceremony. A contemporary and vivid description of the occasion is preserved.[1]

Three 'chambers of pleasance' had been prepared for Lord Grautehuse. The walls were hung with white silk and linen cloth and all the floors laid with carpets. The ambassador's bed, curtained in white sarsanet (a kind of silk, introduced into England by the returning Crusaders), was of the finest royal swansdown, with coverlet and canopy of shining cloth of gold. In addition, a couch of down 'hanged with a tente, knytt like a nette' and a cupboard were placed in the adjoining chamber. Foot posts to beds were not introduced until the early sixteenth century and the canopy was customarily attached to the ceiling (Pl. 1). The third room contained two 'Baynes', or baths, likewise covered with tents of white cloth; and there, about nine o'clock, 'the sayde Lord Grautehuse accompanied with my Lorde Chamberlein whiche dispoyled hym' took his pleasure in bathing. Refreshment, consisting of green ginger, syrups, sweetmeats, and hippocras (a spiced wine), was served to them before retiring. There is scant mention of furniture. Apart from the luxury of great beds, notable mainly for their rare and costly hangings and bedding, which were regarded as property of importance to a comparatively late date, and which were enduring as land and, as such, specifically named in wills (as possessions worthy of inheritance), little bodily comfort was then to be obtained in the interior even of a royal residence.

Even the largest dwellings were sparsely furnished; the smaller, and the homes of the common people, contained little that we should now call furniture and that they could themselves have greatly valued; and their living conditions were very primitive. It was not unusual, for instance, for the whole family (and guests) to be confined to the same bedchamber. Such domestic furniture as existed in the Middle Ages was crudely constructed, most often without the use of glue.

The chest, although primarily intended for the storage of clothes or valuables, served also very frequently as a seat, as a table or, on occasion, as a bed. It was the main piece of furniture.

The food cupboard,* the 'aumbry' or 'ambry', was another storage piece. In two rare Gothic examples now in the Victoria and Albert Museum, both of which may be dated about 1500, the shelves are enclosed by fronts composed of sections pierced with differing designs in the form of geometrical tracery and fitted with small central doors, also pierced. These 'windows' formed of open Gothic tracery served to give ventilation to the contents. The food was delivered (*livrée*) from these cupboards; they are, in consequence, usually referred to as 'livery' or 'dole' cupboards. Early cupboards were always constructed with a central door; interlocking double doors originated at a considerably later date. Rough tables and stools, benches, settles or forms were of course in general use.

At best these few pieces, more or less essential for living, had a rude strength. Tapestries and fabrics of the most varied description, on the other hand, were fine indeed, imparting to the great castles a certain barbaric splendour,

* The term 'cupboard' was in origin 'cup borde' or open shelf.

enhanced by gilding and by the common practice of painting the walls and woodwork of rooms in bright, gay colours (Pl. 1).

The chest is almost the only piece of furniture of fourteenth-century date or earlier to have survived. The chest was, at first, in its most rudimentary form, no more than a portion of hollowed tree trunk bound with iron, and was produced by the arkwright and the smith. The carpenter-made chest, which consisted of six boards or slabs of wood nailed together and strengthened by iron bands, existed

Figure 1 – Chest of boarded construction, with a carved decoration on the front of roundels flanked by tracery. Fifteenth century

contemporaneously with the 'hollowed tree' chest at a very early date (Fig. 1); its solid front was rebated into the ends, which formed the feet or supports of the piece and protected the contents from damp. This 'boarded' type of chest persisted up to the seventeenth century when it was composed of thinner boards fixed by wooden pegs and decorated with carving (Pl. 7).

'Joined' chests, however, are extant from the thirteenth century. Many chests were at one time the property of the Church, which accounts in part for their preservation; and many more domestic specimens containing gold and silver plate or muniments, and deposited in the churches for safe keeping, later became ecclesiastical property. They were used as receptacles for the jewelled ornaments, vestments, and altar cloths. Chests held the offerings to the Church, and specimens fitted with three locks and having a money slot in the lid are thought to be of ecclesiastical origin (Fig. 2). The construction of the joined chest was of the simplest kind: broad stiles, shaped below on the inner side and extending below the chest to form the feet, framed the heavy single boards which constituted its front and back. The lid, also a single board, and strengthened with rails on the under side, was attached to the body of the piece by means of a pin

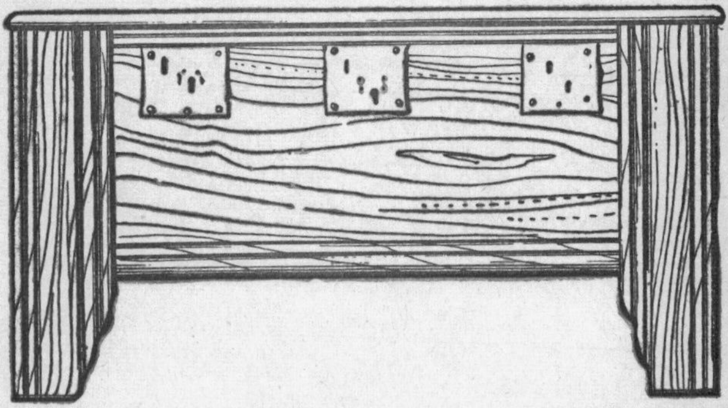

Figure 2 – Chest of early joined type; the single panel which forms the front is flanked by broad stiles, grooved and shaped

hinge. Joints were fixed by dowel pegs. The front and back of the chest were tenoned into the stiles. When decoration was employed it sometimes consisted of roundels or boldly carved geometrical patterns or of grooving at the borders of panels and stiles (Figs. 1 and 2). A heavy iron strap hinge was adopted from the close of the thirteenth century, and decoration became more elaborate; often the chest front was carved with an all-over tracery deriving directly from Gothic Church architecture (Fig. 3). A series of interlacing circular heads, which together form an arcading of pointed arches, is a *motif* found in late fifteenth-century work. After about 1450 tracery is occasionally found to be applied and not carved from the solid.

Figure 3 – Detail of carved tracery; above an arcading of cusped arches are contained six roundels within arches, and above these are three larger roundels within pointed arches. Fourteenth century

About 1500 various linenfold patterns (Fig. 4) were used singly and in combination with such Renaissance *motifs* as heads within medallions, also introduced via Flanders.

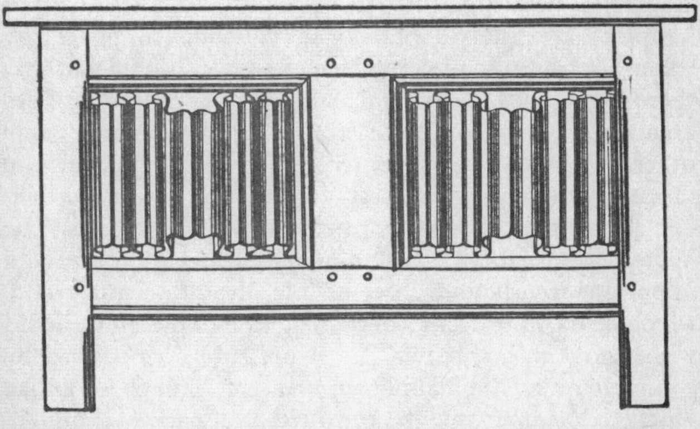

Figure 4 – Chest of framed construction; the two panels of the front carved with linen-fold. Early sixteenth century

Some extant examples bear traces of their original paint. Bright colours, as vermilion or green or olive, were favoured.

The panelled framing of chest fronts (or of cupboard doors) did not become general until early in the sixteenth century. Panel construction, which necessitated the use of tenon, mortise and dowel pins, was the work of a joiner. The panels were thin and were set loosely in the grooves of the framing in order that the effect of the shrinkage of the wood should be minimized. The joiner, in early periods, was with reason a craftsman of greater skill and higher status than the 'arkwright' and was formerly employed on work such as the making of church screens and panelling. The carving of panels, which called for the highest degree of skill, was done independently by the wood sculptors. Elaborate carving is occasionally found on the fourteenth-century chests of framed construction in which the front was tenoned into very wide uprights. The Victoria and Albert Museum collections contain a chest-front panel, of distinct interest, which is carved with a detailed representation of the legend of St George slaying the Dragon. The third scene illustrated is the Princess leading the wounded Dragon into Memphis – which has the aspect of a medieval walled city of the Low Countries, with high-pitched roofs and castle towers. The sculptor was perhaps a Fleming or Walloon. This panel may never have been made up into a chest. It is significant that there is a similar, but complete chest at York (dating from about 1380) which has the same subject in reverse; and other chests of similar character were to be found in Belgium down to the time of the first World War. Scriptural incidents were often alternative to mythological subjects. The Victoria and Albert Museum acquired in 1948 a rare and important iron-bound chest of late fifteenth-century date which bears on its front a representation of the Fall, carved with vigour in low relief. The figure subject is flanked by two large roundels of flamboyant tracery. This chest, unlike the York example, may be regarded as of native origin.

The tripod stool was without doubt a common enough article in the late Middle Ages. Primitive seats of circular form, supported on three legs roughly driven into sockets on the under side, were made at all periods. The stool as depicted in seventeenth-century Dutch 'Interiors of Low Life' (pictures painted by the Van Ostade brothers serve well to illustrate the fact), resembles that to be seen in some medieval illuminated manuscripts. Examples of early date have not survived, presumably because of their very mean construction, but a few Gothic stools and forms of more enduring type, some of the late fifteenth century, are however extant (Pl. 9A). In these, the seat rests on solid splayed ends, tied by a heavy shaped underframing, sometimes decorated with ogee shaped arches and mouldings (Fig. 5). Noticeably, the turned leg is not employed for stools (or chairs)

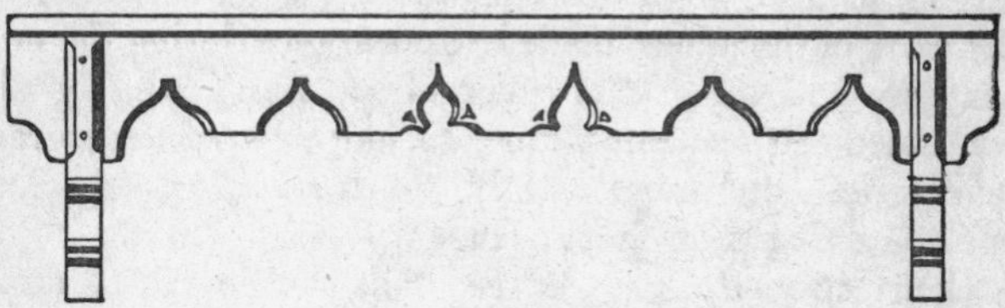

Figure 5 – Form, with solid, shaped end supports, the underframing decorated with ogee arches. Fifteenth century

until the end of the Tudor period – a development which, as we shall see, post-dates the corresponding development in tables by at least a generation. Their hardness was in many cases mitigated by the provision of fitted cushions. X-shaped stools were usually draped with silks or damasks.

During the medieval period until more secure social conditions made the castle and fortified house obsolete, it was customary for the household to assemble for meals in a spacious but barely furnished hall, the common living-room. The lord, his family, and guests of rank dined at the high table set across the hall on a dais. Ranged at this end, often before a fixed canopy of wood covered with fabric, they were seated on one side only of the table (a narrow table, therefore, perhaps two feet wide); they overlooked the company at the great trestle table or tables placed at right angles to the high table down the length of the hall. A ceremonial chair, emblematic of authority, was later reserved for the master of the house, who presided over the gathering. The chair, as an article of domestic furniture, did not come into general use until the seventeenth century. It is, in origin, ecclesiastical, being developed from the choir stall or pew. Chairs in the thirteenth and fourteenth centuries were unwieldy and cumbersome objects. They were made by the carpenter from solid slabs of wood, and, normally being loosely covered by fabrics (the 'banker' for the seat, and the 'dorcer' for the back), were unornamented by the carver. One cushion was placed on the seat, another customarily serving as a footstool. The chair of panelled construction, the work of the joiner, made its appearance during the next century, and the use of chair cloths was gradually discontinued. At the same time, to judge by contemporary inventories, the more lightly constructed turned chair enjoyed a degree of favour (Pl. 4A).

Court etiquette long decreed that the Sovereign alone should occupy a chair, other persons present being seated on stools. The same rule was followed in the halls of his subjects; indeed the stool retained popularity until well after the Restoration period. It was only during the eighteenth century that it became a comparatively unusual seat, with a decorative function as part of a large suite of seating furniture. This is clear from the very numbers of the oak 'joint' or 'coffin' stools of seventeenth century date which have survived (Pl. 9B). 'Stool' was in fact a general term denoting a seat for one person.

Other seating at the high table and in the body of the hall consisted of wall settles, which were usually in the nature of permanent and structural wall fixtures, or of movable forms. If some form of serving or side table was available, it resembled a long chest with pierced front and hinged lid, raised from the ground to a low height on square legs. Numerous serving men assisted at the meal, hurrying to and from the kitchens with the many dishes. Table linen was provided for use on ceremonial occasions from an early date. Instruction with regard to more elaborate procedure involving the use of the surnape, or extra cloths, is contained in the regulations approved by Henry VIII for the proper governance of his household. And by the sixteenth century, napery was customarily laid at most tables – '... shadow these tables with their white veils, and accomplish the court-cupboard.'[2]

At the conclusion of the meal, the table top was lifted from the trestle supports and removed by the servants; made of great planks of oak or other indigenous timber, it was firm because of its weight. The supports, which were not tied by a connecting framework or by stretchers, were stowed away as was convenient. This useful arrangement survived late, to a time when tables of joined construction (Fig. 11) and indeed those with a draw leaf (first introduced about 1550) (Fig. 9) were already plentiful. 'Away with the joint-stools, remove the court-cupboard, look to the plate ...' cries the 1st Serving-man in the opening act of *Romeo and Juliet* (*c.* 1593); and his words are followed, as the music plays and they dance, by Capulet's order – 'More light, ye knaves; and turn the tables up.'

From additional evidence afforded by inventories it may be concluded that to the early Stuart period, the trestle table was used in large houses conjointly with that of framed construction, and that it was in the fifteenth century the more usual form of table. A trestle table of the earlier type was very heavily constructed and often of unwieldy dimensions. Some tables were 25 feet long. The top, which consisted of boards of the greatest length and thickness available, was supported at its ends by solid blocks or trestles, buttressed and set at right angles to the length of the table; in some cases an intermediate support also was required. As a later development trestles were tied by one or more centrally placed stretchers running lengthwise down the table and were made stable by the addition of a cross-piece. They were then of an inverted T-shape.

Small tables with fixed tops and pegged supports, con-

Figure 6 – Side table of semi-circular shape, with double hinged top and turned baluster legs; the frieze carved with strapwork. When opened, the table is circular, the upper flap being supported on a movable gate formed of half of one of the three fixed legs. Early seventeenth century

fined in general to the private rooms, were in use from an early date, and being readily movable served a variety of purposes. They had become, in consequence, quite numerous by the end of the Elizabethan period. Tables often of semi-circular or semi-octagonal shape with (usually) three or four fixed legs respectively, fitted with folding tops and a form of gate support (Fig. 6), were possessed by most early Stuart households of substance. Sometimes these tables had elaborately carved arcaded underframings; the legs were united to a platform, or to a shaped stretcher. Another variety was the early gate-legged table, in which two hinged flaps were supported by movable gates (Fig. 7).

In the Middle Ages the chamber, the private living-room of the master, contained an upholstered bed which, with little or no exposed woodwork, was almost entirely covered with fabrics. It served as a couch during the day, when the curtains were looped back. There was little privacy for most members of the household, and few were allowed a separate apartment in which to sleep. At the close of the Gothic period (say about 1550) even the great chamber, by its nature the most comfortably appointed room of the dwelling, was by later standards lacking in fine pieces of furniture. Hangings in bright colours covered perhaps the walls, carpets were placed on cupboard or press and on the short joined table, and there might be a couple of chests, stools, a chair, and the many embroidered cushions (used very freely from medieval times) and other small objects in silver or brass as andirons, firepan, ewers, and basins.

Italian influence on the design of furniture was not appreciable in England before about 1530–5. Furniture of the Gothic period made by English craftsmen was on the whole inferior to that from the hands of the French, of Germans and, certainly, of Italians. The sea barrier to travel was formidable. Although a guild of carpenters had been in existence in England since the early fourteenth century, and a charter was granted to the same guild about 1475, it is probable that during the fifteenth century, and later, very little decorated furniture was in use in private houses and that much of the finest furniture belonging to the palaces and monasteries was obtained from abroad. Inventories of the furnishings, made in 1547, of the King's many palaces, among them Westminster, Hampton Court,

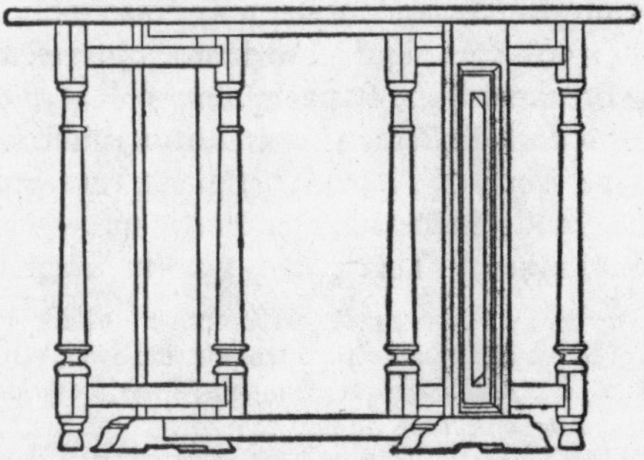

Figure 7 – Gate-leg table, with solid end supports resting on trestle feet, tied by a broad, horizontal stretcher. The flaps of the top are supported on swinging gates with baluster legs. First half of the seventeenth century

Richmond, Greenwich, Windsor, Nonesuch, Oatlands, and Woodstock, show that comparatively few of the thousands of items listed were entirely of native workmanship and that many were directly imported. Likewise the vast collections of Cardinal Wolsey, who was notoriously rapacious in the acquisition of such property, were gathered from many sources. Agents were active in the furthering of these interests.

Textile furnishings were of the greatest importance. Numerous entries refer to tapestries, carpets, embroideries and fine fabrics. A chair is denoted by its upholstery: 'Item one chere of riche clothe of Tissue Tawney fringe wt fringe of Venice gold and tawney silke.'[3] In the house of the ordinary citizen, the hangings, although of plain material (woollen cloth, worsted, say, or painted linen) were yet gay coloured. The woodwork of furniture, when exposed, was often painted walnut colour and parcel gilt.

Renaissance ornament began to appear in the early years of the sixteenth century. Ecclesiastical furniture was at this date closely allied to the domestic: the form of the canopied settle, for example, was similar to that of the choir stall. Thus comparison of the Gothic lower-tier choir stalls of the Chapel of Henry VII in Westminster Abbey, *c.* 1506, and the later magnificent work in King's College Chapel, Cambridge, in pure Renaissance style, may reasonably be made in this connexion – with significant contrast between the two.

Until his break with the Papacy, Henry VIII encouraged Italian artists and craftsmen to come to this country. In particular the work of Pietro Torrigiano revealed at first hand in England the beauty, hitherto unknown, of the Italian Renaissance.* Torrigiano was in England from

* Pietro Torrigiano (1472–1528), a Florentine sculptor who, stated Vasari, 'was of so proud and choleric a temper, and so violent and overbearing, that he was continually attacking his fellows, both in deeds and in words', is notorious because he one day 'gave Michelagnolo such a blow on the nose that he broke it, and the artist was disfigured for life'. He was, wrote Vasari, 'taken by merchants to England. Here he did a number of works in marble, bronze and wood for the King in competition with the masters of the country'.[4]

1511 to 1518, and again for a few months after 1519, working on the tombs of Lady Margaret Beaufort, Henry VII, and Elizabeth of York at Westminster Abbey, and on the monument of Henry VIII at Windsor. The sculptured tomb of Henry VII is his most notable work. Few Italians of his talents travelled as far as Britain. Nevertheless the employment by Henry VIII of foreign artists, architects, and workmen (Flemings, French, Italians, and Germans) in such a building as the great unfinished palace of Nonesuch (Pl. 2) (and the immigration to these shores of the many French and Flemish Huguenots who fled from religious persecution) was responsible in large part for a changed standard of taste and some luxury, at least in London-made pieces. There must have been several score foreign joiners and carpenters resident in London by the latter half of the century. Much of the better furniture had, however, formerly been made for ecclesiastical use. From the thirteenth to the fifteenth century, the services of medieval artists had been spent primarily in satisfying the requirements of the Church. It followed that the abolition of the monasteries was succeeded by a decline in craftsmanship. For a generation or more after 1540, many of the pieces produced by native joiners were of comparatively poor construction and ornament.

A period of transition in English decoration and woodwork came to an end soon after the death of Henry VIII in 1547, when the Gothic was belatedly absorbed into a native version of the Renaissance style. The style was ill understood and much adulterated, being generally derived from Flemish and German sources. In the latter part of the century and during the early seventeenth century, a florid Flemish interpretation of the Renaissance here prevailed. Flemish furniture had been brought into the country in great quantities since the later fifteenth century. Ornament in the form of strapwork (Fig. 8, A and B), lozenge decoration, masks, grotesques and fruit and flower *motifs* became characteristic. Grape and vine leaf ornament was of common occurrence (Fig. 8C). Strapwork, in particular, was abused during the first part of the seventeenth century,

Figure 8 – Details of carved decoration: (A and B) strapwork; (C) grape and vine leaf

when a profusion of carved detail in very low relief was fashionable. A book of designs entitled *Architectura*, by Johannes de Vries, is perhaps the best known of several foreign publications which inspired the more ambitious efforts of English designers; this work was published in 1577.

The complex nature of the decoration of the front and sides of the large oak chest illustrated in plate 6 exemplifies this tendency towards over-elaboration. The chest makes a striking contrast with the earlier linenfold chest (Pl. 5). Rails and stiles are inlaid with small chequer patterns. Floral inlay is used to ornament the three arched panels of the front which are framed and divided by the terminal figures of men and women. It was clearly the intention of the designer to produce an architectural piece. Ornate chests with applied terminal figures to the stiles were in favour during the reigns of Elizabeth and James I.

To certain pieces of inlaid furniture of the second half of the sixteenth century – often chests of architectural character, and boxes or small writing desks – the term

'Nonesuch' is applied. These pieces are decorated with conventionalized representations of an ideal building which bear stylistic resemblance to the Palace of Nonesuch near Cheam (Pl. 2).*

There is a writing desk of this type at the Victoria and Albert Museum (Pl. 3) which is inlaid with holly, bog oak, and various stained woods. The sloping lid is hinged and decorated with intricate chequer ornament. The inside is fitted with small drawers. Representations of the building (with its high-pitched roofs and fantastic towers and steeples, cupolas and flying flags) which occur on front, back and sides of the desk, are enclosed by further geometrical and chequer ornament. These representational designs are comprised of various small pieces of wood, assembled to form a pattern; the technique resembles marquetry. Inlay, properly, is let *into* the solid ground, being therefore distinct from marquetry or parquetry. These 'Nonesuch' pieces are decorated in a style akin to that of

* Nonesuch, a palace 'without equal', and a building which appealed enormously to the imagination of the Elizabethans, being symbolic perhaps of the resources and new-found riches of the age, was built for Henry VIII after the designs of the Italian, Toto del Nunziata. The palace later suffered several changes of ownership. At the end it came, a royal gift of 1670, into the hands of Lady Castlemaine (who also acquired the title Baroness Nonesuch) and by her was gutted and destroyed. It was a rich prize, as may be inferred by Pepys' description of 1665 (when the Exchequer was removed thence, because of the plague): '... a great walk of an elme and a walnutt, set one after another in order. And all the house on the outside filled with figures of stories ... one great thing is, that most of the house is covered, I mean the posts, and quarters in the walls ... with lead and gilded. I walked into the ruined garden....'[5] Evelyn, who supped at Nonesuch, 'tooke an exact view of ye plaster statues ... and punchions of the outside walles of the Court; which, must needs have ben the work of some celebrated Italian [Pl. 2]. I much admir'd,' he wrote, 'how it had lasted so well and intire since the time of Henry VIII, expos'd as they are to the aire; and pitty it is they are not taken out and preserv'd in some drie place; a gallerie would become them. There are some mezzo-relievos as big as the life. The storie is of ye Heathen Gods, emblems, compartments, &c. The Palace consists of two courts, of which the first is of stone, castle-like ... ye other of timber, a Gotiq fabric, but these walls imcomparably beautified.'[6]

contemporary German work and examples not imported are probably the work of immigrant craftsmen.[7] A number of Nonesuch chests date apparently from the period when Queen Elizabeth first took up residence at the Palace (1591) to her death in 1603.

Various contemporary descriptions of the furnishing of the Royal Palaces during the late Elizabethan period, and later, have survived, and as eye-witness accounts are extremely interesting, although not particularly informative as to everyday furniture. The writers were primarily concerned to record what appeared to them to be extraordinary.

Thus, Jacob Rathgeb,[8] at Theobalds Palace, commented in 1592 on certain painted and gilt ceilings, 'skilfully wrought in joiner's work'; several 'tables of inlaid work and marble of various colours' and, in a garden summer house, a table of black touchstone or marble 'fourteen spans long, seven wide, and one span thick'.[9] And at Hampton Court Palace he remarked the 'masterly paintings, writing-tables inlaid with mother-of-pearl, organs, and musical instruments, which her Majesty is particularly fond of'. He observed all the apartments to be 'hung with rich tapestry, of pure gold and fine silk, so exceedingly beautiful and royally ornamented that it would hardly be possible to find more magnificent things of the kind in any other place'.

Similarly, Paul Hentzner, another foreigner, in an account of his travels in England in 1598,[10] praised there certain curiosities in the Hall: 'a very clear looking-glass, ornamented with columns and little images of alabaster ... an artificial sphere; several musical instruments; in the tapestry ... Negroes riding upon elephants ... numbers of cushions ornamented with gold and silver; many counterpanes and coverlids of beds lined with ermine ... a certain cabinet called *Paradise*, where besides that everything glitters so with silver, gold and jewels, as to dazzle one's eyes, there is a musical instrument made all of glass, except the strings.'

At Windsor he noted: 'two stove-rooms ceiled and wainscoted with looking-glass ... Queen Elizabeth's bedchamber, where is a table of red marble with white streaks ... the royal beds of Henry VII and his Queen, of Edward VI, of Henry VIII, and of Anne Boleyn, – all of them eleven feet square ... Queen Elizabeth's bed, with curious coverings of embroidery, but not quite so long or large as the others ...'*

And at Whitehall: 'two little silver cabinets of exquisite work, in which the Queen keeps her paper, and which she uses for writing-boxes. The Queen's bed, ingeniously composed of woods of different colours ... a little [jewel] chest ornamented all over with pearls ... a small Hermitage, half hid in a rock, finely carved in wood. ... A piece of clock-work, an Æthiop riding upon a Rhinoceros, with four attendants, who all make their obeisance when it strikes the hour; these are put into motion by winding up the machine.'

This quantity of fine goldsmiths' work was produced at a time when most articles of wooden furniture were clumsily made and variously used, if only by reason of scarcity. The value of plate and textiles greatly exceeded that of furniture. Belief that the well-to-do possessed such luxuries in plenty is supported by Hentzner's observation that 'all sorts of gold and silver vessels [were] exposed to sale' in the street of the

* The great beds of the time had a weight and consequence which did not belong to other furniture. They were, apart even from the valuable hangings, costly. Arcaded decoration and pilasters in the form of terminal figures often divided the head-board of the bed into formal compartments. After about 1560, substantial foot posts, with heavy bulbs supported on massive, free-standing pedestals and plinths of square section, were a distinguishing feature. The exposed woodwork of head-board, posts and tester provided a field for the display of a wealth of boldly carved ornament. Beds of this description remained fashionable in England for some years after the death of Elizabeth. Uncurtained low or 'stump' beds of a traditional type were made for common use. These were severely practical and were constructed without posts or ceiling. A very clear picture of a primitive but well-ordered dormitory for the sick is given in a panel painted by the Master of Alkmaar in the early sixteenth century and entitled *Visiting the Sick* from the *Seven Works of Charity* in the Rijksmuseum, Amsterdam. It is noticeable that the beds are lacking in ornament of any description and that the head-boards are formed apparently of nailed planks. Nevertheless low beds were frequently carved with some elaboration.

goldsmiths 'as well as ancient and modern medals, in such quantities as must surprise a man the first time he sees and considers them'; as also the same writer's tale of a certain Leonard Smith, a tailor in the city, who possessed 'a most perfect looking glass,* ornamented with pearls, gold, silver, and velvet, so richly as to be estimated at 500 *écus du soleil*'.

Although the oak furniture made by native craftsmen and numerous foreigners domiciled here was limited in type, people were ambitious of comfort and of display: 'The furniture of our houses ... is grown in manner even to passing delicacy: and herein I do not speak of the nobility and gentry only, but likewise of the lowest sort. ... Certes in noblemen's houses it is not rare to see abundance of arras, rich hangings of tapestry, silver vessels, and so much other plate as may furnish sundry cupboards to the sum oftentimes of a thousand or two thousand pounds at the least, whereby the value of this and the rest of their stuff doth grow to be almost inestimable. Likewise in the houses of knights, gentlemen, merchantmen, and some other wealthy citizens, it is not geson to behold generally their great provision of tapestry, Turkey work, pewter, brass, fine linen, and thereto costly cupboards of plate. ... But, as herein all these sorts do far exceed their elders and predecessors ... so in times past the costly furniture stayed there, whereas now it is descended yet lower, even unto the inferior artificers and many farmers, who ... have, for the most part, learned also to garnish their cupboards† with plate, their joined beds with tapestry and silk hangings, and their tables with carpets and fine napery, whereby the wealth of our country ... doth infinitely appear.'[11] By the account he gives of 'such furniture', it would seem clear that William Harrison (whose *Description of England*, published with Holinshed's *Chronicle* in 1587, provides an entertaining, contemporary commentary on Elizabethan life) was thinking less of pieces of furniture than of accessories – the ornaments and new refinements to the house. The mention

* Probably burnished metal.

† Unenclosed 'cup boards' or shelves.

of 'costly cupboards' is incidental: they serve for a display of plate. Furniture was scarce, although solidly made; and, if decorated, was floridly carved in the Flemish manner or commonly was inlaid with various native woods. Walnut was sometimes chosen for the finer work. Deal and chestnut were comparatively rare woods and correspondingly prized. (Henry VIII had set much store by a room at Nonesuch which he had caused to be panelled in deal.) Many pieces, among them chests with drawers and dressing tables, were non-existent. Mirrors of glass were of extreme rarity and were obtained from Venice. The carved chimney piece was perhaps the most prominent and elaborate decorative feature of the room; the tapestries and hangings, needlework cloths and embroidered cushions, gold, silver, and pewter vessels, and above all the painted and gilt ornament of walls and ceiling, gave it colour and warmth.

Nevertheless, a statement by Emanuel van Meteren that the English had not 'so much furniture or unnecessary house ornaments' as the people in the Low Countries was founded on personal observation.[12] Van Meteren, an Antwerp merchant, held the office of Dutch consul until his death in 1612; he lived in London for nearly thirty years and was well qualified to make a comparison between the two countries.

About the middle of the sixteenth century the framed table was introduced and continued to be made throughout the Stuart period. The heavy turned legs on which it rests are tenoned into a framing at the corners and are further secured by outside stretcher rails towards ground level.* Such tables were framed together by a joiner; they were for this reason referred to in contemporary documents as 'joint' tables. They vary considerably in size and many remaining specimens have been cut down. Walnut or oak, ash or elm, were used for their construction. The last wood, in particular, was readily accessible and doubtless fre-

* At first, in the late sixteenth century, stretcher rails were made with a projection on the top surface, and were 'T'-shaped in section; later they were of plain square section.

quently employed, but being a perishable wood has not survived in any quantity, although some tables of elm with single tops 9 feet by 3 feet wide and of a thickness of some inches are extant. Specimens are found with four, six, or eight legs. The top has often a distinct overhang.

The draw-top table (Fig. 9), wherein a subsidiary and additional leaf might be drawn out at each end of the table top, provided an ingenious and popular refinement on the type. The area of the board was by this means almost doubled. The two end leaves, attached on graduated or raking bearers, lay, when not in use, under the main centre

Figure 9 – Draw table; the legs of heavy, baluster form, with bulbous body, tied below by four moulded stretchers. About 1600

board. This centre necessarily allowed vertical movement, was tied by tongues fixed on its underside to an immovable cross bar and was not therefore free to move laterally; when the end leaves were withdrawn to their full extent (rising because of the graduation of the bearers to which they were fastened), the centre fell, by its own weight, into its original position and became flush with the drawn ends.

The most significant feature of style of these framed tables lies in the design of the massive legs and the type of turning chosen by the craftsman making them. In some instances, accompanying forms or sets of stools still survive with the tables to which they were complementary. Tables are lighter in design by the middle of the seventeenth

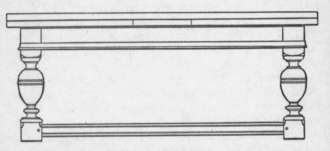

century and their ornament is more restrained in character – a tendency common to other pieces of furniture after the early Jacobean period. The heavy bulbous leg (Fig. 10A) of exaggerated form introduced towards the end of the reign of Elizabeth and used, at first with extreme richness of carving, in other pieces such as beds and in the legs of court

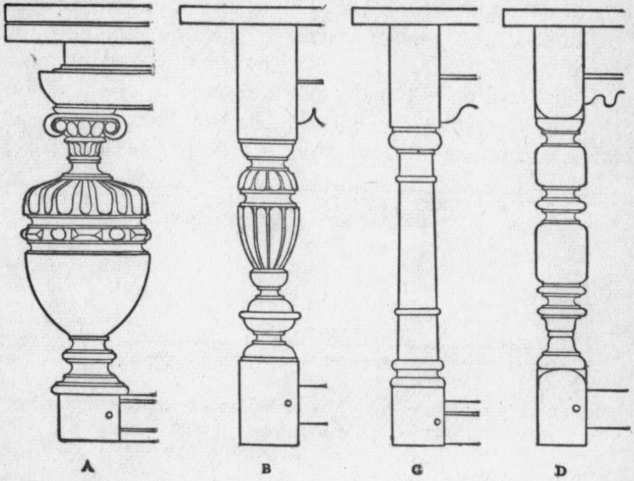

Figure 10 – Details of legs of dining tables: (A) bulbous leg, of 'cup and cover' form, with modified Ionic capital above, and, below, a turned base; carved with gadrooning and baluster and jewel ornament; late sixteenth century; (B) baluster leg of modified bulbous form; carved with gadrooning; early seventeenth century; (C) columnar leg; (D) bobbin-turned leg; mid seventeenth century

cupboards and chairs, while popularly associated with a rather earlier period than that of the late Elizabethan and early Stuart, in fact persisted, in an attenuated and less gross form, for the best part of three-quarters of a century (Fig. 10B). For some years previous to the accession of James I, it was matched in popularity by a graceful columnar leg (Fig. 10C). This latter, and a vase turned leg, dating from the later seventeenth century, endured until the end of the oak period. The three types overlap considerably in date. Bobbin turning, on the other hand, enjoyed a comparatively brief spell of popularity, principally under the Commonwealth. It was, as might be expected, a severe and plain style and its vogue was limited (Fig. 10D). Table tops were thinner at this time and set in narrow boards clamped at each end. This cross-framing at the ends was intended to prevent warping. The frieze of the table was often fluted or carved with lunettes and shallow brackets were placed at the angles formed by the junction of the legs and frieze (Fig. 11). The similarity that exists between numbers of these tables is usually one of district;

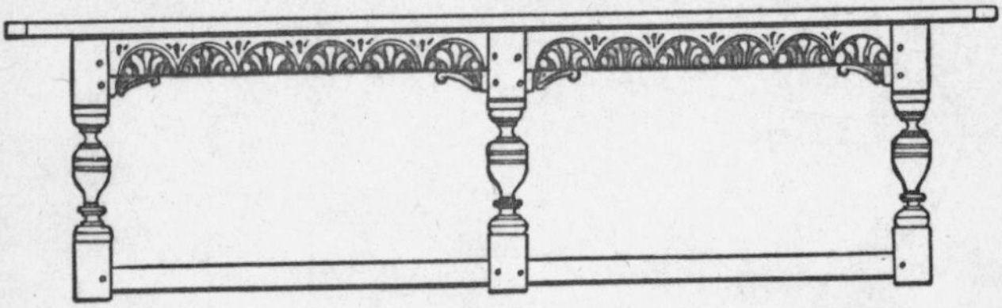

Figure 11 – Framed dining table; supported on six turned baluster legs united by stretchers; the frieze carved with lunettes. Mid seventeenth century

they may be grouped because of the influence of locality on furniture style. From 1600, the secular style of English Renaissance pulpits, screens, and other church woodwork sometimes provides valuable corroboratory evidence when a particular style of decoration is associated with one district – although the Gothic style persisted in some churches (and persists to the present day), after it had fallen into general disrepute.

The processes of wood turning were well known to Tudor craftsmen; nevertheless most chairs, and long and short stools with turned legs, and other pieces of furniture with turned members, were made after the accession of James I; and remaining pieces of this sort antedate his accession by a few years at most (Figs. 12 and 13). Tables are an excep-

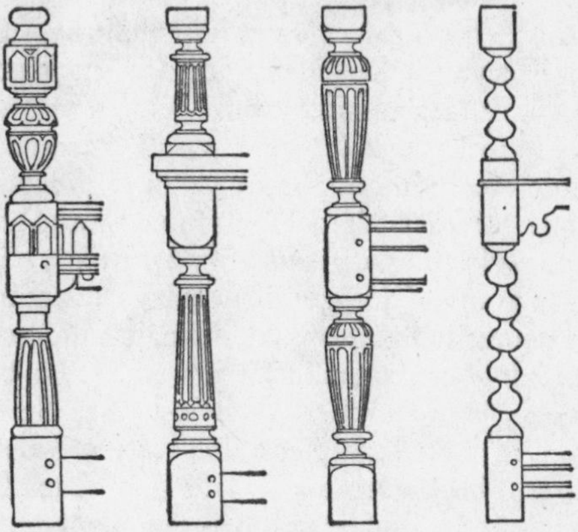

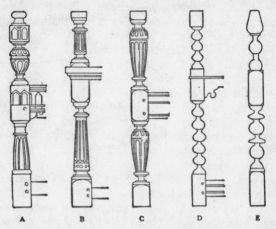

Figure 12 – Details of legs and arm supports of chairs: (A, B, and C) turned and fluted legs; beginning of the seventeenth century; (D and E) ball turned legs; middle of the seventeenth century

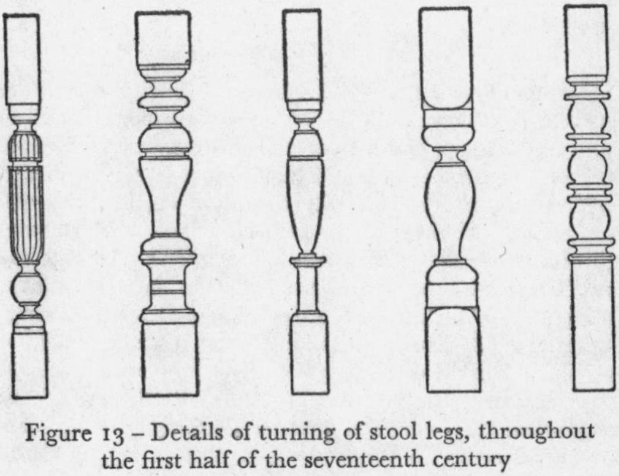

Figure 13 – Details of turning of stool legs, throughout the first half of the seventeenth century

tion, as are also the curious and rather monstrous 'turneyed' chairs of the type shown in medieval illuminated manuscripts but of which no examples earlier than about 1500 appear to have survived. The chair illustrated in plate 4A is made of yew and is of triangular form. It is said one time to have been in the Bishop's Palace at Wells. Turned chairs of this description were formerly associated in particular with the 'Gothic' ages. Horace Walpole was interested to acquire specimens, and writing to a friend from Strawberry Hill in 1761, stated: 'I am now doing a dirty thing, flattering you to preface a commission. Dickey Bateman has picked up a whole cloister full of old chairs in Hertfordshire. He bought them one by one, here and there in farm-houses, for three-and-sixpence, and a crown a-piece. They are of wood, the seats triangular, the backs, arms, and legs loaded with turnery. A thousand to one but there are plenty up and down Cheshire too. If Mr and Mrs Wetenhall, as they ride or drive out, would now and then pick up such a chair, it would oblige me greatly. Take notice, no two need be of the same pattern.'[13]

A year earlier, in August 1760, Walpole had visited Hardwicke, where he found 'nothing but triste grandeur'; it was a house with 'no grace, no ornament, no Gothic in it'.[14]*

* The notes of his journal read thus: 'The great apartment as it was furnished for the Queen of Scots. The first room her Council chamber, immense; at the upper end a State, with the arms of the second Earl & Countess of Devonshire, an inlaid table before it, with a rich covering embossed with gold. Freeze of Stucco very deep, in relief, with Stag-hunting, as is the chimney in the next chamber.... A Cabinet of oak carved, with two tables to the sides, & made with side steps like a confessional. There are other Tables & cabinets in the apartment in better taste, supported by Lions, like Kent's tables, & tortoises for feet. Screens like Stands to brush Cloaths, with long pieces of Carnation velvet hanging over them, fringed with gold; the velvet now turned yellow. On all the tables are magnificent coverings, embroidered and embossed with gold on damask & velvet. The next the Queen's Dressing room. Then her State bedchamber. A very costly bed all in tatters, of Cloth of gold and silver paned, with pieces of different patchwork & embroidery, & one piece of grotesque embroidered like John d'Udine, in very good

In the medieval period, the ruling classes had found it convenient to possess, as far as was practicable, valuables of a movable type. Holdings of land were dispersed; and whole households moved at intervals from one part of the country to another. Iron-bound coffers or 'standards' were particularly useful for transporting the costly materials which covered the bare structure of much of the furniture of the time – bed hangings, wall hangings (costers), and carpets or covers. Coffers were of wood covered with leather and fitted with handles or rings for ease of carrying. They were frequently constructed with curved or gabled lids. In the seventeenth century travelling trunks of wood covered with leather and decorated with brass-headed nails arranged in an intricate pattern were of lighter but not dissimilar form.

By the later sixteenth century, the hall, although still an integral part of the architecture of the great house, had diminished in importance. The long gallery was used for walking and for the playing of games; and it would seem that it held a selection of the best furniture of the house – often of walnut, and inlaid. Much of this walnut furniture has since perished. An inventory taken at Arundel Castle about 1580 provides information in some detail.[16] The gallery contained as many as six inlaid walnut chairs, three chairs covered with black leather, and but six joined stools. There were, in addition, an inlaid, square, framed table and a walnut cupboard. The furniture of the great hall, on the other hand, was intended for hard service and was presumably of a wood less highly valued than walnut. Of eight trestle tables listed, two, perhaps, may have functioned as side boards or serving tables, and were made 'of firre'. Seating accommodation was provided by two chairs, two

Taste, as is the Cloth on the table . . . the hangings of the room, reported to be embroidered by the Queen . . . on black & white velvet with allegoric & historic figures large as the life. The private bedchamber was certainly the Queen's, her Style & arms are over the Door . . . Gallery 60 yards long. a small Couch with a Canopy, bad tapestry, & worse pictures, mentioned in her Will. . . . Many of the doors & much wainscot is inlaid.'[15]

joined forms and sixteen joined stools ('stooles of waynes-cotte'), as well as a number of benches probably constructed with solid backs and placed permanently against the walls. There were many wall hangings and 'Turkie carpetts'. Of the latter, one was reserved for use under the high table, and one for use upon it, and one was placed also on each of the two cupboards which, with long and small cushions and two pairs of andirons, made the sum of the recorded contents of the room.*

The typical Tudor chair, with tall straight back and solid arm supports, sometimes called a 'settle chair', was of box form, the space contained below the seat often being utilized as a cupboard – the door opening either at the back or the front of the piece and the seat being hinged so as to form a lid. The chair was weighty and not readily movable.

Panelled joined chairs with turned legs and open arms were not in use until the latter half of the sixteenth century, and were then frequently enriched with carved or inlaid decoration (Pl. 4B). Comparable in importance with the standing cupboards and chests, they were often carved with the initials of their owners and dated. The decoration was Renaissance and not Gothic in character. Linenfold panels were frequently incorporated into the framing. The form of the turning of front legs and arm supports provides some indication of date (Fig. 12).

From the Elizabethan period a greater variety of good furniture was made. Also, much plain furniture came to us from the Mart of Antwerp, as well as pieces of a more luxurious and unusual nature. It is certain that quantities of chests and chairs were exported thence to England during the hundred years from about 1540. And as late as the Commonwealth period, Mr Robert Spencer, in exile in Flanders, was writing: 'I cannot meete with an Ebony

* The bedchambers were sparsely furnished. The 'Chambre at the Hall-End' is typical of many: 'Item, hangings of the storie of king David v peeces. Item, one other peece of the same storie. Item, 1 bedsteede of oke, 1 bedd and boulster, 1 Venice rugge, 1 olde quilte of silke tawnie, and 1 olde tester of redd and russet satten. Item 1 cubberd of oke, wth a Turkey carpett.'

Cabanet that 's good, I can have choice of Tortus Shell, garnished out with very thin silver or guilt Brasse which I like much better ... *the best choyce is at Antwerp*.'[17]

The court cupboard was produced contemporaneously with the large press, constructed in two stages and fitted

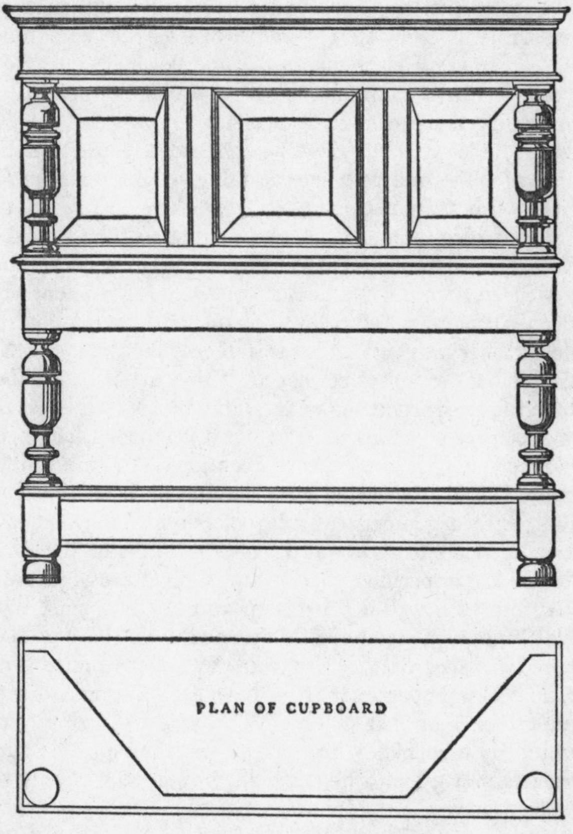

Figure 14 – Court cupboard; the tiers supported in front by bulbous columns of attenuated 'cup and cover' form; the upper part contains a recessed central cupboard, with canted sides. Early seventeenth century

with enclosing doors. By its smaller size, the court cupboard was perhaps intended for use in the dining parlour rather than the hall. In appearance it resembled a stand in three stages and was supported at the two back corners by plain posts; often a central recessed cupboard with canted sides, flanked by carved bulbous columns at each front corner, was contained in the upper part (Fig. 14) – although an open form was alternative – and a drawer was sometimes contained in the frieze beneath the middle shelf. This piece was referred to at its time of origin as a 'court cupboard', a term which has since been inaccurately applied to the 'press'. The '*court*' (i.e. 'short') cupboard was used for the display of plate and as a service table – 'court-cupboards planted with flaggons, cans, cups, beakers ...'.[18] In the summer of 1604, James I gave a banquet to the Constable of Castile at Whitehall Palace. According to a contemporary written account,[19] a choice collection of 'ancient and modern gilt plate' was displayed on one of these cupboards; while on a second, various 'vessels of gold, agate, and other semi-precious stones' were placed. These articles, together with certain cushioned chairs and tabourets of rich brocade, were specifically remarked. The court cupboard had been introduced early in the sixteenth century. The fine walnut example (Pl. 8), decorated with carving and, on the open shelves, with a geometrical inlay of ebony, boxwood and fruitwood, dates from about 1600. The bulbs at the front which tie the uppermost and central shelves are vigorously carved and of a well-defined 'cup and cover' form,* with typical Ionic capitals above thin turned necks. The piece is designed in accordance with contemporary architectural rule. The straight supports at the back are ornamented with palmated or laurelled carving. The upper frieze is surmounted by a cornice with oblique gadrooning. The cupboard is about 3 feet 6 inches high, but stood formerly on low feet.

* By the later seventeenth century, the 'cup and cover' form is generally undefined, although the bulb is sometimes grooved.

Plainer enclosed cupboards of similar proportions to the court cupboard, but in form intermediate between it and the enclosed press, are also found (Fig. 15).

Presses, made in two or three tiers and developing towards extreme width, were, too, in more or less general use throughout the seventeenth century; and, later, plainer

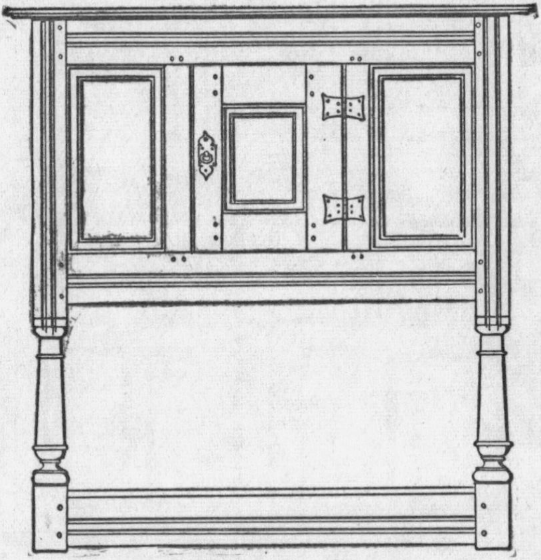

Figure 15 – Enclosed cupboard, with central door, supported on turned columnar legs. Early seventeenth century

examples were made for farmhouses and small houses in the country. They varied greatly according to district. The upper portion was commonly recessed, the frieze being supported at each end by turned columns (and in later cupboards by the pendant bosses which usurped their place) which rested on the ledge formed by the recession and which framed the upper compartments. Drawers and cupboards were contained below (Fig. 16).

A decorative use of turning is met with in simple and comparatively small hanging cupboards, sometimes made of fruitwood or deal, which were used for the distribution of

Figure 16 – Press cupboard, in two stages; there are two cupboard doors in the upper part, and a central panel; the frieze, which projects and is carved with lunettes, rests on bulbous supports; the lower part is enclosed by panelled doors. First half of the seventeenth century

liveries, at least until the end of the reign of Charles I. These cupboards were fitted inside with shelves and were often designed with one row or more of open balusters so arranged as to provide an open screen behind which perishable food was kept (Fig. 17)

Inventories show that upholstered furniture was in use under Elizabeth and had attained some measure of popularity by the next reign.* In this variety of furniture (which included such pieces as the low, wide chair (Fig. 18), the stool or tabouret, the couch and double chair or settee) the visible woodwork was of a relatively undistinguished character. The fashion for upholstery was neglected under

Figure 17 – Hanging livery cupboard; enclosed by two pierced doors, each with two rows of turned balusters. Early seventeenth century

the Commonwealth, when luxury, as indeed ornament, was regarded as indecorous. A few chairs, supplied originally to palaces and great houses, in which the frame and the legs are of beech or soft wood, still may be seen in original condition. These chairs are of X-frame construction and are entirely

* Sir John Harington, it is recorded, questioned if it would not 'become the state of the chamber to have easye quilted and lyned formes and stooles for the lords and ladies to sit on, which fashion is now taken up in every merchant's hall, as great plank forms . . . and waynscot stooles so hard that since great breeches were layd aside, men can scant endewr to sitt upon'.[20]

covered with velvets, trimmed with fringed galon and studded with large brass-headed nails (Fig. 19).*

The farthingale chair was an outcome of an extreme fashion in ladies' dress whereby under James I the farthingale or hooped petticoat increased to fantastic proportions. A peculiar type of chair was evolved to suit such a dress. Farthingale chairs, which were generously upholstered, frequently in 'Turkey' work or with costly foreign velvets, were made without arms and with a widened and very high seat, and supported usually on plain columnar legs. The padded back was correspondingly low. 'Turkey' work chairs commanded a comparatively high price, even after the Restoration. A west country physician, Dr Claver Morris, recorded, among his household expenses for 1686 (the result of his marriage the preceding year to 'Mistress Grace Green of London'), the purchase secondhand of a dozen and a half of such chairs for the sum of £7. 2*s*. 6*d*. He was, however, required to pay £1 only for the ten leather chairs which he obtained from the same source.[21]

Comparatively large sums were paid for English knotted woollen pile or 'Turkey' carpets. According to the Verney papers, Lady Sussex proposed in 1640 to buy two such carpets for the sum of £40, but considered that 'the flowers or workes in them' might prove to be of not very pleasant colour and feared lest the ground prove too dull 'to suet with my haninges and chers'. Carpets were put to various uses. These, wrote Lady Sussex, 'woulde bee very fine for a bede'. A small one, if not serving for a window, would 'sarve for a fote carpet'.[22]

The art collections of Charles I were among the finest in Europe; and by his care and interest the furniture and furnishings of the many Royal palaces were much increased during the second quarter of the century. His personal taste too must have influenced a section of the court. The Royal collections, however, were dispersed by order of the Council

* The Tudor folding X-framed chair (which has hardly survived because its value almost entirely resulted from the fabrics which comprised its back and seat) was revived in the early seventeenth century.

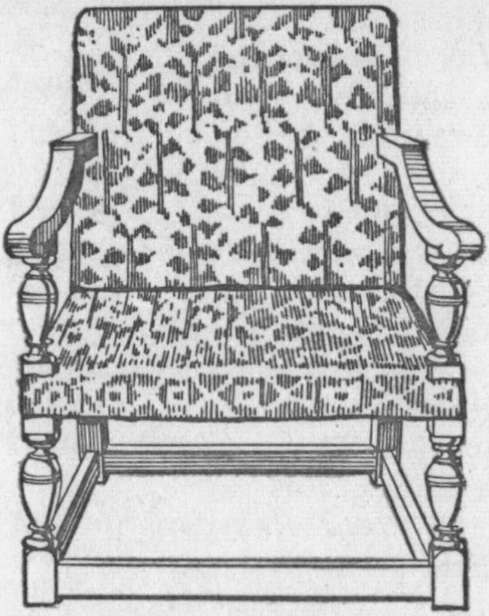

Figure 18 – Arm chair, with covered back and seat; the front legs and arm supports are turned. First half of the seventeenth century

Figure 19 – Arm chair of X-frame construction; the framework is covered with fabric and studded with ornamental nailing. Early seventeenth century

of State, and there was heavy destruction of property of all kinds during the Rebellion and afterwards. Particularly did the early upholstered furniture suffer. When Dame Mary Verney revisited Claydon after four years' absence she found its condition appalling, largely by the quartering of soldiers upon it; she wrote: 'I feare they will make us very poore as beggers; I protest I know nott which way we shall live if the countrey may allwayes quarter soldiers.' The house was 'most lamentably furnished, all the linnen quite worne out ... the spitts, and other odd thinges so extreamly eaten with Rust thatt they canot be evor of any use againe ... the cloath of the Musk-coloured stools spoyled, and the dining-room chairs in Ragges'.[23]

Joined arm chairs of panelled construction have survived in larger numbers. In this type of chair, evolved from the Tudor box chair, the back consists of a solid carved panel, framed and surmounted by a cresting. The chair is supported on baluster turned legs tied by moulded stretchers. Alternatively, the legs are of columnar form or designed with a modified bulbous turning (Fig. 12). The wooden seat is comparatively thin. Noticeably from the beginning of the seventeenth century, and even earlier, there was a tendency for the top rail of the chair back, which supports the cresting, to be placed *upon* the uprights, and not, as formerly (although there are exceptions to the rule) to be contained *within* them; the arms had a marked downward slope; ear pieces were attached to the sides of the uprights and formed pendent brackets to the imposing and very decorative scrolled cresting of later specimens (Pl. 4C). The back panels of many specimens made after the middle of the century were thinly but richly carved over the greater part of their surface with varied *motifs*, as scroll work, floral arabesques or strap work (Fig. 8).* With the

* Deep cutting is characteristic of the carving of the Elizabethan and early Jacobean periods (see the bold gadrooning on the seat rail of the chair illustrated in Pl. 4B); shallow carving and a repetitive use of such forms as the *guilloche* and the *lunette*, which occur in later work, indicate a decline in the standards of craftsmanship.

exception of the turned front leg, which was continued as the arm support, and the seat rails, other parts were usually undecorated.

The oak stool typical of the period was of rectangular form with turned legs of round section (Pl. 9B and Fig. 13). Legs in earlier examples were commonly of modified bulbous shape and decorated with flutings. The connecting stretcher rails were placed rather low.

The most pleasing use of bobbin turning is to be remarked in the otherwise severe design of many Commonwealth chairs, now frequently made without arms. Turning was permitted as decoration, whereas carving, as upholstery, was by the harsh standards prevailing not generally approved. The low backs and the seats of chairs were covered with strips of leather (cow hide) strained over the framing of seat rails and uprights and secured by rows of large brass-headed nails. Alternatively, baluster and, slightly later, a simple twist turning were employed with good effect on the more prominent front rails and legs of chairs of the period immediately preceding the restoration of Charles II to the throne.

The numerous chests produced during the seventeenth century served principally for the storage of clothes and linen. The chest often formed part of the marriage dowry. The 'boarded' construction was sometimes retained, as in a chest of elm, made, according to the carved inscription, by one James Griffin in 1639 (Victoria and Albert Museum) (Pl. 7). The chest is said to have been formerly in the Old Castle Inn, at Old Sarum, Wiltshire, and to have been connected with the Pitt family of Stratford Castle in that place. This piece is pleasingly decorated in low relief with scrollwork and lozenge ornament and bears traces of red and green paint.* A framed and panelled construction was the more fashionable, and in the early years of the century many specimens of a decadent Renaissance design were

* Many Tudor pieces had been painted, but the practice had declined under Elizabeth; yet painted furniture and panelling continued to be supplied in the seventeenth century.

decorated with an elaborate inlay of floral arabesques in brightly coloured woods on a light ground (Pl. 6). An arcaded front was a popular feature, the panels below the frieze sometimes being divided by stiles framing the arches

Figure 20 – Press cupboard, in two stages; the end bosses, pendent from the frieze of the recessed upper part, derive from the bulbous supports found in earlier specimens (*cf.* Fig. 16); the front of the piece is decorated with bevelled panels in deep projection, with applied lozenges and split baluster ornament. Mid seventeenth century

carved with terminal figures or in the form of projecting corbels, and the whole front being enriched by a profusion of carving in low relief. The flat pilasters supporting the arches of the arcading were usually squat in form and occasionally of a bulbous outline somewhat at variance with their architectural character. Chests of this florid character present a remarkable contrast to those specimens of panelled construction with linenfold decoration, dating from the sixteenth century (Pl. 5).

The provision of a lower compartment or drawers at the base of the chest led to specimens with this added feature being described as chests 'with drawers' and, ultimately, to the evolution of the chest-with-drawers proper and again to the tallboy. Chests containing this innovation are recorded in inventories of the later sixteenth century.

Earliest examples of the complete chest of drawers date from the mid-seventeenth century. The drawers contained in the main or lower body of the chest are enclosed by two doors. A shallow drawer lies above or, in some instances, an upper portion which comprises one shallow and one very deep drawer. The geometrical, panelled decoration of these oak chests was mitred and new in conception, being marked by strong projection at the centres. Applied pendants (split baluster forms, which were usually stained black) and bosses, lozenges, strap work, and bold key pattern mouldings were characteristic of the style, and are found also in the oak presses which were among the more substantial pieces of furniture of the time (Fig. 20). Bone and mother-of-pearl inlaid ornament was occasionally introduced, and decorative use was made of ebony and of partridge or zebra wood in the bevels of panels.[24]

NOTES TO CHAPTER I

1. The 'Cominge into Englande of the Lorde Grautehuse', the MS. narrative of a Herald, printed in *Archaeologia*, vol. 26 (1836), pp. 265–86.
2. George Chapman, *A Humourous Day's Mirth*, 1599.
3. See article by I. C. Goodison, *Furniture of Hampton Court* etc., in *Journal of the Society of Arts* (1925).
4. Vasari's *Lives of the Painters, Sculptors and Architects*, trans. by A. B. Hinds (Everyman's Library), 1927, vol. II, pp. 209–10.
5. *The Diary of Samuel Pepys*, ed. by H. B. Wheatley, 1923, vol. v, p. 82.
6. *Memoirs of John Evelyn*, ed. by William Bray, 2nd edition 1819, vol. I, p. 383. Diary for 3rd Jan., 1666.
7. See article by W. A. Thorpe, *Country Life Christmas Annual*, 1951.

8. Jacob Rathgeb, as private secretary to Frederick, Duke of Württemberg, visited Theobald's Palace in 1592.
9. W. B. Rye, *England as seen by Foreigners in the days of Elizabeth and James the First*, London, 1865. (The Journal of Frederick, Duke of Württemberg, trans. from the German.)
10. Rye, *op. cit.* (Hentzner's Journal of his travels in Germany, France and England, penned in Latin, was first printed at Nuremberg in 1612. Horace Walpole published, in 1757, for private circulation, the portion relating to England.)
11. *Elizabethan England: from 'A Description of England', by William Harrison (in 'Holinshed's Chronicles')*, ed. by L. Withington, 1889, p. 118.
12. Rye, *op. cit.* (Extract from Van Meteren's *History of the Netherlands*, edit. of 1614, trans. from the Dutch.)
13. *Letters of Horace Walpole*, ed. by Peter Cunningham, 1861–6, vol. III, p. 429. To George Montagu, from Strawberry Hill, Aug. 20th, 1761.
14. Cunningham, *op. cit.*, vol. III, p. 340. To the Earl of Strafford, from Strawberry Hill, Sept. 4th, 1760.
15. *Horace Walpole's Journals of Visits to Country Seats etc.*, ed. by Paget Toynbee, *Walpole Society*, vol. XVI, 1927–8.
16. M. A. Tierney, *History and Antiquities of Arundel*, 1834, vol. II, pp. 729–30 (appendix No. 2).
17. *Memoirs of the Verney Family*, by Frances Parthenope, Lady Verney, and Margaret M. Verney, 1892–4, vol. III, p. 50.
18. George Chapman, *May-Day*, 1611.
19. Rye, *op. cit.* (Descriptive pamphlet, printed at Antwerp, 1604, trans. from the Spanish by W. B. Rye.)
20. *Nugae Antiquae:* being a collection of original papers in prose and verse by Sir. J. H. and others, 1804 edition, vol. I, p. 202.
21. *Diary of a West Country Physician*, ed. by Edmund Hobhouse, M.D., 1934.
22. Verney, *op. cit.*, vol. I, pp. 255–6.
23. Verney, *op. cit.*, vol. II, pp. 285–6.
24. See also for this chapter, and succeeding chapters, *The Dictionary of English Furniture*, by Percy Macquoid and Ralph Edwards, 1924–7; revised edit. by Ralph Edwards, 1954. The *Dictionary* is a comprehensive work of reference indispensable to any study of this subject.

Note. The majority of the drawings illustrating this chapter (Figs. 1–20) are based on pieces of furniture in the Victoria & Albert Museum.

CHAPTER TWO

THE EARLY WALNUT PERIOD (1660–1690)

'THIS day the month ends ... and all the world in a merry mood because of the King's coming.' Thus wrote Pepys at the end of May 1660, when he expressed the feelings of everyman. The restoration of Charles II to the throne was, in effect, a welcome revolution; and such exultation, although perhaps short-lived, was general in the country.

With the Restoration, foreign influences in furniture design were at once predominant. The heavy oak furniture of the preceding period found small favour at court, and there was no pronounced development of native styles. Instead, the fashions abroad were reflected in furniture and decoration at home as in architecture, and with much benefit. A taste for luxury, which had been acquired by the Royalist exiles, was stimulated both by our admiration for the manners of the court of Louis XIV, in common with most of Europe, and by our commercial intercourse with the Dutch. The arrival of French and Dutch immigrants in the country further contributed towards a changed state of affairs. The considerable quantity of fine oak furniture, of sound construction, which was destroyed in the Great Fire of London was perforce replaced, but often by walnut pieces of entirely different character. (It is estimated that more than 10,000 dwelling houses were lost in the Fire.) 'Joyners, cabinetmakers, and the like, who from very vulgar and pitiful artists,' wrote Evelyn, 'are now come to produce works as curious for the fiting, and admirable for their dexterity in contriving, as any we meet with abroad.'[1] Fortunes, indeed, were spent in the furnishings of houses, and such extravagance spread surely to the middle classes.

Defoe has stated that in the summer of 1665, when the plague was raging in London and all who could afford to do so had fled from the city, trade was brought to a standstill; he then listed the classes of people who suffered as a result of this: 'all master-workmen in manufactures, especially such as belonged to ornament, and the less necessary parts of the people's dress, clothes, and furniture for houses ... upholsterers, joiners, cabinet-makers, looking-glass makers, and innumerable trades which depend upon such as these; – I say, the master-workmen in such stopped their work, dismissed their journeymen and workmen, and all their dependents.'[2] There is, in his words, sufficient confirmation of the recent growth of the industry.

Floral marquetry, which well exemplifies the exuberant nature of Restoration taste, would seem to have been a Dutch importation of about 1670. It was brilliant, decorative, and colourful. This type retained favour in England until about 1690 – and on long-case clocks well into the eighteenth century. Floral marquetry was applied to such pieces as the oblong table with twist legs, the cabinet on stand or base, the chest-of-drawers or chest-on-stand, the mirror frame and the lace box (Pls. 13 and 16). The technique of marquetry, distinct from the earlier practice of inlaying different coloured woods *into* a ground wood such as oak or walnut, consisted in the application of an overlay of variegated veneer *on to* a prepared carcase wood. Floral patterns and designs of flowers with birds were at first reserved in panels (Pl. 12); all-over decoration of the surface followed (Pl. 13). Early English and Dutch pieces coincided in appearance; but, twenty years later, the patterns of English work, finer and more complex than the Dutch, often incorporated cupids and acanthus leaf *motifs*. Light woods were set on a dark ground – walnut, lignum vitae, coromandel or ebony, which were effective as a base for the brilliantly coloured flowers and leaves of ivory, stained green. Many different coloured and unusual woods, increasingly imported from the East and West Indies, were used. Of the number were the fruitwoods, beech, yew, bog oak, sycamore, holly and, for flowers, orange and citron. The occasional employment of a light ground, as also the use of shading and a crude contrast of ground and ornament appeared in Dutch work. A coarse and debased form of floral marquetry persisted in Holland throughout the course of the next century.

The beds made for the Royal palaces and for state apartments in the houses of the nobility were excessively expensive, particularly when one considers the high purchasing power of money at that time. It had become customary for Royalty to give audience in the bedchamber. Ladies, too, held receptions whilst in bed. John Evelyn, attending Charles II one morning in 1683, recorded following his Majesty 'thro' the gallerie ... into the Dutchesse of Portsmouth's *dressing-roome* within her bed-chamber, where she was in her morning loose garment, her maids combing her, newly out of her bed, his Majesty and the gallants standing about her ...'.[3] The bedchamber as a consequence was filled with rich furniture and many costly trifles. The light and satirical commentary in verse on the fashions of her day entitled *A Voyage to Marryland, or, The Ladies' Dressing Room* is informative in this respect.*

'You furnish her apartment
With Moreclack tapestry, damask bed,
Or velvet richly embroidered:
Branches,† *brassero,*† *cassolets,*†
A *cofre-fort,*† and cabinets,
Vasas of silver, porcelan, store
To set, and range about the floor:
The Chimney furniture of plate
(For iron's now quite out of date);

* Written by John Evelyn, or possibly by his daughter, Mary.

† '*Branches:* Hanging candlesticks, like those used in churches.'
'*Brasiere:* A large vessel, or moving-hearth of silver, for coals, transportable into any room, much used in Spain.'
'*Cassolet:* Perfuming pot, or censer.'
'*Cofre-fort:* A strong box of some precious or hard wood, &c bound with gilded ribs.'

Tea-table, skreens, trunks, and stand,
Large looking-glass, richly japann'd;
An hanging shelf, to which belongs
Romances, plays, and amorous songs;
Repeating clocks the hour to show
When to the play 'tis time to go,
In pompous coach ...'[4] *

It has been suggested that the marriage of Charles II with Catherine of Braganza resulted in a temporary vogue for open walnut bedsteads in the Portuguese manner, constructed with ornamental posts and rails of spiral turning and an elaborate carved back. These were designed without ceiling or tester. There is, however, no evidence that this was in fact the case.

Oak bedsteads of box form, with panelled head and foot ends and with curtains which were used to close the sides, corresponded to a type in general use on the Continent, while low or 'stump' bedsteads of panelled construction and simple truckle bedsteads on wheels (which, as the term 'truckle to' implies, were formerly used by servants and which could be stowed conveniently under some other piece of furniture during the day) must have existed in most households. 'Trussing' or folding bedsteads were taken from house to house when travelling.

The small tables with drawers which at this time were probably the type most favoured as toilet tables in bed or dressing rooms were made in walnut and oak and, according to contemporary inventories, were covered with a carpet or a cloth, sometimes referred to as a 'toilet'. They vary considerably in style; no one kind was yet definitely termed a 'dressing' table. Two or three drawers were usual; these contained the numerous cosmetics used by men and women alike. Painting, rougeing, and patching were fashionable and elaborate sets for the dressing table, comprising boxes for the combs and brushes, powder and perfumes, etc., were to

* *The Fop-Dictionary* 'for instruction of the unlearned' was provided as an appendix to the poem for the elucidation of the 'Hard and Foreign Names and Terms of the Art Cosmetick'.

be encountered in silver plate or in Japan work. Among the many modish accessories listed in *The Ladies' Dressing-Room* were the

> '... implements,
> Of toilet plate, gilt and emboss'd,
> And several other things of cost.
> The table miroir, one glue pot,
> ... boxes more,
> For powders, patches, waters store,
> In silver flasks, or bottles, cups
> Cover'd, or open, to wash chaps;
> ...
> Baskets of *fil'gran*,* long and round,
> Or if *Japonian* † to be found, ...'[5]

Jewels were kept in caskets of various shapes and fine materials, with flat or domed lids, lined handsomely in brightly coloured silks. Decoration of these caskets was often in the form of shell or filigree work. Frequently mirrors were set in the lids.

Many of the mirrors with supports which were made to stand on the dressing tables formed part of the toilet set. Some silver-framed examples were chased and engraved in the Chinese manner and stump work or japanning was not unusual.

The extensive use made of walnut throughout the late Stuart period necessitated the importation of additional supplies from the Continent (from France especially) and from Virginia. Both the 'English' walnut (pale brown in colour, with brown and black veining) and the 'black' variety (grey-brown in colour, with dark markings and veining) were grown in England, many of the trees attaining considerable size. The 'black' wood was the harder and less liable to attack by worm.

Walnut wood was variously used in the cabinet work of

* '*Fil-grain'd:* Dressing-boxes, baskets, or whatever else is made of silver wire-work.'

† '*Japonian:* Anything varnished with laccar, or China polishing, or that is old or fantastical.'

the Stuart period, both in the solid and as a veneer. (1) 'Straight cut' walnut was generally resorted to for work in the solid. Walnut is said to be 'straight cut' when cut lengthways from the trunk; the grain then follows the length of the plank, and the wood lacks full figure. (2) By cutting across the smaller branches of the tree at an oblique angle a decorative oval figure can be obtained; and the small, thin sections produced by this means, when arranged to form a flat pattern, are particularly suitable for veneering. 'Oyster shell', as it is called, was much in vogue until it was superseded by (3) 'burr walnut' veneer early in the eighteenth century (Fig. 21).

Cross-banded borders were made use of in many pieces. Such borders are commonly found on the fronts of larger drawers or on cabinet fronts. This border, which contrasted with the ground veneer, was made up of short sections of veneer in each of which the grain ran across the width and not the length of the strips. An inside banding of 'herring bone' pattern added to the decorative effect thus contrived (Pl. 14). The width of border tended to decrease as the century advanced.

Walnut, with its rich and varied figuring, and laburnum, as a most satisfactory alternative, were selected for many of the finer pieces of veneered furniture; while cedar, olive, kingwood (then termed 'princes wood') and coromandel were in subsidiary use. The geometrical patterning of oyster shell parquetry was defined by lines of inlaid holly or box wood (Fig. 21).

During the Restoration period, a most ornamental grouping of side table, mirror, and candlestands was introduced and developed. Movable candlestands, *torchères* or *guéridons* were frequently made in pairs. The tops of the stands were usually of veneered walnut, octagonal in shape, and of tray form; their plain baluster or twist stems in walnut, elm, fruitwood or olive were supported on a tripod base. Their height varied between 3 and 5 feet. Gilt, silvered, and marquetry stands also enjoyed a degree of popularity, and some examples were very ornate. The tapered stem is a feature of later stands and was introduced shortly before *c.* 1690.

Silver chandeliers were rare; brass was commonly employed. Mention is made in 1667 of a crystal chandelier

Figure 21 – Cabinet on stand, decorated with a parquetry of oyster shell veneers; the cabinet, with small drawers and central cupboard, is enclosed by two hinged doors, and supported on a stand of five spiral turned legs, tied by flat stretchers. Late seventeenth century

at Whitehall. Silver wall sconces, however, contributed much to the richness of decoration of late Stuart interiors and considerable skill and care went to their making. The screen, or back plate, was variously decorated and was sometimes engraved or embossed with flowers or foliage. In one form of sconce, the candlestick is held aloft on a branch in the form of a human arm or supported by a hand alone. Numerous plainer examples in pewter, brass, and in enamel have survived (as is the case with movable candlesticks); it may be recalled that Pepys in his *Diary*, in the year 1662, refers to his new 'pewter sconces'.

Some silver candlesticks were made with a stem of cluster column form. Wax candles, newly introduced into private houses in the late seventeenth century and a considerable item of expense, would probably have been burned in these. In 1664 Pepys recorded that he began 'to burn wax candles ... at the office, to try the change, and to see whether the smoke offends like that of tallow candles'.[6] Towards the end of the century the grease pan was placed lower on the stem of the candlestick.

Cast brass was commonly used for the andirons which raised the logs above the hearth. Alternatively andirons of silver and, in the country districts, of wrought iron are to be found. The coloured enamels applied as decoration to the brass included a light turquoise, white, green, purple, red and black.

Chairs of Charles II's reign were often of walnut or beech, and were constructed with backs and seats of caning – which was at first of noticeably coarse mesh. The caned panel (or panels) of the back was framed by turned uprights connected by a cresting rail tenoned between them. Caned chairs were first produced in both England and Holland about the year 1665, and gradually displaced in fashion the more expensive 'Turkey-work' and other chairs made by the upholsterers. At the Restoration, a low oblong back was in vogue and, for a short while, chairs bore a close resemblance to those depicted in the paintings of interiors by the popular Dutch and Flemish masters of the middle years of the century and to those in use at home during the immediately preceding period of the Commonwealth, except that spiral, or twist, turning (also an introduction of about 1665), or a combination of spiral and ball turning, was used for legs, rails and stretchers, and a framed caning began to replace the use of velvet fabrics, leather and Turkey work (Pl. 10A). Chairs were said to be turned 'all over', and were made in sets of perhaps two armchairs and six or more single chairs. The part played in chair-making by the turner was now very considerable. From the first years of the new reign the back tended to become higher and then to be enriched with shallow carving. The Royal crown, sometimes flanked by *amorini*; eagles' heads; flowers and foliage; husks and rosettes – all these were early favourite *motifs* of carved decoration. That of cupids supporting the crown (Fig. 29) was particularly prevalent and perhaps may have been intended to suggest the happy Restoration of the King. After 1665, a flat front stretcher rail, carved to correspond with the deeper cresting, succeeded that with a plain spiral twist. Some chairs show a strong continental influence, more especially those elaborate examples which were intended for the large houses.* Many of the chairs were dished for flat squab cushions, the front legs then projecting above the framing of the seat so as to hold the cushion in position (Pl. 10B). The arms of armchairs have usually a very graceful sweep and scrolled ends. Beech wood, painted black, was commonly used for plainer chairs, being a much less costly wood than walnut. Innumerable beech chairs of the period survive, despite the very perishable nature of this wood. In some upholstered chairs use was made of the fine damasks and figured velvets of Italy, and of tasselled fringes, and many chairs which were originally caned have now been renovated by means of a cushioned back.

The design of chairs made during the latter part of the reign of Charles II became increasingly elaborate. Whereas in early examples the carving was on a solid ground, pierced work later became usual; and the frame of the back panel, as well as the cresting rail and front stretcher, was carved (Pl. 10B). After about 1670, baluster turning enjoyed

* Richard Price, joiner, who supplied walnut chairs to the Royal Palaces in 1681 and 1683, described them in his account as being 'turned of the Dutch turning'.

renewed favour and sometimes replaced the spiral twist. Front legs were frequently scrolled and the ornamental S-scroll form became a prominent decorative feature. By about 1685 an arched cresting, replacing the earlier square shape, was supported *on* the uprights, instead of being, as formerly, tenoned between the squares of the balusters (Pl. 10C). The scrolled 'Portuguese' front stretcher was sometimes used in combination with inward turning scroll feet. The backs were narrower and very tall, and seats, often upholstered and supported on turned cupped legs linked by serpentine X-shaped stretchers with an ornamental central finial, were smaller. Though at this time chairs were not so strongly constructed, the proportions were graceful.

Upholstered armchairs with wings were introduced in the reign of Charles II. A few examples still survive with their original velvet covering. The carved woodwork of chairs was gilded and painted in emulation of French models, and the chairs were covered with velvets or needlework, with rich effect. Often the curtains and hangings, if of damask or velvet, were matched with the coverings on the furniture. The cost of the stuffs, mostly imported from Italy, was entirely disproportionate to the value of the frames on which they were used. Wool needlework on canvas, as an alternative, was frequently worked for furniture by the gentlewomen of the period, and was, moreover, an exceedingly durable material. Curtains and hangings were embroidered in crewel work on a twill ground, especially during the half-century from about 1650: bold and effective leaf designs were shown in strong blues, greens, and browns in imitation of the printed cottons which had been brought from Masulipatam by the East India Company.

Tapestries were hung in many of the great houses (Pl. 17). In England the Mortlake tapestry industry was revived in 1662 and received a yearly subsidy of £1,000; subsequently looms were set up at Lambeth. Their production was excellent, although Evelyn has praised the French tapestries in the apartments of Louise de Kerouaille,

Duchess of Portsmouth, at Whitehall Palace as being 'for designe, tendernesse of worke, and incomparable imitation of the best paintings, beyond any' he had ever beheld. 'Some pieces had Versailles, St German's, and other palaces of the French King, with huntings, figures, and landskips, exotiq fowls, and all to the life rarely don.' [7]

Oak was extensively used, in particular by country makers, and oak panel back chairs of a traditional type were made throughout the period. Many were of pleasingly austere appearance, although some later examples were over-elaborately carved. The back panel was sometimes set high above the seat; and it is not unusual to find twist turning employed for the supports and front stretchers.

A large proportion of children's chairs have survived, presumably owing to their solid construction. They were made in oak in imitation of the panel back chairs of their elders.

Derbyshire and Yorkshire chairs of the early years of the Restoration were comparatively lightly made (Figs. 22 and 23). The design of the back took the form of an arcading of turned balusters resting on a central rail, sometimes with the addition of knobbed finials. Alternatively, two heavy crescent-shaped carved rails of distinctive form were substituted for the arcading. Frequently a man's head, with a pointed beard (a similar *motif* to that present on stoneware of the period), was carved on the top rail. The uprights, often bearing split baluster decoration, terminated in inward turning scrolls. Some chairs were dished for squab cushions. Baluster turning was common to those oak chairs which were upholstered in leather.

Day beds or couches became very popular during the Restoration period. Being fashionable in court circles, they were made also for large houses throughout the country; but of the large number produced, comparatively few have survived. The day bed was more usually of walnut, sometimes of beech painted black, with seats and back rests caned and the uprights, stretchers, and legs of spiral form. The day bed was often supplied to match a set of chairs and stools; consequently the back rest resembled the chair back in a squatter form, and in the detail of its carved decoration followed a parallel course of evolution to that of the chair. The provision of a long squab cushion or mattress and of

Figure 22 – Chair, of Yorkshire or Derbyshire type; the filling of the back within the uprights (decorated with split balusters) consists of two crescent-shaped rails, heavily carved; the front legs are turned and tied by a turned stretcher rail. Third quarter of the seventeenth century

various head cushions rendered the day bed comparatively comfortable. The rake of the head piece was in many cases made adjustable by means of hooks and chains.

The walnut day bed illustrated in plate 11 has flat stretchers 'carved with Boyes and Crownes' and this conventional device is repeated in the pierced crestings. The style of ornament suggests that the piece was made about 1670. Day beds with double ends are extremely rare; this example has a further unusual feature in that the feet are fashioned in the shape of a lion's paw. Oak day beds of a plainer sort, in some cases upholstered in leather, which was

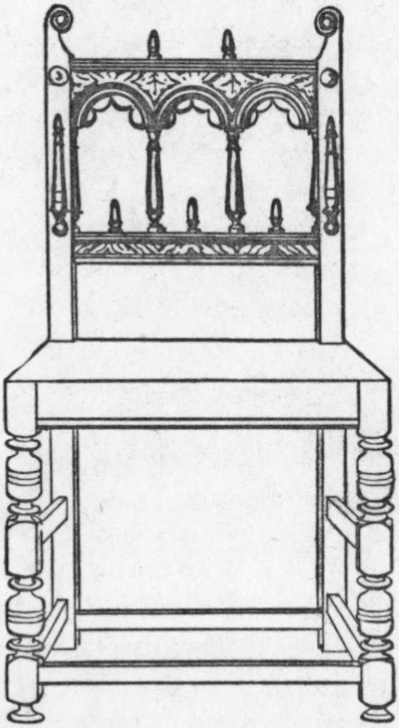

Figure 23 – Chair, of Yorkshire or Derbyshire type; the arcading of the back rests on a horizontal rail above the seat level; the front legs are turned. Third quarter of the seventeenth century

stretched over the framework and lightly padded, had not much to commend them on the score of comfort.

Some of the later upholstered day beds of walnut, introduced towards the end of the reign of Charles II, were carved with great elaboration and covered in richly coloured damasks and silks. Caned back panels and seats continued to be made throughout the period and, as with chairs, the mesh of the caning gradually became finer. The hinged back, on the other hand, was perhaps found to be a weakness in construction. In later examples the back was a fixture, and the piece was frequently constructed with eight legs of scrolled form.

The small settee in the form of a double chair, with caned seat and turned and carved woodwork, which is now extremely rare, was more or less superseded by a comfortable variety of high-backed upholstered couch. The settee, again, was normally made as part of a large set of seating furniture. After a short space of time, wide wings were added and backs become lower. Padded arms added appreciably to the comfort of the piece.

Evelyn looked back with regret to the days of his forefathers when 'they had cupboards of ancient useful plate, whole chests of damask for the table ... and the sturdy oaken bedstead, and furniture of the house, lasted one whole century; the shovelboard, and other long tables, both in hall and parlour, were as fixed as the freehold; nothing was moveable save joynt-stools, the black jacks, silver tankards, and bowls ...'. He deplored our adoption of foreign manners and the 'luxury (more than Asiatick ...)' which had prevailed and was 'corrupting ancient simplicity'.[8] Furniture was desired to be something more than useful in the houses of the rich. Decorative marquetry pieces had attained an extreme popularity; *guéridons*, which were essentially ornamental pieces, and cheval fire-screens with ornately carved and gilded frames, and with panels of colourful velvet, taffeta or tapestry work, were both recent introductions; many mirrors of the finest quality were still imported – and for large sums; and much furniture was gilded in imitation of the taste which had obtained at Versailles. Evelyn, however, moved in the small world of the court. In general, change was gradual throughout the country. Oaken chests and cupboards followed the traditional form. In the seventeenth century and well into the eighteenth, fixed and draw-top dining tables of oak and yew were supplied with accompanying sets of joined stools.

The household possessions of the ordinary country gentleman were largely inherited; the bulk of his furniture had already served earlier generations. Robert Nicholas, Chief Baron of the Exchequer under the Commonwealth, lived on for a few years after 1660 in retirement in Wiltshire. The inventory of goods at that time in his house at Seend, near Devizes, is informative if only by reason of the traditional nature of most of the items listed therein.[9] The compiler of the inventory attached importance to the hangings and fabrics of the various rooms; and chairs, stools, and couches were, as was then usual, particularized by their upholstery. The hall was furnished with a long trestle table with a leather cover, a livery cupboard, more than a score of chairs and stools (one chair described as having twisted legs, and therefore a contemporary piece, and one other, with panelled back, of 'wainscoat'), a leather couch (perhaps made during the Commonwealth period), a round table, three green carpets (covers) and seven cushions of 'Turkey' work. The trestle table and the livery cupboard (Fig. 17) were both outmoded pieces at that date. The furniture of the parlour was very similar, with nearly corresponding items and included three carpets of the 'Turkey' work with which the house had been liberally supplied, probably at a recent date. It is likely that Judge Nicholas' private chamber was situated above the parlour; herein were two bedsteads with green hangings, a couch, a round table, a stand for water, and as many as thirteen chairs and stools. One of the two bedsteads of the main guest chamber was of the wheeled truckle variety, so constructed as to be run under the large bed during the day, and perhaps intended for the use of a body servant. The six remaining rooms were scantily furnished; all had bedsteads with feather pillows and mattresses, and one, by the provision of a needlework chair, a screen, round table and chest of drawers, may be surmised to have been in occupation.

The stool was perhaps still the customary form of seat. In *A Journal of the Plague Year*, however, Daniel Defoe, describing the difficulties experienced by a band of persons in flight from the plague-stricken city and encamped in Epping Forest, relates that 'the gentlemen who dwelt in the country round about ... sent them chairs, stools, tables, and such household things as they wanted', with the implication that chairs, even perhaps of the cruder sort, were not wanting in the country at that time. Stools in walnut and beech, caned or from *c.* 1675 upholstered, existed concurrently with those coarser examples having a wooden seat with shaped underframing and turned baluster or columnar legs (Pl. 10B and C). For the wealthy, stools were supplied as part of a great set of seating furniture, or to match the state beds, and while varying in shape (being square, rectangular, and, rarely, circular), their development corresponded exactly in appropriate features to that noticed in chairs. They were covered with identical fabrics and embroidered in gold and silver thread. The front and back stretcher were usually carved; stools were not designed as wall furniture.

The *tabouret* etiquette was strictly observed at court and, on occasions of ceremony, in private houses. In the course of his *Travels through England* in 1669, Cosmo III, Grand Duke of Tuscany, visited Wilton. Count Lorenzo Magalotti then recorded: 'There was prepared for his highness, at the head of the table, an arm-chair, which he insisted upon the young lady's taking; upon which the earl instantly drew forward another similar one, in which the serene prince sat, in the highest place; all the rest sitting upon stools. His highness obliged the earl to take the place nearest to him, though in his own house; and there were at table, besides all his highness's gentlemen, the sheriff and several other gentlemen, in all sixteen. The dinner was superb, and served in a noble style; they remained at table about two hours.' Again at Althorp in the same year 'his highness sat in the place of honor, in an arm-chair, he having previously desired that my lady, the wife of the earl, might be seated in a similar one; the earl also was obliged by his highness to take his place close to him, the gentlemen of his retinue sitting separately upon stools'.[10] In some large houses children and guests of inferior standing were seated on stools until as late a date as *c.* 1750. This formal practice was observed in imitation of court etiquette.

Long stools with six or even eight legs continued to be made. Footstools were similar in style to the larger stools used as seats.

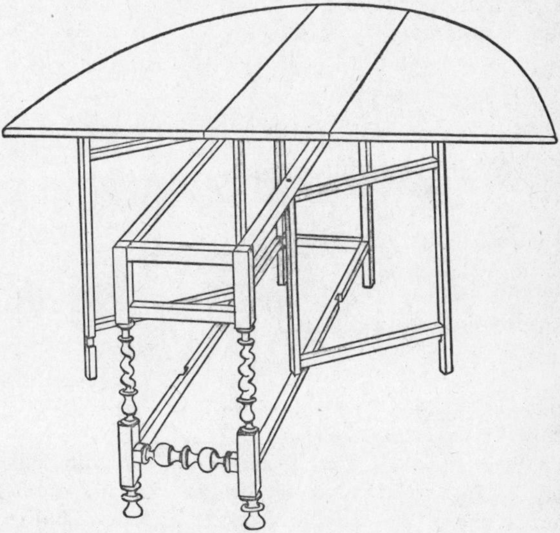

Figure 24 – Gate-leg table (showing construction), with twist-turned supports and turned stretchers. Second half of the seventeenth century

After the Restoration it became fashionable for meals to be eaten in rooms set aside for dining; the older draw-top tables (some, *c.* 1660, with fluted frieze and turned baluster legs) were gradually replaced by oval or round gate-legged tables in oak or, more rarely, walnut (Fig. 24). The tables were usually constructed with two flaps and provided with two, and sometimes four, gates; and leg turning was very varied (Fig. 25). Often a large company dined intimately at several small tables – a French custom which was adopted because of its greater convenience. It would appear from the 1679 inventory that the 'Great Eating Room', at Ham House, converted into the 'Gallery' early in the eighteenth century, contained as many as eight small tables of cedar wood and eighteen walnut chairs of crimson velvet.[11] Gate-legged tables, however, were made in all sizes, some to seat a large number of people. Small fruitwood tables were probably not intended for dining.

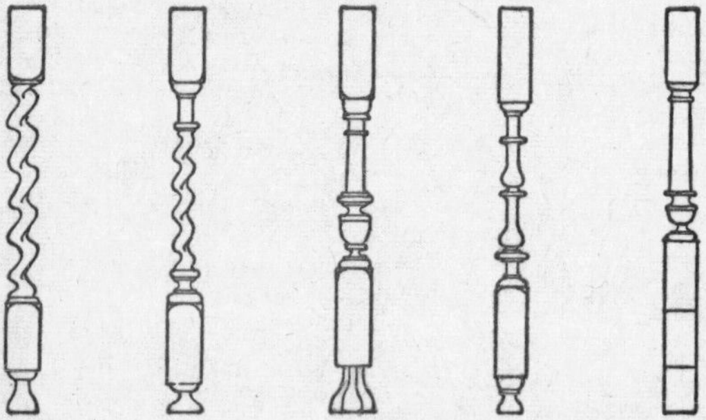

Figure 25 – Details of turning – the supports of gate-leg tables

Count Magalotti's description of the splendid banquet given on the eve of departure by his master, Cosmo III, Grand Duke of Tuscany, in honour of King Charles II, treats of a formal yet singular occasion. '... the saloon ... the largest apartment in the house ... suitably ornamented, was chosen for the supper, in preference to the others which the house contained. From the ceiling was suspended a chandelier of rock chrystal with lighted tapers. In the middle of the room the table was set out, being of an oval figure, convenient both for seeing and conversing. ... Having sat down, his majesty called the Duke of York to set by him on his right hand, and the prince on his left; ... [others] to the number of seventeen, were accommodated round the table, some on one side and some on the other, and there were as many knives and forks, which, when they had sat down, they found before them, arranged in a fanciful and elegant manner. The rest of his highness's gentlemen, with some who belonged to the king's court and that of the duke, stood round the table, near their masters. ... The supper was served up in eighty magnificent dishes; many of which were decorated with other smaller ones, filled with various delicious meats. To the service of fruit, succeeded a most excellent course of confectionary, both those of Portugal and other countries famous for the choiceness of their sweetmeats, which was in all respects on a par with the supper that preceded it. But scarcely was it set upon the table, when the whole was carried off and plundered by the people who came to see the spectacle of the entertainment; nor was the presence of the king sufficient to restrain them from the pillage of these very delicate viands, much less his majesty's soldiers armed with carabines, who guarded the entrance of the saloon ...'.[12] The spectacle was no doubt an extraordinary one. Magalotti observed in England and did not scruple to remark elsewhere in his account: 'a great want of that neatness and gentility which is practised in Italy; for, on the English table, there are no forks, nor vessels to supply water for the hands, which are washed in a basin full of water, that serves for all the company ...'.[13]

Gaming was prevalent during the Restoration. Dicing (for high stakes), ombre (a game for three players), quadrille, piquet, basset, and loo, as well as chess and backgammon, were all popular. Nevertheless, few of the gaming tables doubtless made during the period are extant. Their rarity may in part be explained by the fact that cards were still played on any small table, covered with a 'carpet' or cloth.

Similarly, few shovel – or shuffle – board tables remain. The game was, however, played throughout the century – mainly in the countryside. Tables remained *in situ* in the panelled halls or galleries of the larger country houses. Owing to the great length of table top required, elm was frequently chosen as the wood for their construction.

Tables of various woods were used indiscriminately for writing, tea, or for cards. Those with tray tops were probably used as work tables, especially for the bead work which was then a fashionable diversion.

At first oak was used in the construction of small tables of ornamental appearance, with stretchers and uprights of spiral turning, which in many cases were intended to stand in the middle of a room. After about 1670 oyster-shell parquetry of walnut, olive, or laburnum, or the employment of marquetry decoration became usual in the case of many

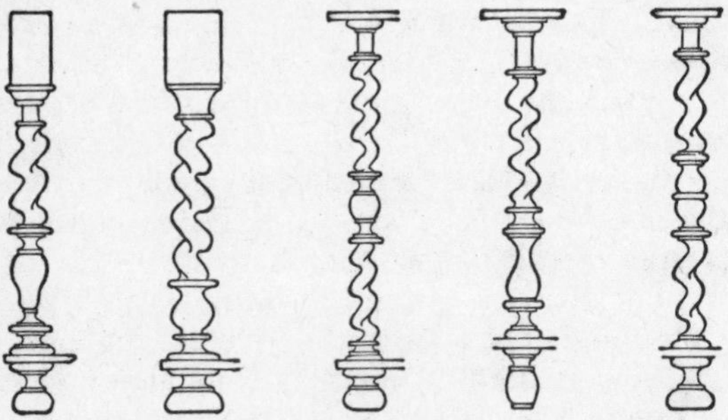

Figure 26 – Details of twist-turning – the supports of side tables and stands

of the finer examples of these centre tables. Some small tables were made with rectangular caned tops; they formed perhaps part of large suites of cane furniture.

'Side' tables were similar in form to 'centre' tables, but ornamented on three sides only (Pl. 12). The veneered oblong top was supported on four or five legs united by flat shaped stretchers, also veneered – and cross banded. In front, one or two drawers were contained in the frieze. As with other pieces, baluster succeeded twist turning (Fig. 26) and was itself followed by a revived baluster turning. Fluted pillar legs, with square or mushroom cappings, were fashionable in the last decade of the century. The S-scrolled form was rare. In certain plainer tables with tops veneered in straight cut walnut, the legs are of elm or fruitwood.

Until the early seventeenth century Venice had enjoyed what had virtually amounted to a monopoly in the making of glass plates for mirrors. A patent taken out by Sir Robert Mansel, however, for their manufacture in England in 1618 had proved successful. With the help of 'many expert strangers from foreign parts beyond the seas' he had made satisfactory looking-glass plates. The venture had been conducted on a large scale at Southwark and for a few years (1620–4) importation of the Venetian glass had been prohibited by law. Renewed activity after the Restoration led to the establishment of the Glass House at Vauxhall. The promoters were assisted by foreigners in this enterprise – as was Colbert in the manufactory established in Paris in 1665, when a party of Venetian immigrants had been installed in the Faubourg St Antoine. Free importation of glass into England had again been denied the previous year. Apparently prices were then much lower, for in December 1664 Pepys recounted going by coach with his wife to the Old Exchange and there buying 'a very fair glasse' which cost him '£5. 5*s*., and 6*s*. for the hooks'.[14] It was not so long since £40 had been asked Sir Ralph Verney for a great glass from Venice.[15]

On 19 September, 1676, John Evelyn recorded in his *Diary*: 'We also saw the Duke of Buckingham's Glasse-worke, where they made huge vases of mettal as cleare, ponderous and thick as chrystal; also looking-glasses far larger and better than any that come from Venice.' [16] The latter statement was open to question. The plates were small and in all likelihood did not exceed 3 feet in length. This was at Vauxhall; on a visit to 'the Italian Glass-house at Greenewich' some years earlier (1673), Evelyn had found the glass to be 'blown of finer mettal than that of Murano at Venice'.[17]

The King's favourite, the Duchess of Portsmouth, possessed the luxury of a glass-lined room. It was not unexampled. Celia Fiennes, in the course of her journeys to various great country houses, mentioned seeing a similar use made of the material at Chatsworth: '... at the end of the dineing roome is a large door all of Looking-glass, in great pannells all diamond cutt, this is just opposite to the doores that runs into the drawing roome and bed chamber and closet, so it shews the roomes to look all double ...'.[18]

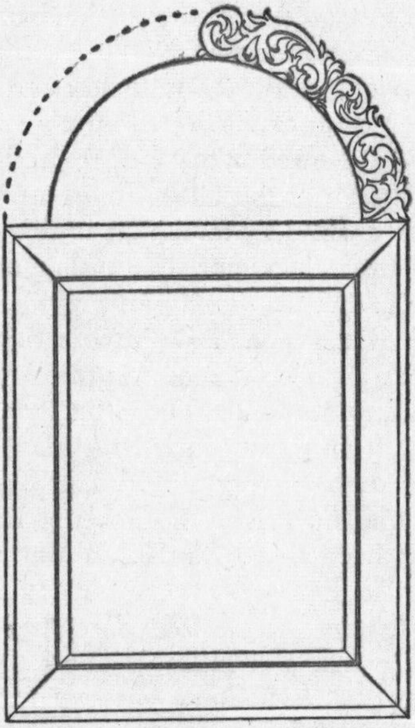

Figure 27 – Mirror frame, of convex section, surmounted by a pediment of semi-circular shape. Late seventeenth century

And this employment of looking-glass was again noted by her in rooms at the house of Admiral Russell, victor at La Hogue and newly created Lord Orford,[19] which was situated about three miles from Newmarket.

The frames of the early square or oblong mirrors were of plain half-round moulded section, broad and in strong projection (Fig. 27). They were the work of the joiner or cabinet maker, in distinction to the carver. Examples are found with or without a decorative semi-circular cresting piece or hood which was attached to the body by means of two wooden tongues. Frames were made in straight cut walnut veneer, in oyster-shell parquetry of walnut, kingswood, olive or laburnum, in floral (and later, arabesque) marquetry, lacquer, tortoiseshell, ebony, enamels, chased silver, and in the amateur stumpwork or beadwork. A rich appearance was imparted to mirrors by virtue of the nature of these various materials used in the construction of the frame.

Picture frames, by contrast, were often ornately and floridly carved with a wide variety of designs (Pl. 18). Acanthus leaf, twisted ribbon and water leaf patterns, and the employment of flat auricular scrolling were of frequent occurrence. Carved gilt frames were indeed costly items. The name of Grinling Gibbons, 1648–1720, is associated with much elaborate carved woodwork. He was employed by Wren at St Paul's and the City churches, at the Royal palaces and the town and country houses of the nobility, but most of the decorative carving that survives in Gibbons' manner is by members of the master's school.*

* John Evelyn, seemingly, was responsible for introducing the young Grinling Gibbons to Charles II: 'This day [18th Jan., 1671] I first acquainted his Majesty with that incomparable young man Gibbon, whom I had lately met with in an obscure place by meere accident as I was walking neere a poore solitary thatched house, in a field in our parish, neere Say[e]s Court [Deptford]. I found him shut in; but looking in at the window, I perceiv'd him carving that large cartoon or crucifix of Tintoret, a copy of which I had myselfe brought from Venice, where the original painting remaines. I asked if I might enter; he open'd the door civilly to me, and I saw him about such a work as for ye curiosity of handling, drawing, and studious exactnesse I never had before seene in all my travells. I questioned him why he worked in such an obscure and lonesome place; he told me it was that he might apply himselfe to his profession without interruption, and wondred not a little how I had found him out. I asked if he was unwilling to be made knowne to some greate man, for that I believed it might turn to his profit; he answer'd he was yet but a beginner, but would not be sorry to sell off that piece; on demanding the price, he said 100*l*. In good earnest the very frame was worth the money, there being nothing in nature so tender and delicate as

Gibbons was a wood-carver of quite remarkable ability and in his hands frames decorated with profuse and heavy ornament (a medley of flying *amorini* and swags of fruit and flowers, naturalistically treated in high relief) were lightly rendered, with great delicacy and skill (Pl. 18). Much of his work was as ornament to rooms panelled in oak, walnut or olive wood, and was executed in lime or pear wood which, uncoloured and disengaged from the background, showed to great advantage. His reputation remained high after death. Horace Walpole's description of Petworth may be cited: 'There is one room gloriously flounced all round with whole-length pictures, with much the finest carving of Gibbons that ever my eyes beheld. There are birds absolutely feathered; and two antique vases with bas-relieves, as perfect and beautiful as if they were carved by a Grecian master.' [22] Grinling Gibbons was 'Master Carver to Charles II'. He was, as well, an able draughtsman and designer. He and his followers frequently used limewood, which has an even texture and works crisply and easily. A number of elaborately carved tables in his style are constructed in this wood, then newly introduced into England. Vertue was of the opinion that though 'a most excellent Carver in wood he was neither well skilld or practized in Marble or in Brass – for which works he imployd the best Artists he

the flowers and festoons about it, and yet the worke was very strong; in the piece were more than 100 figures of men, &c. I found he was likewise musical, and very civil, sober, and discreete in his discourse. There was onely an old woman in the house. So desiring leave to visite him sometimes, I went away.

'Of this young artist, together with my manner of finding him out, I acquainted the King, and begg'd that he would give me leave to bring him and his worke to Whitehall, for that I would adventure my reputation with his Majesty that he had never seene any thing approch it, and that he would be exceedingly pleased, and employ him. The King said he would himselfe go see him. This was the first notice his Majestie ever had of Mr Gibbon.' [20] The carving was not, in fact, bought by the King. But, Evelyn was instrumental in bringing Gibbons to the notice of Christopher Wren and setting him to a career followed with merited success for a space of fifty years. 'From thence,' remarked George Vertue, antiquary and engraver, 'Mr Gibbons took his Rise.' [21]

coud procure' [23]; and names Francis Bird, Dievot, Laurens, and Nolder as being among his one-time workmen.

Musical instruments included virginals, spinets, and harpsichords. Unfortunately, very few examples are now extant of the rectangular virginal; the spinet, belatedly introduced from the Continent, ousted it from favour. The cases of these instruments were usually of oak, and were about 5 feet in length. The insides of the lids were decorated.

Linen and clothes were, by the majority of people, still stored in chests. Some of oak, plain and simply carved, were decorated with applied balusters; others were inlaid with bone and mother-of-pearl, and occasionally partridge wood. Walnut chests were often inlaid with coloured woods.

Many leather-covered travelling trunks, studded and patterned with brass nails, have survived.

Some of the early oak chests of drawers (about 4 feet in height) closely resemble those chests, placed on stands and fitted with a long drawer, from which they were evolved. The ornamentation was similar – use being made of ivory, bone, or of mother-of-pearl inlay, of geometrical panelling and of facings of other woods such as sycamore. Many veneered walnut chests of drawers were inlaid with lines of holly, boxwood, or sycamore in geometric patterns. The plain and graceful piece illustrated in plate 14 is supported on a low stand which contains one long drawer. Five twist turned legs are connected at the front and sides by shaped stretchers, and at the back by a straight stretcher. The drawer fronts are veneered with walnut of good figure, and in the upper portion are decorated with broad 'herring bone' borders. The half-round moulding, applied after veneering to the carcase and framing the drawer fronts, is that which was in general use from *c.* 1660–1705 (Fig. 28A and B). (The double half-round moulding did not appear until after 1700.) As was the normal practice from *c.* 1660–1690, in good pieces of English workmanship, the rather coarse dovetailing of drawers is taken through as far as the veneered face of the chest. The sides of drawers are nailed

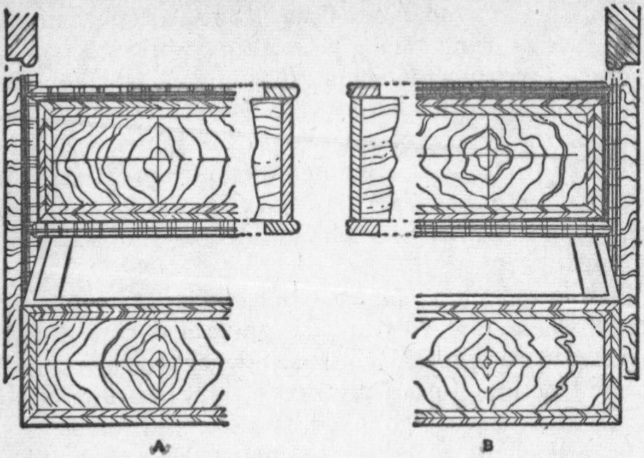

Figure 28 – Details of mouldings surrounding the drawer fronts; (A) the half-round (c. 1660–1705); (B) the double half-round (after c. 1700)

to their bottoms, to which, in this case, strips of wood have been affixed as runners. The grain of the carcase wood runs from back to front of the drawer bottom, and not from side to side; this last feature persisted throughout the first half of the eighteenth century. Chests of drawers were on occasion placed on stands of yew or chestnut.

Marquetry, as with chests of drawers, was the more usual decoration for the finer cabinets on stands (or on bases of drawers) which were now being increasingly made; walnut veneer was chosen for the simpler pieces. Numerous small drawers, grouped usually around a central cupboard, were enclosed by solid doors. The larger cabinets were supported on stands with five or six legs. Cabinets with shelves and glazed doors, some of which were designed to display newly acquired collections of Chinese porcelain, are rare. Cabinets of olive and princes wood (the contemporary term for king-wood) were owned by Charles II and William III. Evelyn mentions that the latter wood was used by the inlayer.

Cabinets on chests of drawers, with drop fronts which let down to disclose pigeon holes, drawers, and cupboards, served for writing. Their vogue was of brief duration in England; they were, however, popular on the Continent, the form persisting with modification throughout the eighteenth century. Bureaux were not made until after the reign of Charles II; and small desks with fitted interiors designed to stand on tables were still very generally employed. Those of walnut with floral marquetry were intended to be placed on a walnut table, similarly decorated. Oak specimens were numerous, but the carving on these was more or less stereotyped.

Reference can now be found to bookcases: to Pepys in the summer of 1666 comes 'Sympson, the Joyner' contriving presses in which to set books now growing numerous, and lying in disorder, so that within a few weeks Pepys may have 'as noble a closett as any man'.[24] Twelve of the bookcases are now in the Pepys Library at Magdalene College, Cambridge; they are probably the earliest documented examples of English domestic bookcases extant (Pl. 15). They are constructed of oak. The doors of a tall upper stage are glazed and subdivided by heavy bars. The boldly projecting cornice surmounts a coved frieze decorated with acanthus carving. A low base is also glazed and enriched by carved mouldings.

Boxes intended for many different purposes were made – boxes to hold Bibles or documents, boxes to hold chessmen, jewellery, lace, ruffles, gloves and other articles. Craftsmen employed a wide variety of materials, including ebony, tortoiseshell (with mounts of silver), as well as marquetry (Pl. 16), oyster-shell veneers, the popular stump work and oak. Some boxes (usually with flat lids and sloping fronts) were placed on stands, a drawer being incorporated in the lower part of the box. Silver, pewter, or brass were occasionally used for candle boxes.

In farmhouses in the country oak cupboards or presses, simply carved and fitted with drawers in the lower portion, were put to varied use; while court cupboards of walnut or oak, although primarily intended for storage and to hold the cups, goblets and silver, and to display the contemporary earthenware dishes, were to be met with in hall, parlour and bedroom. Their form was traditional and they were decorated with incised floral or chain patterns, with split baluster ornament and fluting. By 1660, pendants were displacing the columnar supports of earlier examples (Fig. 20). Many pieces contained two or three small cupboards in the upper section, with a large cupboard beneath. About 1680, the cupboard doors were often composed of one horizontal and two vertical panels. The cupboard tended, as the period advanced, to become lower and longer. Oak dressers, also used to display plate and earthenware, contained three and sometimes four drawers. Plainer than those of an earlier date and lightly carved, they were designed without superstructure.

In some parts of England, particularly in the Northern and Western areas, furniture styles remained constant throughout the course of the century and the new fashions, materials and methods of construction which prevailed in London and elsewhere at the Restoration were disregarded by traditional craftsmen.

NOTES TO CHAPTER 2

1. John Evelyn, *An Account of Architects and Architecture. The Miscellaneous Writings of John Evelyn*, ed. by William Upcott, 1825, p. 361.
2. Daniel Defoe, *A Journal of the Plague Year* (Everyman's Library), p. 108.
3. *Memoirs of John Evelyn*, ed. by William Bray, 2nd edition, 1819, vol. I, p. 563.

4, 5. John Evelyn, *Mundus Muliebris, or The Ladies' Dressing Room Unlock'd & her Toilette Spread*, 1690.

6. *The Diary of Samuel Pepys*, ed. by H. B. Wheatley, 1923, vol. IV, p. 287.
7. Bray, *op. cit.*, vol. I, p. 563.
8. John Evelyn, preface to *Mundus Muliebris*, etc.
9. See *Wiltshire Notes and Queries*, vol. VI.
10. Count Lorenzo Magalotti, *Travels of Cosmo the Third, Grand Duke of Tuscany, through England, during the reign of King Charles II (1669)*, trans. of 1821, pp. 150 and 248–9 respectively.
11. Ralph Edwards and Peter Ward-Jackson, *Ham House Guide*, 1950, p. 25.
12. Magalotti, *op. cit.*, pp. 376–8.

13. Magalotti, *op. cit.*, p. 464.
14. Wheatley, *op. cit.*, vol. IV, p. 288.
15. *Memoirs of the Verney Family*, by Frances Parthenope, Lady Verney, and Margaret M. Verney, 1892–4, vol. I, p. 259.
16. Bray, *op. cit.*, vol. I, p. 487.
17. Bray, *op. cit.*, vol. I, p. 462.
18. *The Journeys of Celia Fiennes*, ed. by Christopher Morris, 1947, p. 99. The Northern Journey, 1697.
19. Morris, *op. cit.*, pp. 153–4. Journey from London through East Anglia to Ely, 1698.
20. Bray, *op. cit.*, vol. I, pp. 433–4.
21. *Vertue I. Walpole Society*, vol. XVIII, 1929–30, p. 40.
22. *Letters of Horace Walpole*, ed. by Peter Cunningham, 1861–6, vol. II, p. 179. To George Montagu, from Strawberry Hill, Aug. 26th, 1749.
23. *Vertue V. Walpole Society*, vol. XXVI, 1937–8, p. 59.
24. Wheatley, *op. cit.*, vol. V, p. 385.

Figure 29 – Detail of carving: 'Boyes and Crowne'

CHAPTER THREE

THE LATER WALNUT PERIOD
(1690–1720)

'After dinner,' wrote Evelyn one day in August 1678, 'I walk'd to Ham, to see the house and garden of the Duke of Lauderdale, which is indeede inferior to few of the best villas in Italy itselfe,* the house furnish'd like a greate Prince's; the parterres, flower gardens, orangeries, groves, avenues, courts, statues, perspectives, fountaines, aviaries, and all this at the banks of the sweetest river in the world. ...'[1] The baroque splendour of Ham House (which a hundred years later Horace Walpole was to find in a 'state of pomp and tatters', the furniture 'magnificently ancient, dreary and decayed')[2] was at the close of the seventeenth century emblematic of England's well-being. 'The politer way of living' which had come with the Restoration, with a thorough-going change in the design of furniture, was rooted in the increased prosperity of England, in the towns and throughout the countryside. Trade was flourishing. Good cloth, for instance, was being made in the West Country, in Yorkshire, Westmorland, and elsewhere; the serges of Exeter were celebrated, as was glassware from Stourbridge in Worcestershire; and the earthenware of Staffordshire was used far afield. In the neighbourhood of Ham, as elsewhere, building was going on apace, and smaller houses or villas, variously designed in the Dutch manner, were introduced in many of the villages near London. Fine manors and solid farms were to be found in the wider countryside, especially in the more wealthy southern and south-western counties. London itself was

* Alterations to the house had been made 1673–5.

growing fast and houses were going up in areas where hitherto had been only open fields. Nicholas Barbon (*c.* 1640–98) was responsible for many of the new streets and squares, and largely for the standardization of the town house. His houses, tall and narrow, with high casement windows, conformed to pattern. Tapestry hangings were replaced by panelled walls. Wainscoting, of long panels of a larger size than formerly used, with bolection mouldings, lined rooms which were loftier and admitted more light. The panelling, which in some cases was made ready by joiners in London, was taken to the house for which it was destined and there carved, so giving rise to work for the skilled carvers. Grinling Gibbons and his school were no doubt concerned in a good deal of work of this nature.

Furniture of the period of William and Mary was enormously influenced by Dutch (and French) taste and by the further influx of Dutch cabinet-makers, who came to England in quite considerable numbers after William's accession to the throne. The effect of their activities was widespread and certainly beneficial to us. Dutch craftsmen, among them the notable Gerreit Jensen, were employed on work at Hampton Court and Kensington Palaces – which William III much preferred to Whitehall – as well as at Ham House (Pl. 25B).

At the beginning of the reign chairs were in general of lighter form and weaker structure, although a confusing multiplicity of chair types then existed and had existed indeed for some years. Chairs with turned uprights, turned legs and stretchers (sometimes of double twist form) were made contemporaneously with those constructed with cross stretchers and legs of scrolled form; and flat, serpentine X-stretchers, often surmounted by a central finial, are found used in conjunction with the straight leg, which had been revived about 1690. This latter support, sometimes baluster-shaped and turned, sometimes square and tapering, was headed by a square or bulbous capping (of mushroom or pear shape) and was enriched by fluting and gadrooning. Small, shaped aprons appeared on the seat rails of chairs about the same time – a common feature which persisted for many years.

Tall upholstered chairs without arms were designed with rectangular backs; occasionally the tops were shaped. The woodwork was frequently gilded and a rich Genoa velvet used as a covering material. Upholstered winged armchairs were made throughout the period, those dating from the end of the century often with padded, scrolled arms and legs with pear-shaped cappings, and with an embroidery in wool.

Caning, however, fell very gradually into disfavour and innumerable tall, narrow caned chairs were supplied to most households long after the introduction of more fashionable types. The industry was firmly established, persisting until as late as about 1740. 'Cane-Chair Shops' in St Paul's Churchyard survived to that date, selling chairs with richly carved walnut frames at 10*s*. to 15*s*. apiece, and chairs of beech at a few shillings only. There is a passage in *Gulliver's Travels* (1726) which gives a good indication of the popularity of caned furniture, largely perhaps because of its cheapness: 'I desired the Queen's woman,' says Gulliver, 'to save for me the combings of her Majesty's hair, whereof in time I got a good quantity; and consulting with my friend the cabinet-maker, who had received general orders to do little jobs for me, I directed him to make two chair-frames, no larger than those I had in my box, and then to bore little holes with a fine awl round those parts where I designed the backs and seats; through these holes I wove the strongest hairs I could pick out, just after the manner of cane-chairs in England.' [3]

At the end of the century, in the last years of the reign of William III, a new type of chair, described as 'in the style of Daniel Marot',* made its appearance. The type was

* Daniel Marot, Minister of Works to William of Orange, styled *architecte de Guillaume III, roy de la Grandes Bretagne*, was born in Paris about 1660; he studied under Lepautre and subsequently was influenced by André Charles Boulle. Marot was a Huguenot who had entered the ser-

distinctive and in several features foreshadowed coming fashions. A narrow back of curved outline (which often enclosed a vase- or fiddle-shaped central splat of wood) was supported on cabriole front legs, in imitation of French and Italian models. An early form of cabriole was the French *pied de biche*. The chair illustrated in plate 19, which belongs to the early eighteenth century, is a particularly fine example in which the uprights are scrolled and the splat is carved in open-work with strapwork and cartouches. The legs, which finish in hoof feet, are tied by shaped stretchers. A large set of similar chairs is known to have been supplied to Hampton Court Palace in 1717 by Richard Roberts, Chairmaker to George I.[4]

Subsequently, hoof-shaped and scrolled feet gave way to club, and claw and ball feet (*c.* 1710), and on most fashionable chairs the stretcher was discarded. The cabriole leg was often carved on the knee, sometimes with a husk and later with a shell *motif*, the decoration in some cases being repeated on the centre of the seat rail, which later is found connected with the shoe piece. The solid type of splat which was adopted was accompanied by a plainer cresting rail. Chairs were more comfortable, apart from the upholstered seats, as the backs were shaped to support the user's body, matching the curvature of the chair legs. Veneering, a normal technique for cabinet furniture during the reign of Anne, was applied to some chairs, and marquetry is found on more elaborate specimens. Upholsterers preferred a broad galon, without fringing.

Chair backs were noticeably lower by the time of George I. Gilding was sometimes used to enrich mouldings and details of the carved decoration; and the honeysuckle *motif* was a popular form of ornamentation. The cabriole leg was frequently 'hipped' – or carried above the corners of the seat-rail.

vice of the Prince of Orange on the Revocation of the Edict of Nantes, 1685. His magnificent designs for furniture and for the decoration of rooms, conceived in the style of Louis XIV, strongly affected contemporary taste in England, which he visited from 1694–7 and again in 1698.

Upholstered stools were made in large numbers, in particular for the Royal Palaces, where they were still the most usual form of seat. Walnut and painted beech wood were generally employed for stools, as for chairs, and coverings were of velvet or in some cases of needlework. The seats of most specimens were rectangular or square, although those of circular and oval form are also found. The drop-in seat was not uncommon. The rush-seated stool was probably supplied by the country maker. In a certain passage in *The Compleat English Tradesman* Defoe was concerned to examine the furniture of the house of 'a middling tradesman' at a place such as Horsham, in Sussex, 'where very few, if any manufactures are carried on'. He wrote: 'Come next to the furniture of their house; it is scarce credible to how many counties of England, and how remote, the furniture of but a mean house must send them; and how many people are everywhere employed about it; nay, and the meaner the furniture, the more people and places employed. ... The chairs, if of cane, are made at London; the ordinary matted chairs, perhaps in the place where they live. Tables, chests of drawers, &c., made at London; as also looking-glass. ...' [5]

Settees of the reign of William and Mary followed a similar evolution to chairs and stools and were extremely graceful articles of furniture; they exhibit the rich taste of the period, with its sense of elaborate display. The high padded backs, some with wings at either side, padded arms and seats with squab cushions, the whole covered in sumptuous velvet, damask or needlework, made for a standard of comfort hitherto unknown. Backs were frequently in the form of a double chair. Cane settees, which were cheaper and less comfortable, must have been made in large numbers although comparatively few of these have survived. Most settees were small in size, but some, which would be termed 'sophas', were long enough to lie on and conformed to a fashion which emanated from France. In the first years of the eighteenth century arms were usually of C-scroll form.

The high back was outmoded during the reign of Anne and replaced by a low straight back, and a few years after the adoption of the cabriole leg, stretchers were discontinued. About 1710 wooden arms are found on upholstered settees and the double chair form of wood again appeared. The settee illustrated in plate 21 may be dated *c.* 1710. (The painted coat of arms on the exceptionally wide, veneered cresting has been identified as that borne by Wadham Wyndham, who married a daughter of the Helyar family in the early years of the eighteenth century.) The covering is of Barcheston tapestry (*c.* 1585) from the manufactory established by a Warwickshire squire, William Sheldon. One long panel depicting the Three Virtues has been cut to fit the back of the settee; the small hunting scene which forms its upper border is incomplete. Two separate cushion covers, *Justicia* and *Temporantia*, have been used for the seat. The cabriole is inlaid on the shoulder with marquetry and decorated with a square ringing below. This unusual settee is about 4 feet in width.

Following the Royal example, settees were frequently covered in needlework, in designs influenced by French taste, by the ladies of a household. Celia Fiennes, describing a visit to Hampton Court, recounted: 'Out of the dressing-roome is the Queens closet, the hangings, chaires, stooles and screen the same, all of satten stitch done in worsteads, beasts, birds, images and fruites all wrought very finely by Queen Mary and her Maids of Honour. . . .'[6] The fashion was continued in the eighteenth century. Vases of flowers were specially popular, and armorial devices, small repetitive patterns and *bergeries* were also chosen as subjects.

'Love seats' (a modern term) were introduced during the reign of Queen Anne, and were similar in style to the settees then in vogue, with cabriole legs, low backs, and padded seats.

Plain oak settles were still being made in the country, many having the owners' initials and the date carved on them. They were pieces well suited to the farmhouse interiors for which they were destined. The panels of the back were sometimes 'fielded' – that is, the centre was raised and the surround bevelled off within the framework.

Day beds, covered in imported silks and velvets, were made usually for the large houses of the wealthy. A remarkably fine day bed (Pl. 20) and a settee supplied to the first Duke of Leeds, *c.* 1695, and bearing his cypher and coronet on the crestings, have been acquired by Temple Newsam House, Leeds. These pieces, formerly at Hornby Castle, Yorks, exemplify the luxurious appearance and fine quality workmanship of the best furniture of the period. The legs are tapered and connected by oval stretchers; the woodwork is painted black and gilded. The coverings are of Italian cut velvet, trimmed with tasselled fringing. At a later date, the cabriole leg was used in conjunction with straight turned stretchers. Few day beds were made in the reign of George I, but couches then took their place.

The home manufacture of silks engaged considerable attention at this period. As early as 1697, Celia Fiennes observed in the 'flourishing town' of Canterbury the 'great number of French people ... employ'd in the weaving and silk winding'; she saw '20 Loomes in one house with severall fine flower'd silks, very good ones ...'.[7] Subsequently Defoe remarked the improvement and increase of this trade: 'now,' he wrote, 'we make at home, all the fine broad-silks, velvets, brocades, damasks, &c., which formerly came from Italy and France; and above twelve hundred thousand pounds a year, which by the strictest calculation, was formerly paid to the French, Genoese, &c., for wrought silks, is now all kept at home, and expended among our own poor. But,' he adds, '... the ladies will allow nothing but French to be fit for a person of quality to wear ... the richest silk, the most beautiful pattern, the most agreeable colours, if it has the scandal of being English, it must not have the honour to come upon their backs.'[8] The preference for imported fabrics would appear to have been firm. Pierre Antoine Motteux, man of letters and a dealer in 'curiosities', who kept an 'India Shop' in the City, was, in 1711, prepared to sell various 'rich brocades, Dutch *Atlases*, with gold and silver, or without, and other foreign silks of the newest modes'. Trading in Oriental fabrics had recently been impeded by law. As Motteux wrote in explanation: 'Indian silks were formerly a great branch of our trade; and since we must not sell them, we must seek amends by dealing in others.' [9]

One advantage of the new panelled rooms was that cupboards could be built in the wall; and for this reason 'wardrobes' or presses were often dispensed with. Cupboards to hold clothes were fitted with a door. Open alcove cupboards, termed 'buffets', were also incorporated into the panelling, being used to display collections of Chinese porcelain and Delft ware. At Hampton Court Palace, where Queen Mary had 'a Sett of Lodgings, for her private Retreat only, but most exquisitely furnish'd', Defoe remarked a 'Collection of *Delft* Ware, which indeed was very large and fine; and ... a vast Stock of fine *China* Ware, the like whereof was not then to be seen in England; the long Gallery, as above, was fill'd with this *China*, and every other Place, where it could be plac'd, with Advantage'.[10] And Celia Fiennes, when travelling in southern England in the first years of the eighteenth century, noted in one house '... a little parlour wanscoted, white in veines and gold mouldings, a neat booffett furnish'd with glasses and china for the table ...' [11] which would indicate that these alcoves were also put to practical use.

Corner cupboards with fitted doors were also used to store china, probably the dishes used for the drinking of tea, a habit which was now spreading. Small hanging corner cupboards, japanned (Pl. 26) or veneered in burr walnut and often surmounted by a hooded cornice, were succeeded by a larger type in two stages.

Shelves for books were sometimes placed along the walls of rooms, a planned feature, especially in large houses; but straight fronted, free-standing bookcases were also made, in oak and in walnut. Those dating from the reign of Queen Anne were in general of pleasingly austere appearance, being devoid of the somewhat pretentious architectural character which these pieces later acquired. The upper stage of the bookcase was fitted with shelves behind glazed doors, the lower often containing drawers enclosed by solid doors. Walnut veneer was frequently applied to an oak carcase.

Although for country use, Dutch influence is apparent in the oak dresser of about 1690, often designed with fielded panels and front legs of baluster form. Some of the dressers made in the early eighteenth century have a central cupboard and decoration resembling that of contemporary chests of drawers and tallboys; while others were constructed with a superstructure of shelves.

A small number of oak court cupboards of sideboard type were still produced, with supports usually of turned baluster form and carved frieze. They followed a traditional form and could no longer be regarded as fashionable.

Large lacquered blanket chests, with distinctive domed lids, were in vogue towards the turn of the century; some specimens, similar but for a flat top, would appear to have been placed upon a stand. In many instances the lacquer work was of Oriental origin. The oak chest on cabriole stand contained a drawer, or two small drawers, at the base.

Chests of drawers were veneered in a variety of woods such as walnut and kingwood oyster-shell, burr walnut, partridge wood, yew, or tulip; and in some cases both the top of the chest and the drawer fronts were decorated with marquetry. 'Seaweed' or 'endive' marquetry (resembling the arabesque and Persian varieties) was employed on many of the finer pieces of the time, and was closely allied in style to French rather than Dutch work, being in effect a translation into woods of the marquetry of shell and metal of André Charles Boulle and his school. Fine and complex scrolled patterns were executed in holly, box, sycamore, or pear, on a walnut ground, and were usually confined to oval panels, differing in this respect from the arabesque which was generally an 'all-over' decoration, and from the earlier floral marquetry in its minute character. The work called for the greatest skill from the craftsman. A combination of two such woods rendered the work quiet and sober in colour.

Decorative use was made of parquetry, of inlaid lines of light-coloured wood arranged in geometrical patterns, and of lozenges. Burr walnut, finely marked, mottled and cut across the branches of the tree, was much employed as a veneer during the reign of Anne, when a more restrained taste succeeded that of the previous forty years. Seaweed and arabesque marquetry decoration was at the same time confined usually to small panels (Pl. 22). Applied carving was in low relief.

Some chests of drawers were mounted on stands; japanned examples are found, sometimes arcaded. Here, as elsewhere, the peg-top headed leg gave way to the cabriole. A more discriminating construction was apparent in these pieces by 1700: dovetails were stopped a fraction of an inch from the drawer front and were smaller and more numerous; and nailing was infrequent. The double half-round moulding bordering the fronts of drawers (Fig. 28B) remained fashionable until *c.* 1715, when drawers with overlapping moulded edges are found.

The side table was among the most varied and ornate of pieces made at the end of the seventeenth and beginning of the eighteenth century. Its purpose was largely ornamental. Early examples with S-scrolled legs and bun feet were frequently decorated with floral, or later, seaweed, marquetry, and sometimes contained a drawer in the frieze. The type of table with folding top supported on two hinged inner front legs (or gates) of twist, baluster, turned, cupped or tapered form, was more serviceable. French influence was afterwards pronounced, and some gilt side tables, owing their inspiration to the extravagant, but highly attractive, designs of Berain, were doubtless the work of French immigrant craftsmen. Ornate pendants to the frieze and the absence of a drawer suggest the influence of Marot (Fig. 30). Gilding was the rule, partly because of its predominance at the court of Louis XIV. (James II, early in the previous reign, had been supplied with furniture from

Paris. For the Queen's Great Bedchamber at Whitehall, he ordered from Simon de Lobell, the French upholsterer, a great bedstead with matching chairs, stools, cushions, and fabrics, at a cost of more than £3,000. Under William III men such as Francis la Pierre, upholsterer, John Pelletier, carver and gilder, and, on occasion, Nicholas Pic and his partner Peter Michon, cabinet makers, supplied the Great Wardrobe.)

Figure 30 – Side table of carved and gilt wood, supported on pillar legs, tied by scrolled stretchers surmounted by a central finial; pendants depend from a plain frieze. End of the seventeenth century

The side table with tapered pillar legs, headed by gadrooned capitals and united by scrolled and foliated cross stretchers supporting a central finial (or by flat looped stretchers or those of H-form), was by about 1700 already giving place to the table designed with legs of the early cabriole shape. Tops were frequently of finely carved gesso, but marble, purchased in Italy, had become very fashionable early in the eighteenth century; and scagliola, a composition much admired by Evelyn when travelling in

Italy in 1664, was also introduced as an alternative. Some travellers returned with slabs or plaques of marble or mosaic which were then incorporated in tables and cabinets designed for that purpose. 'In the hall & all over the House,' noted Horace Walpole when describing the interior of Castle Howard, 'are fine busts, urns, columns, Statues, & the finest collection in the World of antique tables of the most valuable marble, & some of old Mosaic, & one of Florentine inlaying. There are two fine Cabinets of the same work & materials. . . .'[12]

About 1700, the swing mirror on box stand was introduced, often being placed on the small walnut or japanned tables, with two or three drawers, which served for dressing. The stand, sometimes of two tiers and with gracefully shaped front, contained small toilet drawers (Fig. 31).

Many very elaborate designs for chandeliers, based on French models and in the style of Marot, Lepautre, or Berain, were at this time executed in carved and gilt wood. 'A fine large Carved Wooden Branch with Brass Nozells to hold twelve Candles all Gilt with fine Gold' together with a model is recorded as having been supplied in 1716 to St James's Palace for the sum of 100 guineas, the makers being John Gumley and James Moore.[13] Silver was also used for the Royal Palaces and great houses, and brass more widely. At first the stem was usually gadrooned. Grease pans were often ornamented with the acanthus leaf *motif*, and about the beginning of the new century pendants in the form of inverted pineapples were introduced. In both wooden and brass chandeliers an eagle in many cases surmounted the stem. Some magnificent chandeliers of rock crystal at Hampton Court Palace date from *c.* 1695–1700. The rock crystals were imported from the Continent and cut in this country.

Candlesticks (of silver, brass, wood, or a combination of wood and brass) were, of course, in very general demand. Silver candlesticks, with hammered stem of fluted columnar form, exhibited a wide and ornamental rectangular grease-pan, placed immediately above the base, and becoming, during the reign of Anne, round or octagonal in shape. The alternative baluster stem was cast. Silver candelabra were designed usually with three detachable branches. Iron rushlight holders continued to serve the needs of the poor.

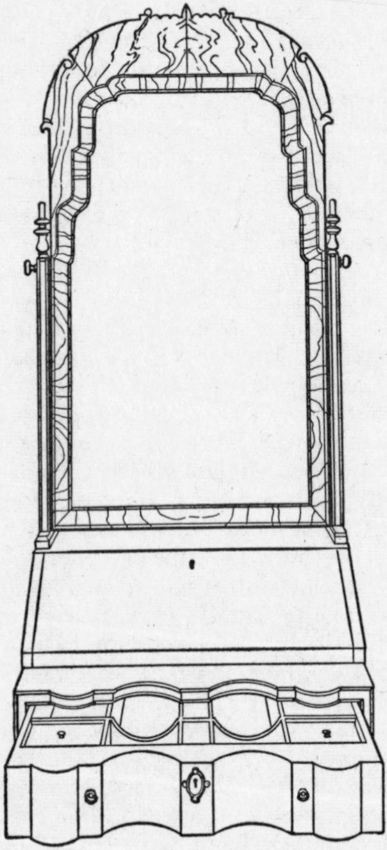

Figure 31 – Dressing glass; the mirror suspended between uprights on a stand of two tiers, with shaped front. End of the seventeenth century

Elaborate workmanship was given to supporting candlestands, often in pairs, which were purposed to match an ornamental side table and the accompanying mirror. Sets of these articles were supplied in profusion to the Royal Palaces. Candlestands were of carved and gilt soft wood, of walnut (at times decorated with an inlay of arabesque marquetry), of olive, 'princes' and Grenoble wood, of gilt gesso, or on occasion were japanned. The stand with scrolled tripod base, tapered shaft, and vase-shaped top gave way during the reign of George I to one of heavier and less graceful form with solid baluster shaft.

Small writing desks were provided with interiors fitted with drawers and pigeon holes in the manner of fashionable bureaux. The lid, when opened, was supported on two slides; and usually a drawer was contained in the lower portion of the desk, below the lid. Desks were sometimes placed on stands and conformed in size with an earlier portable variety. Many were the property of ladies. They were often most finely constructed, and their decoration, either in the form of veneering or of marquetry, accorded with contemporary taste.

Mirrors were important pieces in the decoration of late Stuart rooms. The glass was of appreciably greater size and of better quality than formerly and was more easily procured – largely owing to the increased number of glassworks now in existence in or near London. Glass was rapidly becoming cheaper. It is significant that early in the eighteenth century Defoe referred to one tradesman as possessing 'two large pier looking-glasses, and one chimney glass in the shop, and one very large pier-glass, seven feet high, in the back shop'.[14] On the other hand the splendid glasses which were supplied about 1700 to Hampton Court Palace (a number by Gerreit Jensen) were of considerable value: '4 Glasses for the Peires of 62 inches long and 36 inches broad' are known to have cost £320. During the reign of William and Mary a change is observable in the shape of the mirror. A tall upright glass was adopted; it was of distinctly elegant proportions and was in keeping with the increased height of rooms; and at least two plates of glass were employed for each mirror (Fig. 32). Bevelling was usually done by hand, but machinery was now also in use for this purpose. In this connexion it may be noticed that the *London Gazette*, November 1698, advertised an

Figure 32 – Tall mirror, in frame of wood decorated with gilt carving and gesso; the elaborate cresting centring in a mask form within scrolls and acanthus carving. End of the seventeenth century

'Engine for Grinding, Pollishing, and Cutting Looking-Glass Plates (for which a Patent is granted by his Majesty) by which Glass is truly Ground and Polished with the best black Pollish; And also the Borders cut most curiously hollow, and with a better Lustre than any heretofore done'.[15] The perforated crestings of the frame were now very elaborate and gilding was widely employed (Fig. 32). Frequently, a narrow gilt moulding or a coloured glass banding enclosed borders of glass, bevelled and having raised ornaments at the angles and centre of sides. A mirror made for William III at Hampton Court Palace is of this type. The engraved glass border is decorated with rosettes, and bandings are of a deep sapphire blue. The cresting of

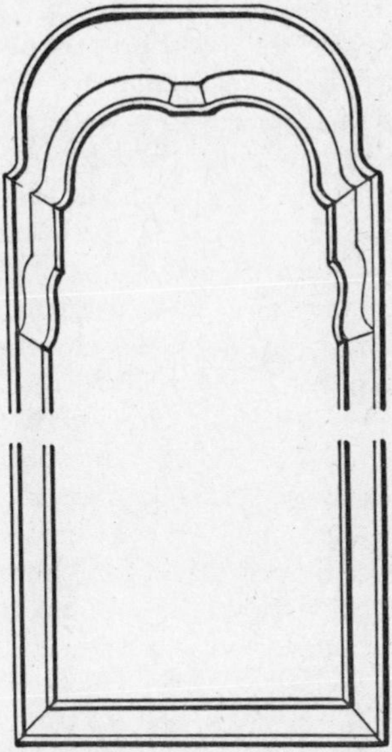

Figure 33 – Tall mirror, with moulded frame of glass. End of the seventeenth century

this fine glass is in the form of the King's cypher and crown. Frames were in some cases decorated in *verre églomisé*: the design in gold was executed on a coloured ground. The unfired colours and gilding were applied to the back of the glass and protected by means of varnish or another sheet of glass. Such a process was followed in the eighteenth century by a certain Glomy, a French framer and gilder, from whom the term '*églomisé*' derives – apparently a misnomer. Borders were sometimes made of plain looking-glass (Fig. 33); and in many of the later mirrors gilt gesso was applied to the frame. During the reign of Anne, the cresting took on a more solid form and a central shell was a favourite ornament; the bottom of the mirror also was often shaped. The heavy, half-round frame of convex section, which had been in vogue about 1680 (Fig. 27), was displaced by one which was flat, moulded and shaped (Fig. 34). Candle branches were often attached to the lower portion of these frames.

Silver was used as a decoration in some cases, being applied either in small pieces to a wooden frame or, more often, as a complete covering, chased and embossed. Celia Fiennes, who visited Windsor Castle in 1698, recorded seeing there in the drawing-room a 'large branch of silver and the sconces round the roome of silver, silver table and stands and glass frames and chaire frames...'.[16] This table and the three stands, given by the citizens of London to Charles II and William III, survive.*

By the time of William III the woodwork and upholstery of fashionable beds were almost indistinguishable (Pl. 17). The slender posts, of oak or beech, and the woodwork of the back and tester were covered with material – often silk damask or figured velvet, which were used also for the full-tasselled fringed bed covers and hangings; while trimmings of silver added to the general richness of appearance. (The state bed of William III at Hampton Court Palace is hung with crimson velvet, trimmed with silver galon.) Care was devoted to the arrangement of the folds of draperies. The value of beds, depending almost entirely on the materials with which they were covered, was often excessive. 'Pontadre' (Pintado) and 'Cantoon' (Canton) stuffs would seem to have been popular, and woollen materials, serge, camlet and mohair, were all employed on occasion. Because of the increased height of rooms – and they were 'soe lofty its enough to breake ones neck to looke on them', wrote Celia Fiennes of the 'large dineing-roome' at Windsor[17] – beds were higher, and deep valances were

* The royal apartments, having been largely rebuilt, were refurnished by Charles II.

Figure 34 – Mirror, in carved and shaped frame decorated with gesso; the broken pediment encloses a conventional shield form. Early eighteenth century

adopted. The vase-shaped finials which usually surmounted the four corners of the tester were also covered and, in some cases, the cornice. Great plumes of feathers were placed in the cups at the corners of the tester. According to the

Palace inventories 'feather dressers' were employed to keep them in good order.

The fine bed of crimson Italian brocade, believed to have been made in 1694 for the visit of William III and his court to Boughton House, Northants, when newly redecorated and rebuilt by Ralph, Duke of Montague, and now in the Victoria and Albert Museum, is 14 feet high – 6 feet less than the lofty 'King's Room' for which it was designed; while the great baroque bed from Melville House, Fife, lately given by the Earl of Leven to the same museum, is even higher and more magnificent.

Queen Anne's state bed, at Hampton Court, is hung with Spitalfields velvet, patterned in rich colours on a cream ground; and the cornice is surmounted by four urn-shaped finials. A chair, stool, and footstools of the same date are covered with a matching velvet. Some great houses retained mourning beds, draped in black.

A new half-tester type of bedstead (without footposts) began to be made towards the end of the seventeenth century, and is referred to by Celia Fiennes: '... thence a dineing roome the Duke of Norfolks appartment [at Windsor] a drawing-roome and two bed chambers, one with a half bedstead as the new mode ...' and again '... thence into the King's constant bed chamber being one of the halfe bedsteads of crimson and green damaske inside and outside the same hangings, and chaires and window curtaines the same ...'.[18]

The small bureau on a stand, a piece newly introduced and one of delicate proportions, was usually of walnut. The example illustrated in plate 23 is supported on a stand of a wood, darker than the desk itself, which is perhaps French walnut; the solid turned legs, which screw both into the blocks of the frieze and into the hollow bun feet, and flat curved stretchers, follow the fashion prevailing about 1700. This bureau is little more than 30 inches wide. The sloping front is hinged to fall forward upon slides, disclosing an interior with small drawers and a central well.

The type generally adopted during the reign of Anne was

constructed with a base of two or three long and two short drawers and was supported on bracket feet; the desk was enclosed by a sloping front which, when let down, revealed a more ample interior of small drawers, central cupboard, pigeon holes, a well, and often two or three secret drawers or compartments.

Tall bureaux in two stages were frequently based on a lower stage following the foregoing form. These pieces usually exhibit very fine execution, and are in many cases found japanned or with decoration of seaweed marquetry. (Floral marquetry was already out of fashion at the date of their introduction. The large, rather coarse bureau or bureau bookcase with floral marquetry and with a *bombé* front is of Dutch origin, often dating from as late as *c.* 1750.) The doors of the upper part, which enclosed an interior of great elaboration and refinement, were sometimes inset with mirror glass. Surmounting cornices were variously serpentine, pediment-shaped, straight or double hooded (Fig. 35). A writing cabinet at the Victoria and Albert Museum, by tradition said to have belonged to Dean Swift, is of walnut with some marquetry enrichment (Pl. 22). The glass doors of the upper section are each framed in two fluted pilasters and surmounted by a straight cornice. The lower stage, which is of greater width, is of a form which appeared about 1700, with recessed central cupboard (or knee-hole) and deep drawers on either side. The drawers of this specimen are concave and are banded with holly and ebony. The interior of the desk portion is contained by a straight fronted flap, falling to provide a writing shelf.

The composite tallboy and writing bureau is similarly constructed: the top drawer of the base pulling out so as to form a desk, its front being hinged.

Small walnut and marquetry fall-front writing cabinets on chests of drawers or stands (in total height between 5 and 6 feet) continued to enjoy popularity (Fig. 36). These pieces, which were then called 'scriptors', or 'scrutoirs', closely resemble those cabinets faced by a pair of hinged doors, opening to display a fitted interior, of which examples

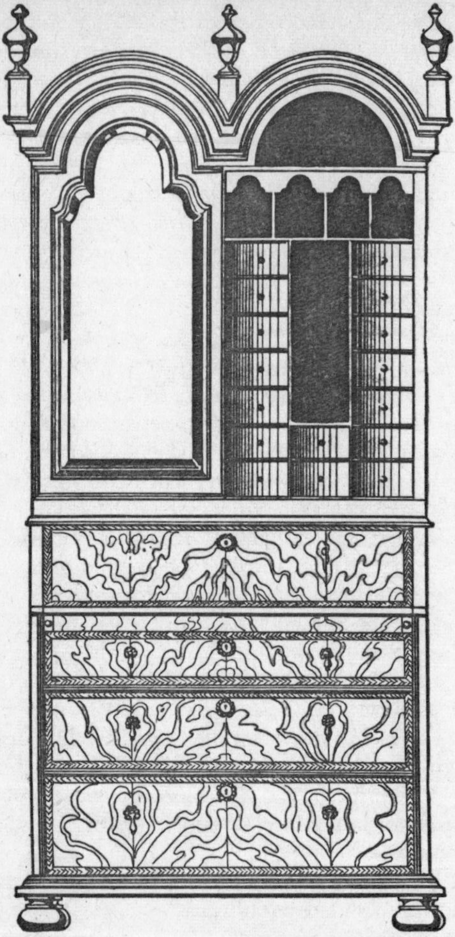

Figure 35 – Writing cabinet, in two stages; the doors of the upper part are inset with mirror glass and enclose an interior fitted with small drawers and pigeon holes; the top drawer of the lower part is closed by a flap forming a shelf for writing, beneath which are slides; the cabinet is surmounted by a double hood, and rests on ball feet.
End of the seventeenth century

Figure 36 – Writing cabinet, based on a chest of drawers; the front falls to disclose a fitted interior of small drawers, pigeon holes and a central cupboard. Early eighteenth century

exist of larger dimensions, supported on stands with six legs, and usually of marquetry. Cabinets veneered in walnut or decorated with marquetry of different varieties, usually are found surmounted by a convex frieze (Fig. 37) in the form of a long drawer.

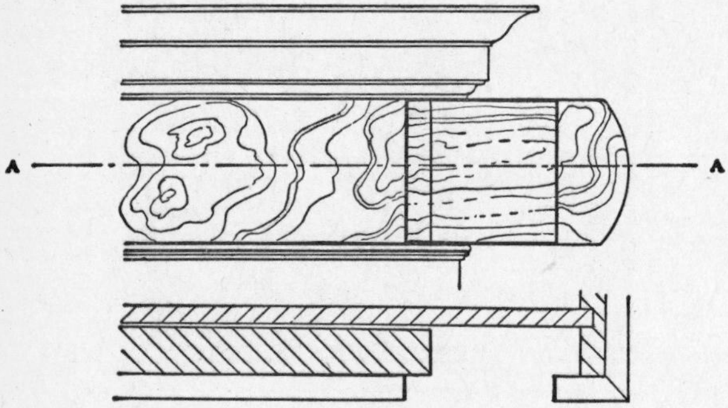

SECTION THROUGH A–A

Figure 37 – Detail of Fig. 36 – convex frieze, below the cornice, facing a long drawer

NOTES TO CHAPTER 3

1. *Memoirs of John Evelyn*, ed. by William Bray, 2nd edition, 1819, vol. 1, p. 500.
2. *Letters of Horace Walpole*, ed. by Peter Cunningham, 1861–6, vol. v, p. 240. To George Montagu, from Strawberry Hill, June 11th, 1770.
3. *The Works of Jonathan Swift*, ed. by J. Hawkesworth, 1778, vol. v, pp. 169–70.
4. Ralph Edwards, *A History of the English Chair*, 1951 (Victoria and Albert Museum), p. 24, item 46.
5. Daniel Defoe, *The Complete English Tradesman* (1745), edition of 1841, vol. 1, p. 266.
6. *The Journeys of Celia Fiennes*, ed. by Christopher Morris, 1947, p. 355. London and the Later Journeys, *c.* 1701–3.
7. Morris, *op. cit.*, pp. 123–4. Tour of Kent, 1697.
8. Defoe, *op. cit.*, vol. 1, pp. 199–200.
9. *The Spectator*, No. 288, Jan. 30th, 1712.

10. *A Tour of Great Britain* by Daniel Defoe, 1927 edition, with introduction by G. D. H. Cole, vol. I, p. 175.
11. Morris, *op. cit.*, p. 345. A house in New Inn Lane, Epsom. London and the Later Journeys, *c.* 1701–3.
12. *Horace Walpole's Journals of Visits to Country Seats, etc.*, ed. by Paget Toynbee, *Walpole Society*, vol. XVI, 1927–8, p. 72. Journey to Castle Howard, Aug. 1772.
13. See article by I. C. Goodison, *Furniture of Hampton Court*, etc., in *Journal of the Society of Arts* (1925).
14. Defoe, *op. cit.*, vol. I, p. 207.
15. See article by R. W. Symonds, 'English Looking Glasses (II)', *Connoisseur*, May 1950, wherein the passage is quoted.
16, 17. Morris, *op. cit.*, p. 279.
18. Morris, *op. cit.*, pp. 277, 279–80.

CHAPTER FOUR

LACQUER FURNITURE WITH SOME MENTION OF GILT AND SILVERED FURNITURE AND GESSO

THE Restoration Court adopted, among other extravagances, the rich 'Indian' taste. The term 'Indian' was then applied without discrimination to objects from the Orient. 'Indian' furniture was lacquer furniture, and continued to be so called in the eighteenth century; geographical knowledge of the East was uncertain on the part of most Europeans.

Lacquer or 'lac' cabinets and screens had been imported here since the days of Elizabeth, and sometimes are listed in inventories of the Jacobean period (e.g. the Northampton inventory of 1614), but it would seem probable that the art of lacquering was known at a much earlier date. There was an interest in this stuff, 'most pleasant to behold'.[1] Van Linschoten, whose voyage to the East Indies was translated into English in 1598, had written 'the fayrest workemanshippe thereof cometh from China, as may be seene by all things that come from thence, as desks, Targets, Tables, Cubbordes, Boxes, and a thousand such like things, that are all covered and wrought with Lac of all colours and fashions'.[2]

The 'taste' set in early in the seventeenth century; it is significant that two small cabinets of that date in the Victoria and Albert Museum are decorated in a pseudo-Oriental style,[3] and there are many references to true Oriental wares in the early records of the English East India Company.

Probably the greater part of the trade was carried by the Dutch armed merchantmen. Evelyn, who was concerned with the East India prizes taken by Lord Sandwich, was informative on this matter, writing in 1665: 'Then I deliver'd ye Dutch Vice Adml, who was my prisoner, to Mr Lo[wman] of ye Marshalsea, he giving me bond in 500*l.* to produce him at my call. I exceedingly pittied this brave unhappy person, who had lost with these prizes 40,000*l.* after 20 yeares negotiation [trading] in ye East Indies. I din'd in one of these vessells, of 1200 tonns, full of riches.'[4]

Similar interest prevailed in France: Richelieu's great collection of works of art at the *Palais Cardinal* had contained hundreds of pieces of Oriental porcelain and a quantity of Chinese lacquers. The luxurious nature of imported lacquer, embroideries, carpets, and porcelain was well known to Charles II by reason of his exile abroad. Catherine of Braganza brought from Portugal as her dowry 'such Indian cabinets as had never before ben seene here'.[5] Reaction against austerities enforced under the Commonwealth was unqualified. 'The Queene's bed was an embrodery of silver on crimson velvet, and cost £8,000.'[6] Rich cargoes were unloaded at the East India House. In the first years of the Restoration period Evelyn mentioned supping 'at my Lady Mordaunt's at Ashted, where was a roome hung with *Pintado* (the East Indian chintz then in vogue), full of figures greate and small, prettily representing sundry trades and occupations of ye Indians, with their habits.'[7] By 1700, 'Mr Pepys at Clapham' had 'a very noble and wonderfully well-furnish'd house, especially with India and Chinese curiosities'.[8] Tea; porcelain or 'chiney-ware'; drugs; embroideries; lacquered tables; lacquered boards for screens; lacquered panels in frames, painted and carved for rooms; lacquered sticks for fans; lacquered trunks, 'escretors' and bowls – all these were brought home by the trading vessels. At Court, presents of considerable value were made; they were sought at the jewellers, goldsmiths, and the 'East India' shops.

Two varieties of Oriental lacquer were brought to England during the late seventeenth century – the very beautiful and most durable incised or 'Coromandel' lacquer, decorated 'for the generality in Colours, with a very small sprinkling of Gold here and there, like the patches in a Ladies countenance'[9] and then referred to as 'Bantam' work (from the Dutch trading post of that name in the Malay Peninsula), and that with raised and gilt decoration on a one-coloured ground. The latter appears to have been the more popular of the two. It is not easy to account for the preference. In 1688, incised lacquer was stated to be 'almost obsolete, and out of fashion'; it was further remarked that 'no person is fond of it, or gives it house-room, except some who have made new Cabinets out of old Skreens. And from that large old piece, by the help of a Joyner, made little ones ... torn and hacked to joint a new fancie ... the finest hodgpodg and medly of Men and Trees turned topsie turvie'.[10] For the most part, importation was confined to large six-fold screens and to boards or plain panels. The mirror frames, table-tops, stands, or cabinet doors found in the incised lacquer were originally made up from these screens or panels which, being decorated on both sides, were the more economical and convenient for cutting up. The mutilation of scenes and figures is often apparent, and the design noticeably incomplete; men are figured, 'angling for Dolphins in a Wood, or pursuing the Stag, and chasing the Boar in the middle of the Ocean ... and such irregular pieces as these can never certainly be acceptable'.[11]

Often, panels portrayed full landscape scenes with figures, buildings, beasts, and flowers, and were bordered by 'the emblems of happy augury', 'the precious objects' and other symbols. The soft painted colours are comparable in quality with the enamelling of contemporary *famille verte* porcelain. Reds, blues, greens, aubergines, and buffs show harmoniously, in profusion and delicacy of taste, on a polished black ground. English imitations were made, but by the use of very different materials. The wood of the ground was usually soft deal; and the over-laying composition of size and whitening was applied in many successive thin coats up to perhaps a depth of a quarter of an inch, allowed to harden, blackened or coloured, and was then varnished and polished. The design, taken from Oriental examples or from pattern books, was traced on the surface, which was cut away with a graver and other instruments, and coloured; gums, or often turpentine, were used as a medium. This was a substitute for the Oriental preparation made of sand, fine clay, fibre grasses and gums, which when uncovered shows a brownish tint, and which was applied to a non-European wood.

By contrast, the raised lacquer, or 'japan', to use the contemporary name, enjoyed sustained popularity. The polished surface of such lacquer made appeal: 'What can be more surprizing, than to have our Chambers overlaid with Varnish more glossy and reflecting than polisht Marble? No amorous Nymph need entertain a Dialogue with her Glass, or Narcissus retire to a Fountain, to survey his charming Countenance, when the whole house is one entire Speculum.'[12] The raised portions of the design were gilded, usually on the effective black ground, or on other coloured grounds. A red ground, in particular, showed to advantage, with a magnificence fitting to the period. All these pieces are now much dulled and tarnished. Contemporary assertion that 'no damp air, no mouldring worm, or corroding time, can possibly deface the work'[13] has proved false.

Merchants were at first encouraged by the vogue for lacquered furniture to send to the East designs for pieces to be copied there for the European market – a procedure paralleled by that which later prevailed in respect of the 'India Company's china'. But although the lacquering was of high quality and retained an excellent finish, the cabinet work was considered inferior. Strength of jointing or of ground wood was not in fact necessary owing to the protective quality of the 'lac'. And dovetailing of joints, when employed at all, was coarse. Captain William Dampier observed in the course of his voyage to Tonquin made in 1688: 'the Joyners in this Country may not compare their Work with that which the Europeans make; and in laying on the Lack upon good or fine joyned work, they frequently spoil the joynts, edges, or corners of Drawers of Cabinets: Besides, our fashions of Utensils differ mightly from theirs, and for that reason Captain Pool, in his second Voyage to the Country, brought an ingenious Joyner with him to make fashionable Commodities to be lackered here, as also Deal boards ...'.[14]

Furniture made by English joiners, therefore, was sent out to the East for lacquering, and subsequently returned here for sale. Bills of lading provide some evidence of the practice. The quantity, however, was insufficient and most lacquered furniture extant in England is of entirely English workmanship; the preponderance of European over Chinese and Japanese examples existed by the early years of the reign of George II, when the increasing demand for 'Lac' had been met by English makers, producing a creditable although inferior imitation of the 'Indian' process. The 'Jappan Cabinets' advertised for sale in the *London Gazette* of the late seventeenth century were of both Eastern and home manufacture; and Celia Fiennes' mention of 'My Ladyes Closet [which] is very fine, the wanscoate of the best Jappan',[15] at Burghley House, is indeterminate, as are indeed other early references made to rooms 'pannell'd all with Jappan' at Hampton Court Palace and Chatsworth (that at Chatsworth was of the Oriental incised variety, some of which was cut up later to form chests). No distinction was made as between the lacquer of China and Japan.

The Eastern lacquer had a hard, dry, glossy surface, with a tendency to chip. Dampier described the basic constituent, the sap from a native tree, to be: 'a Sort of gummy Juice, which drains out of the Bodies of Limbs of Trees ... gotten in such Quantities by the Country People, that they daily bring it in great Tubs to the Markets ...'.[16] It was applied in several coats, each being given time to dry thoroughly. He explained: 'It grows blackish of it self, when exposed to the Air; but the Colour is heightened by Oil and other ingredients mixt with it. When the outside Coat is dry, they polish it to bring it to a gloss. This is done chiefly by often rubbing it with the ball or Palm of their Hands. They can make the Lack of any colour. . . .'[17]

The European substitute was produced by less elaborate methods. True imitation of the Eastern process was not possible. The 'lac' itself could not be imported, owing to its property of hardening on exposure to the air; nor was the climate suitable for its working. First the carcase wood was overlaid with successive coats of a preparation of whitening and a size obtained from boiled parchment shavings. The ground was then treated with varnishes of gum-lac and other ingredients dissolved in spirits of wine, and polished to a high gloss. The varnish was most often 'Black Japan', but other colours advocated were red (of which there were several varieties), chestnut, olive, and blue. The design was outlined on this surface in gold size. The raised decoration of figures, animals, trees, etc., was achieved by the dropping on the ground, by means of a rush pencil stick, a paste of whitening mixed with gum arabic water and fine sawdust. When the raised portions were sufficiently built up and modelled, they were coloured, polished, and gilt with variegated metal dusts. Certain subsidiary portions of the design, such as the flat landscape background, were drawn simply and directly on the ground in gold size. The process presented small difficulty and japanning was taken up by people of leisure as a fashionable accomplishment and amusement as early as the last decade of the seventeenth century.

In 1688, John Stalker and George Parker had produced an illustrated *Treatise of Japaning and Varnishing, Being a compleat Discovery of those Arts. With the best way of making all sorts of Varnish for Japan. . . . The Method of Guilding, Burnishing, and Lackering. . . . Also Rules for Counterfeiting Tortoise-shell, and Marble. . . . Together with Above an Hundred distinct Patterns of Japan-work, in Imitation of the Indians, for Tables, Stands, Frames, Cabinets, Boxes, etc.* (Pl. 24). The authors stated therein that 'our Gentry have of late attained to the knowledge and distinction of true japan'. Salmon's *Polygraphice* followed in 1701, but was little more than an imitation of the *Treatise*. The volume of amateur – and commercial – work increased enormously during the early years of the eighteenth century.

Mrs Pendarves (later Mrs Delany) was an authority on the art. She wrote: 'It put me in mind of the fine ladies of our age – it delighted my eyes, but gave no pleasure to my understanding.'[18] She had been assiduous in its pursuit a few months earlier, writing to her sister: 'Lady Sun. [Sunderland] is very busy about japanning: I will perfect myself in the art against I make you a visit, and bring materials with me. ... Everybody is mad about japan work; I hope to be a dab at it by the time I see you.' Two years later she wrote again: 'You never saw such perfection as Mrs Clayton's trunk; other's Japan is beautiful, but this is *beauty* – it is the admiration of the whole town.'[19]

There were, then, several distinct varieties of lacquer in England: Chinese incised work (largely confined to screens); Chinese and Japanese raised lacquer; European substitutes produced as an industry; and much amateur work. A wide variation in quality between pieces results from the diversity of origin.

Chinese or Japanese work intended for the European market is distinguished by a superior ground, which is lustrous, hard, and impervious to the action of solvents, and which has remarkable preservative qualities. The raised decoration is drawn with facility, but, with time, is inclined to sink into the ground. Landscapes, enlivening figures of animals, birds, buildings, bridges, trees, and flowers are depicted in their appropriate place. The European imitation often consists of various 'Indian' *motifs* taken from several sources, and haphazardly pieced together: the medley of men and beasts, flowering shrubs, and natural objects are painted 'according to fancy' and 'arranged as occasion serves', filling the surface as evenly as possible. A mountainous landscape with a lake and pavilion by the shore is a favourite device for a large panel. The Oriental metal mount, wearing better than the English, is distinctively Eastern in character, and thinner. The clumsy drawing and execution of the English japanned designs are noticeable, particularly in the amateur work.

Amateur japanners were apt to try their skill on any piece of furniture which appeared to present a suitable surface for the work. Chairs, mirror frames, toilet glasses, corner cupboards, boxes, and other small objects answered their purpose. Some such toy as a powder or patch box, a jewel case, a brush handle, or a 'standish for pen, inke & paper wch allso may sarve for a Comb box',[20] must have engaged the passing attention of many a japanner of such trifles. Japanning, during the early Georgian period, and in the later years of the craze, presumably was attempted by enthusiasts even on the veneered walnut furniture of the preceding age, with a ruthless disregard for the unsuitability of the material. The commercial japanning of cabinet makers and joiners was done with more circumspection. By inference from the *Treatise* by Stalker and Parker, 'Japanners, Painters and Guilders' worked on a ground wood such as deal, oak, or pear-tree; and also on new pieces specifically intended for japanning.

Towards 1730 in England, japanning lost much of its character; later work is for the most part undistinguished and the raised decoration is in comparatively low relief. The bold designs derived from Oriental prototypes were replaced by a more conventional delineation of flowers and foliage. The fashion was revived about 1750, when lacquered furniture in the 'Chinese taste' was favoured in the bedrooms and sometimes used, with striking decorative effect, in conjunction with colourful Chinese wallpapers. Robert Dossie observed, in 1758, that japanning was 'not at present practised so frequently', and gave an indication of changing technique: 'one principal variation in the manner of japanning is the using or omitting any priming or undercoat on the work to be japanned. In the older practice such priming was always used ... but in the Birmingham manufacture, it has always been rejected'.[21]

The Ladies' Amusement or Whole art of Japanning Made Easy, with more than 1,500 plates by Pillement and others, was published about this time. The usual designs were supplemented by others for shipping, shells, vases, insects, and borders. These might be juxtaposed. There was small pretence of technical instruction in the art of japanning. The former process of first preparing the ground and then applying several coats of varnishes, allowing each to dry before the next was applied, was doubtless found too tedious, and one sufficed. In this sense japanning was a preliminary to the revival in the next decade of ornamental painting on furniture.

The vogue persisted in the early nineteenth century. Mrs Arbuthnot, who won £80 by a bet on the Duke of Rutland's *Cadland* at the Derby of 1828, wrote: 'I have spent the money in making up a japan cabinet I painted last year, & in putting curtains in the anteroom & one of the drawing rooms. ... The cabinet is really excessively pretty.'[22]

Most of the articles of furniture made in walnut in the early eighteenth century were produced also in English japan, the carcase being constructed of a soft wood as deal, or sometimes oak. Beech was suitable for chairs; deal, more commonly, for other objects such as bureaux, bureaux-bookcases, chests with drawers, tables and dressing tables, corner cupboards, mirrors, and toilet glasses. The doors of bureaux-bookcases, like corner cupboards, were solid and unglazed. The very pleasing hanging cupboard illustrated in plate 26 (one of a pair) is probably English work of the first quarter of the eighteenth century. It is decorated in polychrome: birds, fruit, and flowers are displayed in cream panels against a background of reddish-brown hue; the shelving above for the display of china is coloured green. The total height is rather less than 4 feet.

During the earlier phase of the fashion, square cabinets, and chests with straight or domed lids were (with screens) the pieces most in evidence. These, whether of English or, more usually, of Oriental workmanship, were customarily mounted on English stands or 'frames', of gilt and carved wood, elaborately and crisply cut in high relief (Pl. 25A).

Boldness of carving was characteristic of the late Stuart period and was achieved by the use of the soft woods as fir, lime, and pear. About 1670 a florid apron-piece, profusely carved with ornament – *amorini*, beasts, festoons, and acanthus foliage – united heavy scrolled legs. Rather later, a cresting piece was added to the cabinet; being removable it has, in many cases, not survived. This ornamental feature is, however, preserved on a cabinet dating from about 1695 at the Lady Lever Art Gallery (Pl. 27). The cabinet is japanned in black and gold, with some touches of colour. The gilt cresting is unusually high and extends round the sides; a winged female figure seated on a shell and flanked by cupids bearing cymbals is enveloped by scrolling acanthus in open carving, and forms its central and dominant feature. The cabinet rests on a very splendid stand, in the style of Daniel Marot, with six tapered legs headed by wreathed Ionic capitals, surmounted by a deep frieze. The legs are linked by double cross stretchers. Stands in the style of Marot with pillar legs connected by flat curved stretchers, and those also with lighter S-scrolled legs, were fashionable in the last decade of the century. By the reign of Anne these were displaced in turn by japanned or gesso stands of comparatively simple appearance, with legs of cabriole form. Alternatively, japanned bases with drawers, or fitted with cupboards, were substituted for the less useful but more ornamental stands.

Throughout the first half of the eighteenth century, and earlier, English gilders were producing work of the highest quality in close rivalry of the French. In water-gilding, the ground wood was overlaid successively with a paste composed of size and whitening and, in several thin applications, one of fine red clay and parchment size. Gold leaf was applied to the smoothed and hardened surface after it had been moistened with water: 'Lay on your gold,' enjoins the *Treatise*, '... pressing it gently and close ... if your work be sufficiently moist, you'l perceive how lovingly the gold will embrace it, hugging and clinging to it, like those inseparable friends, Iron and the Loadstone.' [23] A granulated effect might be obtained by a previous addition of sand to the ground. The legs and backs of chairs and settees were frequently 'double-gilded'. The object could be burnished as desired – an advantage not to be obtained if the coarser method of oil-gilding was employed. 'A dog's tooth was formerly lookt upon as the fittest instrument for this business; but of late (1688) Aggats and Pebbles are more highly esteemed, being formed into the same shapes. ... These Pebbles are each valued at 5*s.* I do therefore prefer and recommend 'em before dogs-teeth.' [24]

The gesso worker followed a similar procedure. A composition of finely ground chalk and parchment size was applied in several coats to a surface already roughly carved; when hardened, it was re-carved to a high finish and gilded. French craftsmen applied up to twenty coats of the composition, but Stalker and Parker apparently deemed seven or eight to be sufficient. Gesso was used in part or in whole for the decoration in low relief of gilt centre and side tables, tall mirror frames, *torchères*, chests on stands and, to a lesser extent, chairs and other furniture; it was particularly suitable for the ornamentation (often with floral arabesques incorporating the cypher or monogram of the owner, sometimes on a latticed background) of such large flat surfaces as the tops of tables. Monotony of appearance was avoided by the punching of the background, by sanding, by etching, or by the burnishing of raised parts. Ornament in the time of William and Mary had often the elaborate symmetry of a style which suggests the influence of Boulle and other French decorative artists working under Louis XIV. The excellence of French work was acknowledged; the fashion for gilt furniture came from France to England and did not attain full perfection here until about 1730, when its brief period of ascendancy was almost ended. Some gilding, like japanning, was done by amateurs. Towards the mid eighteenth century, ladies assembled in parties and amused themselves by gilding or regilding the chairs, stools, picture frames, and other small things about the house. In a letter of 1741, Lady Hertford wrote to the Countess of Pomfret:

'Within doors, we amuse ourselves ... in gilding picture frames, and other small things: – this is so much in fashion with us at present, that I believe, if our patience and pockets would hold out, we should gild all the cornices, tables, chairs, and stools about the house.'[25]

Later, moulded composition was introduced by the Adam brothers. It was not dissimilar to gesso when applied to furniture, but was produced by mechanical means and lacked vitality. The invention was greatly used thenceforward.

Silver and silvered furniture, in common with much else of an exuberant and lavish nature, made some considerable appeal. In the Earl of Chesterfield's house at Bretby, Celia Fiennes remarked: 'the bride chamber which used to be call'd the Silver roome where the stands, table and fire utensills were all massy silver'. She added that 'when plaite was in nomination to pay a tax, the Earle of Chesterfield sold it all, and the plaite of the house'.[26] The silver furniture of Louis XIV's bedchamber at Versailles had a similarly transient existence. Solid silver furniture was at source an Italian fashion and rare in England. A notorious exception is provided by that commented on by John Evelyn in his *Diary* for 1683 on the occasion of his visit to the apartments of the Duchess of Portsmouth: 'that which engag'd my curiosity, was the rich and splendid furniture of this woman's apartment, now twice or thrice pull'd down and rebuilt to satisfie her prodigal and expensive pleasures ... chimney furniture, sconces, branches, braseras, &c., all of massie silver, and out of number ...'.[27]

Silvered furniture, being but a variation on gilded, was not uncommon. Many stands of the Charles II and William and Mary periods were silvered; and silvering was often overlaid with gold lacquers in simulation of gilding. The leaf, applied in like manner to the gold leaf, did not repay the full labour of beating and was in consequence considerably thicker.

Furniture overlaid with thin silver plates, heavily embossed with ornament sometimes in scroll designs but of varied character, had some vogue at the end of the seventeenth century; and silver when used in conjunction with ebony was found to make an effective display. The technique was Dutch in origin. The 'Ebony Table garnish'd with silver', which bears the initials 'E.D.' for Elizabeth, Countess of Dysart, on the central silver plaque set in the ebonized top (a renovation), is listed in the 1679 inventory at Ham House (Pl. 25B). The table is supported by four female terminal figures elaborately carved in walnut. This fine piece is one of several of that kind noted as being then in the house. It shows strong Dutch influence and was probably executed by one of those craftsmen for whom a clear preference was shown at Ham. Some of the furniture there resembles contemporary Dutch work. But silver-mounting was, in general, more appropriate to the ornamentation of such smaller objects as table mirrors, sconces or travelling cases, and may be noticed as an expression of the then ruling taste for luxury in all furnishings: it was not a significant factor in the evolution of design in furniture.

NOTES TO CHAPTER 4

1, 2. Quoted by Francis Lenygon, *Furniture in England, from 1660 to 1760*, 1914, p. 271.

3. One cabinet (W.37 – 1927) is decorated with mother of pearl inlay and painted in gold and silver on a black ground, with flowers in vases and arabesques; the other (W.32 – 1919) with flowers, fruit, and birds on a black ground.

4. *Memoirs of John Evelyn*, ed. by William Bray, 2nd edition, 1819, vol. I, p. 381. 29th Sept., 1665.

5, 6. Bray, *op. cit.*, vol. I, pp. 348–9. 9th June, 1662. Evelyn states that the bed was 'a present made by ye States of Holland when his Ma[ty] returned, and had formerly ben given by them to our King's sister ye Princesse of Orange, and being bought of her againe was now presented to ye King'.

7. Bray, *op cit.*, vol. I, p. 382. 30th Dec., 1665.

8. Bray, *op. cit.*, vol. II, pp. 71–2. 23rd Sept., 1700.

9–13. J. Stalker and G. Parker, *Treatise of Japaning and Varnishing ...* (1688).

14. *Dampier's Voyages*, ed. by John Masefield, 1906, vol. I, p. 609.

15. *The Journeys of Celia Fiennes*, ed. by Christopher Morris, 1947, p. 69. The Northern Journey and the Tour of Kent, 1697.
16. Masefield, *loc. cit.*
17. Masefield, *op. cit.*, vol. I, pp. 609–10.
18, 19. *The Autobiography and Correspondence of Mary Granville, Mrs Delany*, ed. by Lady Llanover, 1st series, 1861, vol. I, p. 227 (5th Dec., 1729); vol. I, pp. 212, 213, 285 (23rd Aug. and 9th Sept., 1729, 13th July, 1731).
20. Stalker & Parker, *op. cit.*
21. Robert Dossie, *The Handmaid to the Arts*, 1758.
22. *The Journal of Mrs Arbuthnot, 1820–1832*, ed. by Francis Bamford and the Duke of Wellington, 1950, vol. II, p. 205.
23, 24. Stalker & Parker, *op. cit.*
25. Quoted by Percy Macquoid, *English Furniture, etc.*, Lady Lever Art Gallery Collections III, 1928, p. 93 (item 435).
26. Morris, *op. cit.*, p. 171. The Great Journey to Newcastle and to Cornwall, 1698.
27. Bray, *op. cit.*, vol. I, p. 563. 4th Oct., 1683.

CHAPTER FIVE

THE EARLY GEORGIAN PERIOD

(1720–1740)

FURNITURE produced during the reign of Anne had been characterized by restraint and good proportion; and pieces were enriched principally by a fine figure obtained by the use of selected veneers of walnut. There was some reaction against the Baroque, adopted after the Restoration, in favour of a less exuberant style.

The advent of the Hanoverians to the throne brought little change of taste. Furniture design remained more or less static throughout the first quarter of the century, with the exception of pieces designed by architects for the builders of great Palladian houses. The change which occurred in the fourth decade of the century was due to the introduction of mahogany – a new and costly wood, the ready adoption of which was made possible only by the increasing wealth and prosperity of the country.

In 1720, the walnut wood famine in France, and a consequent embargo placed by the French authorities on the exportation of timber, forced English craftsmen to put greater reliance than formerly on the supply of native trees. The darker Virginian walnut, which resembles mahogany, was imported also. The supply obtained from these sources was insufficient. As a consequence, a number of London makers turned to mahogany. 'Spanish' mahogany had been known in England for more than a century, having been observed, on a voyage of 1595, by the carpenter on board Sir Walter Raleigh's ship. It was admired as one of the many wonders of the Indies and subsequently used on rare occasions. The logs brought to England during the early mahogany period were obtained from the Islands of

San Domingo (Hispaniola), Cuba, and also from Puerto Rico. One writer, in 1757, lists 'the mahogany too, in such general use with us', as being amongst the natural products of Jamaica, and speaks of 'the excellence of everything which is produced in that climate'.[1] Additional testimony to the excellence of mahogany is contained in the export figure for the year 1753, when more than 500,000 feet of the timber were received through Jamaica.

Mahogany began to supersede walnut in general use in the making of furniture in England during the second quarter of the century, and rapidly gained favour. Mahogany was superior to walnut in several respects: (1) while present-day taste appreciates the mellowed brown hue to which time has reduced many extant pieces, in the eighteenth century, the dark reddish colour of the newly polished wood was much preferred.* The taste for strong colour is not inconsistent with the heavy gilding of post-Restoration furniture and woodwork, which is exemplified in the many gilt consoles and side tables, mirrors, chairs, settees, and *torchères* of late seventeenth and early eighteenth century date. (2) Mahogany was found to be very strong. The Cuban variety, especially, was hard, heavy, and close grained. It lasted well, and because of its hardness did not easily mark or scratch, taking a good, lasting, and natural polish without much difficulty, and without the application of varnish. It did not crack or warp; nor was it liable to attack from woodworm.

The very considerable production of walnut furniture throughout the early Georgian period, however, is liable to be disregarded because, by comparison with mahogany or oak, walnut is perishable, and proportionately little survives. Some of the best work of the country craftsman was in walnut; and, although held in progressively diminishing favour, its popularity persisted as late as 1760

* Mention is made in cabinet-makers' receipts for polishing of a desirable red colour, and furniture in contemporary 'conversation pictures' is noticeably, in many cases, of a warm reddish tint. Country makers indeed are reputed to have stained oak with bullocks' blood.

in the provinces. In 1736, one of the Purefoy family wrote to a certain 'Mr King a Chair frame maker at the King & Queen Bircester' in the following terms: 'Mr King. As I understand you make chairs of wallnut tree frames with 4 legs without any Barrs for Mr Vaux of Caversfeild, if you do such I desire you will come over here in a week's time any morning but Wensday. I shall want about 20 chairs. This will oblidge, Your freind to serve you [Elizabeth Purefoy].'[2]

Many early mahogany pieces corresponded exactly in design with counterparts in walnut. 'Spanish' mahogany, however, lacked figure and the process of veneering was not employed. The aspect of such furniture was somewhat austere as a consequence and was relieved in three ways: by the employment of carving as a means of decoration; by the use of mouldings; and finally, at a later date, by the more frequent shaping of pieces in the French or the Dutch manner. Flat surfaces became serpentine, bow, or hollowed. The readiness with which the early mahogany took a natural polish, and its hardness, made it the ideal wood for shaping; and mouldings of it could be laid expeditiously in the solid with small expense and the promise of durability unlike those of walnut which were veneered on a carcase wood and cross-banded. The decorative matched veneers of the walnut period were gradually replaced by carved enrichments. Construction, modified to suit the properties of mahogany, was in the solid, although the seat rails of chairs and settees were veneered, and, on occasion, the splat; in this particular, a return was made to the old method which had been superseded during the walnut period. Fine carved ornament became a distinguishing characteristic of such work. Towards *c.* 1750 the curled and rippled 'Spanish' wood and the Honduras (formerly called 'baywood' to distinguish it from the West Indian) varieties of mahogany were imported.

The large size of the planks was of especial value to the joiner in the construction of the dining table. The gate-legged table, made of oak or walnut, had been formerly in general use. When this was of large size – and examples are comparatively uncommon – each of the three parts comprising the oval top was of necessity made of joined planks. This constructional difficulty was removed if mahogany was used. A few mahogany gate-legged tables are to be found, dating from the second quarter of the eighteenth century, which conform essentially to those tables made some two generations earlier; these are of interest in that they suggest that the conservative section of the public, also, realized the material advantages possessed by mahogany.

During the early Georgian period numerous mahogany flap dining-tables were made. They have rectangular, oval, or occasionally polygonal tops with four legs of cabriole or modified cabriole form. Large examples have six or as many as eight legs. The type presented a logical continuation of the gate principal. The earliest form of mahogany extension table was evolved at this time; the length of the table was increased as required by the insertion of a separate, central section with two wide drop leaves. It was also the custom for a pair of tables (with square flaps) to be placed together when occasion demanded.

The increasing use of mahogany in place of walnut at first hardly affected taste. Chairs of identical design were made in either walnut or mahogany according to the wish of the purchaser; as similarly, but more rarely, a wood such as padouk might be used. The cabriole leg, plain, or sparsely carved with shell ornament on the knee, the simple club foot, shaped hoop back, and unpierced central splat, relieved only by the figure of the veneer and in some cases by the addition of some carved ornament, were features which had given character to the type of chair formerly in popular demand (Pl. 28) – a type which now persisted in more decorated form throughout the half-century. The stuffed-over or upholstered back was retained as an alternative to the shaped, pierced, and carved splat back in wood. In general, the chair back tended to become lower and square, with straight or undulating uprights and bow-shaped top rail (cf. Pl. 28A and B).

Carving of a high quality is exemplified in seating furniture of the early mahogany period, and was confined mainly to front legs, the centre piece or apron of the seat rail, and to such portions of the chair or settee back as the cresting of the top rail or broad central splat. It has subtlety, vitality, and fine surface unobtainable in a soft wood. A carved eagle's head or sometimes a scroll form was favoured for the termination of the arm (Fig. 38), and, like the spiral whorl occurring at the junction of upright and top rail, is frequently found on both mahogany and walnut pieces. The leg in particular was developed into a decorative area; the carving of the knee often being in high relief and extending to the ear-pieces. In some cases the knee was

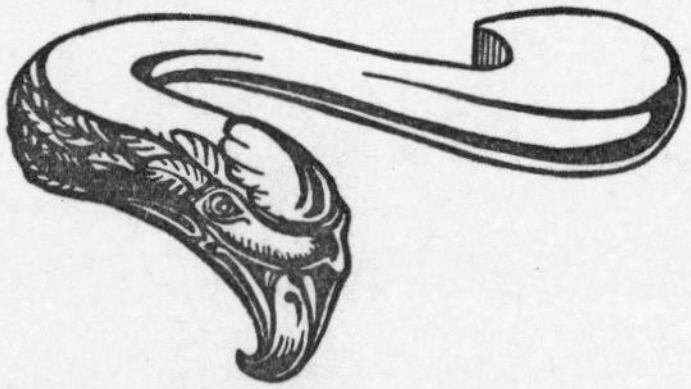

Figure 38 – Detail of arm terminal – the carved eagle's head

'hipped' at the junction with the seat rail; the hipping, a characteristic detail dating from about 1730–50, was also carved (Pl. 28B). The cabriole leg, terminating in claw-and-ball foot (Fig. 40A), is a most satisfactory form. In good examples the leg appears to have an unusual strength and firmness, and the tense grip of claws on ball, conveyed by vigorous carving, is convincing.

The main *motifs* in use were the lion mask, the satyr or human mask, and *cabochon* and leaf ornament (Fig. 39); all enjoyed a term of popularity during the early years of the reign of George II. The lion mask, which may have been inspired by similar decoration on some of the imported Chinese pieces, was properly employed in conjunction with the paw (Fig. 40C), or paw-and-ball foot; in those instances

Figure 39 – Detail of carving – *cabochon* and leaf ornament

the whole leg was often naturalistically carved. The claw-and-ball foot, which had been adopted at the beginning of the century in succession to the simple club foot, either round or pointed, returned to favour during the rococo phase of design when lion furniture, the vogue for which was comparatively brief, was outmoded.* Similarly, the satyr mask and cloven foot are often to be found in association; and one may expect the scroll or 'French foot' (Fig. 40B) to be used with the *cabochon* and leaf *motif*, in so far as it

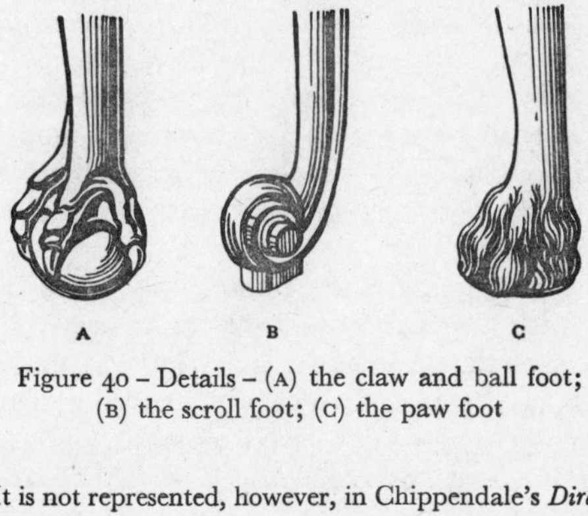

A B C

Figure 40 – Details – (A) the claw and ball foot; (B) the scroll foot; (C) the paw foot

* It is not represented, however, in Chippendale's *Director*.

reflects the imitation of French fashions which appeared strongly and enduringly after about 1735.

These forms, however, were employed without rule at the whim of the chair-maker. Carved ornament was vigorous and not yet of a stereotyped nature, and in most cases expressed an individual preference of the carver who worked by invention and not from measured drawings. With the exception of some country-made chairs, the stretcher was dispensed with and did not reappear until the straight leg came back into fashion *c.* 1750. Stretchers marred the appearance of the boldly shaped cabriole leg and were unnecessary for strengthening purposes.

The popularity of settees of chair-back form was established about 1715. As with the earlier upholstered type, they formed part of a set of seating furniture which, in the case of the wealthy, often comprised as large a number of pieces as two settees, two armchairs, long and short stools, and many single chairs of similar pattern. The settees were of double or triple chair-back form, the number of legs in front varying accordingly from three to four. Upholstered and chair-back settees shared popularity throughout the century. Sets, now rarely complete, are found in walnut and mahogany alike. Regular and uniform disposition of furniture was desired. In Vanbrugh's project, for instance, of a 'Detach'd Gallery' or Greenhouse for Blenheim (quashed, however, by the Duchess of Marlborough's: 'Nothing, I think, can be more mad than the proposal, nor a falser description of the prospect') provision was made for the orderly disposal of books 'in Presses made handsome like Cabinets, And plac'd Regularly along with the Chairs, tables And Couches'.[3]

Spurious examples of the upholstered settee are fairly plentiful; with the exception of the centre leg, which is of a different form, the piece can conveniently be made up out of a chair of the period. The upholstered settee, which corresponds in size to a double chair-back counterpart, will in most cases have been constructed with three front legs; and the larger variety, of triple chair-back size, with four.

The 'love seat' and the winged armchair were customarily fitted with thick squab cushions and were made with rather shorter legs.

Although the chair had by now displaced the stool as the usual seat, stools were made in appreciable numbers, mostly for use in state apartments; and it was not until the latter half of the century that the popularity of the stool declined. The furniture belonging to Celia Fiennes and listed in her will (dated 1738) included 'two square stools that have hook and staples to hang on to the chair as a couch'. She possessed in addition a 'seatee of Irish stitch' and 'an ebony couch'.[4] Stools normally formed part of a set of furniture, breaking the monotonous appearance produced by many identical chairs (Pl. 29). As a consequence those surviving are often of fine quality. The demand for stools by the middle classes was never very great.

Stools were of various types, with both upholstered and drop-in seats, often rectangular in shape, sometimes oval, and more rarely circular. A kidney shape, supported on three legs instead of the usual four, and the X-frame stool were also made. The height of the seat from the ground was approximately 18 inches. Design and decoration followed a course parallel to that of chairs and settees; knees and seat rail were enriched by carved ornament and by parcel gilding. After 1730, there is a preponderance of mahogany over walnut or wholly gilt examples.

The fever for gambling was at its height during the early years of the century and infected all classes of society in England. Ombre and quadrille retained the interest with which they had been welcomed at the Restoration; and picquet and commerce were popular. Numerous card tables of the period survive in some diversity. Many show great ingenuity of construction; there are, of course, wide differences in quality, but the general standard of workmanship is high.

The seventeenth century gaming table had been essentially a chess and backgammon board on supports. This piece was improved for the playing of card games by the provision of a multiple top. Tables were frequently dished for candlesticks and fitted with wells for counters; sometimes a small drawer was contained in the frieze. Card tables were made before about 1700. Development conformed in many regards with that of other pieces: the stretcher had been dispensed with by the opening years of the century; the restrained cabriole leg of the reign of Anne, either plain or carved on the knee with modest shell or acanthus ornament and usually terminating in club or spade foot, tended to be of bolder and more decorated form and to be used in conjunction with the claw-and-ball; mahogany gradually displaced walnut; and during the third decade of the century the paw foot, lion decoration, and satyr and human mask ornament all shared a comparatively brief period of favour.

The circular card table (of about 1700), with a folding top received when open by two back legs which swung out rather in the manner of the gate, persisted until 1720. A square table with cylindrical corners was made concurrently. The latter, as also the circular table, was served by one movable leg only. The corners of the flap were unsupported by this arrangement, however, and a somewhat ungainly and unbalanced appearance was imparted to the opened table. An improvement conceived before 1715 provided for the support of the flap in more sightly manner by the movement of both back legs on a hinged folding framework, when all four sides appeared to be identical. This ingenious type of table has been given the name 'concertina' (Pl. 32). By 1715, the frieze was shaped to follow the lines of the table top; formerly, rounded corner pieces had projected by 3 or 4 inches from the square frieze. A type with square projecting corners was introduced some fifteen years later; this, and the plain square table, remained in favour for a considerable time. A triangular table, supported at each angle and opening to the usual square shape, was made; and early tripod tables were in use at this period, sometimes as card tables.

It seems that card tables were made in a uniform size;

the width of most specimens is about 3 feet, although smaller tables are known, and these, because of their rarity, are extremely valuable. Pairs of tables, when folded, were frequently used as small wall consoles.

The small tripod tea,* or china, table† was made in

* Tea had been introduced into this country from Holland about the time of the Restoration; in 1660, Pepys remarked that he 'did send for a cup of tee, (a China drink) of which I never had drank before'.[5] Tea and coffee were at first drunk by the well-to-do in public places. By the first decade of the eighteenth century it was a fashionable but still very dear drink. Green tea was priced at more than 20*s*. per pound, and the bohea at more than half as much again. By the end of the reign of George I, however, open-air tea gardens in and near London, presently to become very numerous, enjoyed excessive popularity and gradually became unfrequented by people of fashion; the next few years saw a rapid growth of the habit of tea drinking in private houses. Thenceforward the price decreased rapidly and it has been estimated that during the last quarter of the century the yearly consumption per head of the population varied between two and three pounds. In larger houses the company withdrew from the dining table to the 'Tea Room', a smaller room where the porcelain cups and saucers, the silver and other utensils of the tea equipage were kept and which was given up exclusively to the ceremony of taking tea. The habit was indulged by both sexes and contributed towards the softening of manners noticeable in this century. It displaced in part the conventional drinking bout by which the winter hours of darkness after dinner were filled by those who otherwise found them dreary. On first being introduced tea had been regarded as an efficacious antidote to drunkenness, being taken as recommended both before and after over-indulgence in food or drink.

† Later in the century it was customary at some houses for each tea drinker to be provided with a small table. 'Perhaps you do not know,' wrote Hannah More to her sister, in May 1788, 'that a *The* is among the stupid new follies of the winter. You are to invite fifty or a hundred people to come at eight o'clock: there is to be a long table, or little parties at small ones; the cloth is to be laid, as at breakfast; every one has a napkin; – tea and coffee are made by the company, as at a public breakfast; the table is covered with rolls, wafers, bread and butter; and what constitutes the very essence of a *The*, an immense load of hot buttered rolls, and muffins, all admirably contrived to create a nauseau in persons fresh from the dinner table. Now, of all nations under the sun, as I take it, the English are the greatest fools: – because the Duke of Dorset in Paris, where people dine at two, thought this would be a pretty fashion to introduce; we, who dine at six, must adopt this French translation of an English fashion, and fall into it, as if it were an original invention: taking up our own custom at third hand.'[6]

increasing numbers, and rarely in walnut, from about 1730. The form was pleasing, and serviceable – the table stood securely on an uneven floor. The round top was supported by a central pillar on a tripod base of cabriole form, terminating in club, paw, or claw-and-ball feet. The short knee, more often than not, was unornamented. The shaping of the stem and base, especially if undecorated by carving, demanded judgement on the part of the maker. Tripod tables were put to very general use, and were to be found in most households by the mid-century (Pl. 33). Supper tables, of similar form to the tea-table and ringed for as many as eight plates, appeared before 1750. There was also a small but sustained demand for a rectangular tea-table, with tray top, plain frieze, and plain cabriole legs, which apparently was made contemporaneously with the tripod type throughout the third quarter of the century.

The pole screen on small tripod base became fashionable about 1730 as an alternative to the established cheval or 'horse' firescreen. The type was not new. An iron 'screen stick' of this form was listed as an item of the 1679 inventory of Ham House – and is still there. Such screens are, however, seldom found in walnut. The panel, usually of needlework, was adjustable for height. Fire screens were made in considerable numbers and many have survived. The open basket grates threw out great heat into rooms which were commonly ill-ventilated. (The interest of pole screens is now mainly decorative and they are often cut and converted into small coffee tables about 20 inches high.)

Throughout the century, oak and other native woods such as elm, yew, ash, or the fruit woods, were largely used according to local supply for a quantity of simple, useful furniture which satisfied the needs of most of the people; this applied particularly to the furniture of the country districts, where successive fashions in furniture were for the most part disregarded, even by the well-housed. The country was self-sufficient in its way of life. The isolation of some village communities remained undisturbed until the time of the Napoleonic wars. And then change was slow and often unwelcome. We read in *Rural Rides* that on a Thursday evening, 20 October, 1825, William Cobbett paused at Reigate on his progress 'From Kensington, across Surrey and along that county', to record his feelings experienced that day at a farmhouse close by the River Mole. This dwelling had been leased for generations to a family named Charington. The present tenant, now quitting, was breaking a long continuity of tenure. The old furniture which was to be sold and dispersed was, according to Cobbett's description, mostly of oak, plain, useful, and enduring; oak coffers, bedsteads, chests of drawers, long tables, and many joint stools were remarked. 'Some of these things,' he wrote, stressing the traditional nature of most, 'were many hundreds of years old.' But this 'scene of *plain manners* and *plentiful living*' had been spoilt at last by the infiltration of new manners and an assumption of gentility on the part of the Charingtons. 'And, which was the worst of all, there was a *parlour*! Aye, and a *carpet* and *bell-pull* too! ... and there was the mahogany table, and the fine chairs, and the fine glass, and all as bare-faced upstart as any stock jobber in the kingdom can boast of.'

Cobbett was indignant that fashion had intruded in a yeoman's house, where durability and usefulness had long prevailed. 'When the old farm-houses are down (and down they must come in time) what a miserable thing the country will be! Those that are now erected are mere painted shells, with a Mistress within, who is stuck up in a place she calls a *parlour*, with, if she have children, the "young ladies and gentlemen" about her: some showy chairs and a sofa (a sofa by all means) ...' [7]

In the early Georgian period, the Charingtons had, no doubt, gone to the village for their furniture. Most villages possessed a joiner who followed the old models he knew and worked in the traditional way perhaps taught him by his father or his father's father, using their tools. He supplied settles because they gave freedom from draughts and because drawers could be fitted below the seats, or good cupboards contrived behind the high backs; he made many chests, corner and hanging cupboards because they too offered good storage and occupied little space. After the early years of the century, the small hanging cupboard was

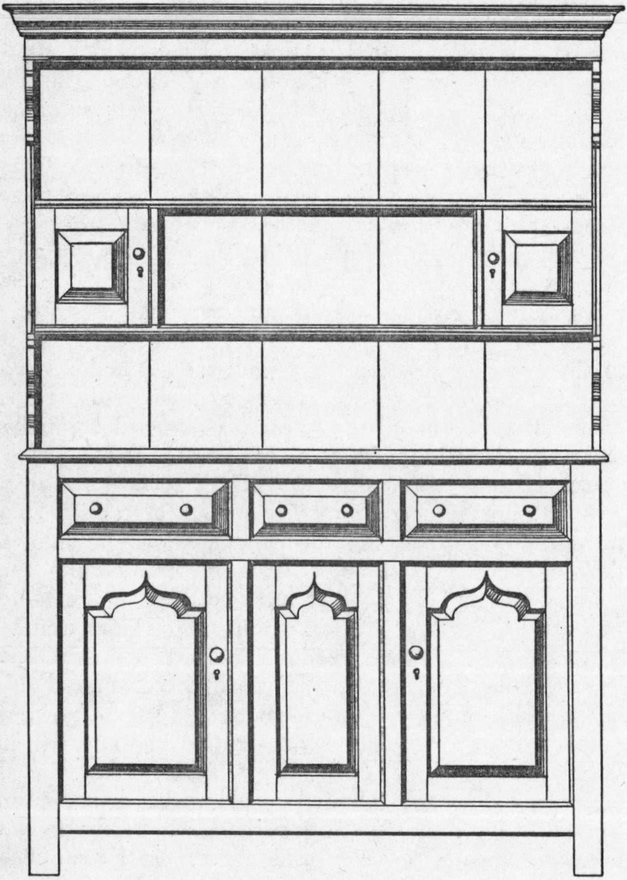

Figure 41 – Dresser, in two stages; the base contains three small drawers above cupboards with fielded panels and supports a superstructure of open shelves

found mainly in farmhouse and cottage and was scarcely affected by the trend of fashion except in the details of ornament. A change of style interested the country joiner little. Published pattern books did not appear until rather later; the information gleaned by him regarding the present taste in his craft was modified to suit his own requirements.

The demands of ordinary townspeople were not exacting. The mass of old furniture, much of which has suffered subsequent mutilation or 'embellishment', may not be dated with the exactitude permissible in the case of exceptional pieces. New fashions arose among the governing class and were adapted for humbler purposes at a later date. The time lag was often quite considerable. Oak cupboards and dressers *in situ*, which are found in outlying districts, are sometimes inscribed with the initials of their first owners, and a date commemorative of their wedding; which may be so late as to be incompatible with the apparent style of the piece. In such cases the latest feature affords a guide to the date. Some oak dressers of the mid eighteenth century and later were fitted with an upper stage containing shelves for the display of pewter or earthenware, and with small side cupboards (Fig. 41). Concession to contemporary fashion was reflected in such details as superimposed ornamental pilasters or in the use of inlaid mahogany borders.

Much of the bedroom furniture, even of the great houses, was simple in character; people passed without surprise from splendidly appointed public rooms to modest bedchambers in which little provision was made for personal comfort. In the standard type town house, which was a notable and English contribution to eighteenth-century architecture, the furnishings of dining and withdrawing rooms differed widely from those of the smaller upper chambers. The distinction between the public and private rooms of the house persisted, to a lesser degree, beyond the close of the century.*

* Catherine Morland, a privileged guest on her arrival at Northanger Abbey, was conducted to rooms in which 'the furniture was in all the profusion and elegance of modern taste ... the dining-parlour a noble

At the end of the reign of Anne, 'furniture not of the latest fashion' was relegated at convenience to an upper floor, while such new pieces as chests of drawers, chests on stands, and tallboys made primarily for use in a bedroom followed an even course of development and were in large part unaffected by the vagaries of fashion. Although mahogany was, of course, used for a number of exceptional pieces, or to special order, the consistent employment of walnut for this class of furniture persisted until the mid-century in many households. Better specimens were as a rule finely veneered with burr walnut, and were constructed with veneered sides and oak-lined drawers. Others were plainly veneered, with deal linings, mouldings worked in the solid, and sides forming part of the carcase. Pieces were mostly straight fronted; serpentine shaping (in mahogany) which added considerably to the interest of the surface – and incidentally to the cost – occurs after about 1740.

Chests of drawers were also made in oak in large numbers, according to the often very pleasing fancy of the country maker, and incorporated ornamental or constructional features of traditional sort.

The 'chest-upon-chest', or tallboy, which was of Dutch inspiration, had been introduced early in the century and stood, like the chest of drawers, on plain bracket feet. The more ornamental ogee bracket foot is not encountered until about 1740. The chest on stand is almost exclusively a walnut piece, and later was superseded by the tallboy. Since the stand contained two long drawers only, it was less commodious. Use of the tallboy imposed, nevertheless, as George Smith, a nineteenth-century cabinet-maker later observed, the disagreeable necessity 'of getting on to chairs to place anything in the upper drawers'.[9] The tallboy was designed with straight hollow cornice or more rarely a

room ... fitted up in a style of luxury and expense'. The General, when she spoke her admiration, 'confessed he did look upon a tolerably large eating-room as one of the necessaries of life'. Catherine found, however, that the furniture in her own apartment was 'handsome and comfortable though not of the latest fashion'.[8]

broken pediment. Canted and fluted corners to the fronts were not unusual (Fig. 42). The feature of a shaped concavity, bearing a star decoration, in the centre of the bottom drawer and plinth moulding was of Dutch origin. In spite of finer dovetailing and such added refinements as the dressing-slide, these walnut pieces appeared plain in comparison with earlier examples. Effective and decorative balancing of veneers on the drawer fronts is confined to a few specimens.

The dressing-table with legs of cabriole form, usually fitted with three drawers, and the knee-hole pedestal dressing-table (Figs. 43 and 44), were used in conjunction with the toilet mirror on stand. Both were small, rarely exceeding 3 feet in width. As early as the second quarter of the century, specimens of the latter type were designed for dressing, with a top drawer containing a hinged toilet glass and divided into numerous small compartments. Ladies' dressing-tables, and the mirrors above them, were often draped. The mode extended over a period of years.*

In the course of the first half of the century, the third Earl of Burlington was occupied in disseminating in Georgian England the architectural principles followed by Palladio in Italy in the sixteenth century. He was aided by William Kent. In the words of Horace Walpole, Lord Burlington, 'the Apollo of arts, found a proper priest in the person of Mr Kent'.[10] A small coterie of *cognoscenti* now made architecture their chosen pursuit. The architect himself was no longer anonymous. The group approved and adopted the Renaissance style introduced into England a

* Hogarth shows a draped table in the *Countess's Dressing Room* of 1744 (Tate Gallery), and the *Modiste*, of 1746, a canvas by François Boucher (Wallace Collection), confirms that a similar fashion prevailed in Paris. *Lady Easy's Steinkirk*, a painting by Francis Wheatley, illustrated an incident in Colley Cibber's revived comedy *The Careless Husband*. The scene is Lady Easy's bedroom. The players wear clothes of about 1790, and the furnishings are in the style of the latter half of the century. Both the dressing table and the gilt mirror, which is supported on it, are draped in a pale soft fabric which extends below a pleated valance to the carpeted floor.

Figure 42 – Chest of drawers in two stages, or tallboy, veneered with figured walnut; the base is supported on plain bracket feet and fitted with a dressing slide; the upper portion is designed with a straight cornice of concave section, and the corners to the front are canted and fluted

hundred years previously by Inigo Jones (1573–1652) – a style which had been incompletely understood in the seventeenth century. The Palladians were interested in the lay-out of the grounds and gardens, and also in interior decorative detail; they believed that, whenever possible, the building should conform throughout all its parts to approved architectural principles. The 'Rules of Taste' were emphatic, pervasive, and inviolable, and might well be applied to furniture.

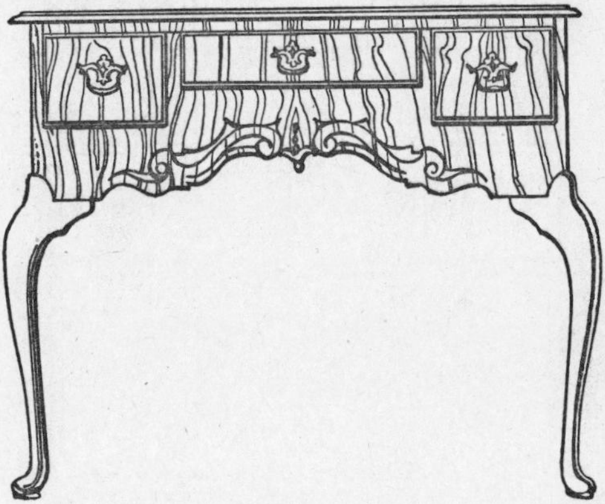

Figure 43 – Dressing table of walnut, with three drawers; the cabriole legs, 'hipped' at the knee, finish in plain pad feet

It is significant that there was a considerable demand for books on architecture; and some included a few plates devoted to furniture. Cabinet-makers did not as yet publish trade catalogues. Leoni, Colen Campbell, and Batty Langley were among the authors of these treatises; such other contemporaries as James Gibbs, protégé of the Earl of Mar, and Flitcroft, one of Burlington's following, were directly interested in the furniture placed in their buildings. George Vertue, the engraver, who laboriously gathered material for his projected but unwritten *History of the Art of*

Painting and Sculpture in England, and to whom we are indebted for the greater part of the first-hand information as to the arts at that period, noted tersely of the latter: 'Mr Flitcroft was a Joyner – now Architect.'[11]

The name of William Kent (1685–1748) is closely connected with the Palladian movement. In his youth Kent was an indifferent portrait and 'history' painter. While in

Figure 44 – Dressing table of kneehole form, supported on plain bracket feet and fitted with short drawers and a central cupboard

Italy between 1710 and 1719, he became acquainted with Lord Burlington, with whom thereafter he lived in close association. As architect, landscape gardener, and furniture designer, he held a high contemporary reputation and was in fact indispensable to the society of his time. The ideas to which he gave successful expression mirrored the cultured but rigid taste of the ruling classes. Horace Walpole's judgement of Kent appears to us not to have been wide of the mark. 'Kent,' he wrote, 'had an excellent taste for ornaments, and gave designs for most of the furniture at Houghton, as he did for several other persons. Yet chaste as these ornaments were, they were often immeasurably ponderous. His chimney-pieces, though lighter than those of Inigo, whom he imitated, are frequently heavy, and his constant introduction of pediments and the members of architecture over doors, and within rooms, was disproportioned and cumbrous. . . . his oracle was so much consulted by all who affected taste, that nothing was thought complete without his assistance. He was not only consulted for furniture, as frames of pictures, glasses, tables, chairs, etc., but for plate, for a barge, for a cradle. And so impetuous was fashion, that two great ladies prevailed on him to make designs for their birthday gowns. The one he dressed in a petticoat decorated with columns of the five orders; the other like a bronze, in a copper-coloured satin, with ornaments of gold.' [12]

In contrast to everyday furniture of the early Georgian period, made by joiner, cabinet- or chair-maker, and for all sections of the population, there was this important class of furniture of architectural character which was influenced by models from France (and, more particularly, Italy) and which was of a semi-movable nature. It was ornate, lavishly enriched with carving, and more often than not gilded, and included side tables, mirrors, and bookcases. These pieces were intended to remain in the houses for which they were designed and to contribute directly to an interior effect. They were complementary to the elaborate doors, windows, chimney-pieces, and cornices of apartments. They had no extensive influence on furniture design, being provided for a small privileged class.

The evidence afforded by conversation pictures and by inventories suggests that the rooms of this period, at least in most houses, were not overcrowded (Pl. 29). The centres of reception rooms were left comparatively free of furniture. The state apartments of great houses were spacious and of lofty proportions, but were perhaps frigid in character and required some relief of colour and warmth. Richly gilt distinctive furniture was essential. Unfortunately, much of the furniture designed by William Kent and his followers, now detached from an appropriate setting, appears cumbersome and in dubious taste.*

Gilt side tables, and the mirrors which usually surmounted them, continued the tradition of Stuart times. They differed, in the absence of shaped stretchers bearing a central finial, from the accomplished pieces made, in many cases by foreign immigrant craftsmen, at the close of the seventeenth century. They were often free adaptations of the side tables then to be found in the Venetian palaces; and their use was ornamental. William Kent had long studied and travelled in Italy; he now, in the capacity of architect, employed a number of carvers, some probably Italian, whose skill and fine execution did much to redeem his designs in this variety of furniture from coarseness.

Side tables displayed great freedom and variety of form. The straight fronted tops, 5 or 6 feet in length, were composed of marble, scagliola, or sometimes of gesso decorated in low relief with all-over patterns or scenes. Monsters, animals, cupids, or sphinxes were introduced as supports, and usurping the place of legs and conventional frieze, occupied the greater part of the area between the table top and ground. Some more extravagant examples may well be regarded as works of sculpture in high relief rather than furniture. Alternatively, less ornate tables, about 1720–5, were supported on legs of scrolled or cabriole form, of square section decorated with scale pattern (Pl. 32); the knee was then often in the form of a volute carved with acanthus. Successively, 1730–40, tables are found with a straight frieze decorated with a popular *motif* of the period

* Vanbrugh was following his normal procedure when, late in his life (April 1724), he wrote to the Earl of Carlisle at Castle Howard, near York: 'I believe four doors will give both Light and View Sufficient, without Windows, and then there will be Space enough for Chairs; the Table I think (as I have mention'd formerly) shou'd stand always fix'd in the Middle of the Room.'[13]

such as the Vitruvian scroll or 'wave pattern', or were designed with a heavy apron piece bearing a central mask of human or animal form. A richly carved mahogany side table of this type, dating from *c.* 1730, is in the collection of the Lady Lever Art Gallery at Port Sunlight. The parti-coloured marble top is supported on scrolled legs which are united by an openwork carved apron piece, displacing the frieze, and composed of *coquillage*, swags of grapes, and, in the front, a central male mask of Bacchic form. The latter feature suggests that this specimen, as many other side tables, was originally in use in the dining-room as a side-board (Pl. 31).

The introduction of the console, originally called a 'clap' table, dated from the first years of the century. Although of bracket construction, the console was in form closely related to the side table and had the same decorative function when used in conjunction with a mirror and often a pair of stands. An eagle with outstretched wings (Pl. 30) was introduced as a support and, like the caprice of two intertwined dolphins, attained wide popularity. Apparently this variety of furniture rapidly became as much the fashion here as at Versailles.

Ornamental candlestands or *torchères* were, for the most part, taller and more imposing than specimens of late seventeenth-century date, with twisted stems. In common with pedestal stands intended to support heavy candelabra, bronzes, or busts, the more fantastic of gilt *torchères* were distinguished by an ingenious fancy and, as with this whole class of furniture, by architectural detail. The mahogany stand, fitted with gallery top and supported on a tripod base, was adopted towards 1740.

Both Vauxhall and Southwark had for some years produced plates of mirror glass claimed to be without blemish and which were certainly of considerable size. In the *Post Man* for 1702, the claims of the Bear Garden Glass House at Southwark had somewhat exceeded those of their rivals at 'the old Glasshouse at Foxall [Vauxhall], known by the name of the Duke of Buckingham's House'. They sold

'Looking-Glass Plates, Blown from the smallest size upwards, to 90 Inches, with proportionable breadth, of Lively Colours, free from Veins and foulness, incident to large Plates that have been hitherto sold'.[14] Mirrors, also, exhibited marked architectural character, in many cases being intended to harmonize with, or to supplement, the windows of rooms. On occasion, details and mouldings of the mirror frame duplicated those of door, window, or cornice. Since the glass was thin, it was a commendable achievement when plates of 6 feet and more in length and of 'proportionable breadth' were ground without breakage.

The suave lines of the mirror frames of an earlier period became formalized. Broken, or alternatively swan-necked, pediments enclosed a central ornament of shell, mask, heraldic cartouche, or plinth, surmounting an entablature of classical form (Fig. 45). The frieze was strongly marked; floral pendants, or similar ornament, edging the sides, relieved the severe lines of a plain oblong or square-cornered inner framing. Candle brackets were still attached to the base. The long pier glasses of the period, purposed to hang between tall windows, were designed in corresponding style.

Similarly, large overmantel mirrors, with arched or serpentine headings, were superseded by those with plainer rectangular frame, or with square corners. Occasionally a sea- or land-scape in oil colours was framed with the glass and formed the upper portion of the overmantel.

Reproductions of a small, simple, and comparatively inexpensive type of mahogany hanging mirror are to-day numerous; the original examples of this lesser glass, designed usually with inner gilt framing and a fretted cresting, were in the main confined to the bedrooms. When of mahogany or walnut, and not of gesso, the mouldings of the inner framing were of cross-grained veneer, either of half-round section or flat with moulded edges. The shaped hood or cresting was either plain or relieved with gilding. Modern glass is comparatively thick and reveals a substantial image; old glass, spotted by age, and with shallow bevelling, is distinctive.

A number of oval glasses were made in this period, as in the succeeding one, an elaborate cresting often centering in a mask form. The design was less rigid than in those oblong specimens.

Library tables of massive open pedestal form were inspired by French pieces in the style of Louis XIV and

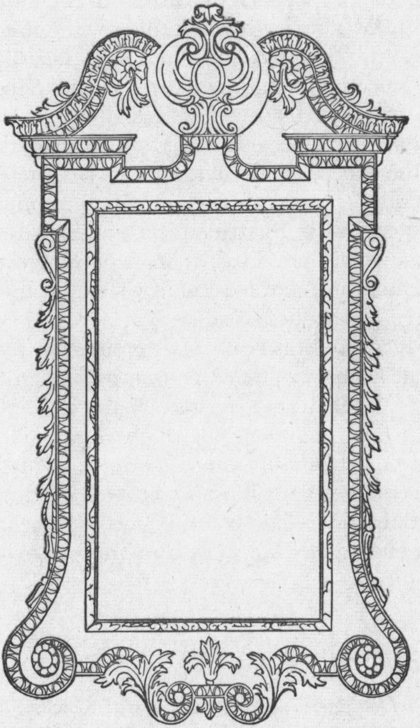

Figure 45 – Mirror; the frame is veneered with burr walnut with carved enrichments in gilt gesso; the heavy scrolled pediment finishes in rosettes and encloses a central *cabochon* and leaf ornament; the glass is bordered by a leaf moulding, while the outer moulding is enriched with gadrooning and edged with floral pendants. The shaped base is ornamented with floral scrolls. About 1730

were intended to stand in the centre of rooms. The technique of Boulle and his followers was not attempted, although some of these mahogany tables bore lavish carved and gilt enrichments having the appearance of ormolu mounts. This manner did not persist much beyond *c.* 1740.

China cabinets and bookcases hitherto had been of good proportion and plain appearance. It is likely that they were interchangeable pieces, used according to the requirements of owners. In later mahogany specimens, the flat veneered surface of the cabinet front was replaced by one with sunken panels and bolection mouldings; their architectural character was emphasized by the free use of detail commonly found in stone or plaster – the classical cornice, the broken pediment, the capital or pilaster, and the Greek key pattern. Certain massive bureau cabinets, in which prominence was given to the central compartment by a shallow recession of the flanking wings, provided a particularly suitable field for the designer, and marked the first stage in the development of large library bookcases.

William Kent and his circle endeavoured to place furniture adapted from Venetian Baroque models in Palladian interiors of classical and formal character. They were successful in this difficult task, which was undertaken for men who were arbiters of taste. The opulent gilt furniture, often of eccentric proportions, which was produced under their direction for a few great houses is, however, very different in character from most contemporary walnut and mahogany pieces.

NOTES TO CHAPTER 5

1. *An Account of the European Settlements in America*, London, 1757.
2. *Purefoy Letters, 1735–53*, ed. by G. Eland, 1931, vol. 1, p. 102.
3. *The Complete Works of Sir John Vanbrugh*, The Nonesuch Press, 1928; the Fourth Volume containing the Letters, ed. by Geoffrey Webb, pp. 35–6.
4. *The Journeys of Celia Fiennes*, ed. by Christopher Morris, 1947, Appendix, pp. 362–4.
5. *The Diary of Samuel Pepys*, ed. by H. B. Wheatley, 1923, vol. 1, p. 231.

6. *Letters of Hannah More*, with an introduction by G. Brimley Johnson, 1925, p. 123.
7. William Cobbett, *Rural Rides*, London, 1830, pp. 241–5.
8. Jane Austen, *Northanger Abbey*, chapters xx–xxi; written during 1798, first published 1818.
9. George Smith, an eminent cabinet-maker, published *Designs for Household Furniture and Interior Decoration*, 1808, and the *Cabinet Maker and Upholsterers Guide*, 1826.
10. Horace Walpole, *Anecdotes of Painting in England*, chapter XXII (Architects in the Reign of George II); first published, Strawberry Hill, 1762–71.
11. *Vertue III. Walpole Society*, vol. XXII, 1933–4, p. 51.
12. Walpole, *loc. cit.*
13. Webb, *op. cit.*, p. 160.
14. *Post Man*, Jan. 13th, 1702. Quoted by R. W. Symonds, *English Looking-Glasses I*, in the *Connoisseur*, March 1950.

CHAPTER SIX

THE PRE-'DIRECTOR' PERIOD (1740–1754)

THE earliest pattern books were produced by architects or builders, and contained comparatively few designs for furniture, although suggestions for the improvement and ornamentation of the interiors of houses were included and we find designs for chimney-pieces, for the decoration of the floors with parquetry, and for such furniture as allowed an architectural treatment.

A book of this nature, a *Treasury of Designs*, by Batty and Thomas Langley, was published in 1740 and is useful in so far as it provides some guide to fashionable taste at the time. The Palladian influence was still strong, but waning. The work was prefixed by a substantial section in interpretation of 'The Five Orders of Columns; according to Andrea Palladio'; and the Orders were explained 'in the most familiar Manner'. A good understanding of the Orders was stated to be essential.*

There were 'upwards of Four Hundred Grand Designs', engraved on '186 large Quarto Plates'. Some were for book-

* 'Cabinet Makers,' observed the authors, 'originally, were no more than Spurious Indocible Chips; expelled by Joiners, for the Superfluity of their Sap ... 'tis a very great Difficulty to find one in Fifty of them that can make a Book-case, &c. indispensably true, after any one of the Five Orders; without being obliged to a Joiner, for to set out the Work. ...' Similarly, 'if these Gentlemen persist much longer thus to despise Study of this Noble Art; the very Basis and Soul of their Trade, which now to many Joiners is well understood; they will soon find the bad Consequences of so doing: and have Time enough on their Hands, to repent of their Folly. And more especially, since that our Nobility and Gentry delight themselves now more than ever, in the Study of Architecture, which enables them to distinguish good Work and Workmen, from assuming Pretenders'.

cases (designated as 'Tuscan', 'Doric', and 'Ionic' – plain, but of pleasing appearance) and for 'marble' side tables*; others, 'enriched after the French Manner', were for a chest of drawers, a medal case, a cabinet of drawers and one impractical dressing-table, liberally bedecked with fabrics. The patterns were advertised as being intended to 'prove useful to Workmen, for whose Service' they were in fact published. The names of many joiners, with carpenters, cabinet-makers, carvers, plasterers, masons and bricklayers, were included in the list of subscribers to the work, notwithstanding its somewhat high cost. There were few private individuals; but *The City and Country Builder's and Workman's Treasury of Designs* was a manual, produced primarily for the guidance of craftsmen. The numerous measured drawings for memorial monuments, for stone garden tables, for niches or 'Buffets', and Church fonts, were intended, for instance, for the mason – as those for ceiling pieces, the plasterer.

Langley acknowledged, with some reserve, Inigo Jones as a source of inspiration in the work, and he depended on him for some of the many designs for chimney-pieces. He was not willing, however, to admit any indebtedness to French models, despite very direct borrowing in the case of one or two ornamental side tables. These tables are freely, even capriciously designed, and foreshadow a general adoption of the Rococo in England. Their inclusion seems to be at variance with the principles Langley had set down.†

Many patrons, however, were tiring of a rigid application of the rules of Palladio and the Five Orders to the interiors of their houses and to furniture, and desired a change of style. The fifth decade of the eighteenth century witnessed a reaction against classicism. 'The cabinet-maker,' wrote R. Campbell in 1747, 'is by much the most curious workman in the wood way except the carver, and requires a nice

* I.e. tables with marble tops.

† He abused such freedom as an 'evil Genious, that so presides over Cabinet Makers, as to direct them' to ignore the 'Rules of Architecture, from whence all beautiful Proportions are deduced'.

mechanic genious . . . the youth who designs to make a figure in this branch must learn to draw, for upon this depends the Invention of new Fashions and on that the Success of his Business. He who first hits on any new whim is sure to make by the Invention before it becomes common in the trade; but he that must always wait for a new Fashion till it come from Paris, or is hit upon by his Neighbor, is never likely to grow rich or eminent in this way.' [1] The French, Chinese, and Gothic tastes (and subsequently a new style of ornament, which often took the form of a blending of these tastes) were adopted in England by makers of furniture as well as by architects and builders. The Gothic was expressed also in sham castles and picturesque ruins, which were placed to advantage in parks; the Chinese in those garden houses, gazeboes and bridges, etc., which enjoyed an equal or greater vogue and which are to be found in William and John Halfpenny's *Rural Architecture in the Chinese Taste* of 1752.

Some continued interest in the Palladians and, more directly, in William Kent is evinced, however, by the appearance in 1744 of a volume entitled *Some Designs of Mr Inigo Jones and Mr Wm Kent.* It was published by John Vardy the architect who, if not a pupil, was at least a follower of Kent, and whose principal building (Lord Spencer's house in St James's Place, begun 1755) continued the Palladian tradition.*

* Vardy was responsible for the fifty measured and engraved plates which comprised the work. Of these about one third (largely composed of designs for chimney-pieces at the Palace at Greenwich, at Lord Pembroke's at Wilton, and elsewhere) were devoted to Inigo Jones. The remainder of the plates, which were given to Kent, were, because of the latter's many activities, more varied and included designs for chandeliers, candlesticks, 'Vases with Pedestals for Mr Pope', cups and other plate, as well as those for seating furniture and some other purely architectural features. 'A Seat in Kensington Gardens' is followed by designs for an ornamental table 'at Lord Burlington's at Cheswick' and another 'for Ld Orford'. Plates 31–33 are of particular interest. 'The Section of Merlin's Cave in the Royal Gardens at Richmond as design'd by Mr Kent' presents a picture of a romantic and picturesque retreat. The cave or grotto is lit by daylight from two round apertures in the roof, and con-

None the less, in general, French influence was already apparent in a light, more lively, manner which succeeded that imposed by the Palladians; and qualified admiration of French taste persisted throughout the greater part of the century, with definite effect on English furniture design.*

French fashions were not approved by all sections of the public. We have such expressions of distaste as those voiced by one critic in the *London Magazine*: 'The ridiculous imitation of the French taste,' he wrote, 'has now become the Epidemical distemper of this kingdom, our cloathes, our furniture, nay our food too, all is to come from France.' [3]

A large sixfold leather screen of about 1750 in the Victoria and Albert Museum (448 – 1865) provides an example of direct imitation. The panels are lacquered, gilt, and painted in oils with numerous small pastoral scenes. The compositions were derived from pictures by French artists; and three of the subjects are identified as being adapted from prints after Lancret – *L'Automne* engraved by N. Tardieu (two subjects), and the portrait of *Mlle Camargo*, the celebrated dancer, engraved by Laurent Cars.

A restrained version of the Rococo† reached England by the middle of the century. The earliest of the designs of Matthias Lock, the first exponent of the style, date from

tains a few pieces of 'rustic' furniture. These, which include a pair of bookcases with pediments and adorned with ornamental busts, are conceived and disposed in the formal Palladian manner. A calculated symmetry is to be observed in the arrangement of the furniture in the succeeding plate also – the interior of the 'Hermitage'.

* Lord Chesterfield wrote thus to Madame de Monconseil (5 September, 1748) concerning the interior of Chesterfield House, South Audley Street, a graceful Palladian building by Isaac Ware: '*Oui vraiment, Madame, j'ai un boudoir, mais il a un défaut, c'est qu'il est si gai et si riant, qu'on n'y pourra jamais bouder quand on y sera seul. ... La boisure et le plafond sont d'un beau bleu, avec beaucoup de sculptures et de dorures; les tapisseries et les chaises sont d'un ouvrage à fleurs au petit-point, d'un dessein magnifique sur un fond blanc; par-dessus la cheminée, qui est de Giallo di Sienna, force glaces, sculptures, dorures, et au milieu, le portrait d'une très belle femme peinte par la Rosalba.*' [2]

† The term 'Rococo' was first used (in a derogatory sense of 'freakish') in the early nineteenth century, and '*Rocaille*', which is to-day a synonymous term, was descriptive of some fantastic grotto or bower of rocks.

1740. In that year Lock published a *New Drawing Book of Ornaments, Shields, Compartments, Masks, etc.* The ornament was lively and elegant. The venture was followed in 1744 by designs for *Six Sconces.* These were in a style which people were then prepared to receive kindly. *Six Tables* appeared after a further interval of two years. The imaginative inventions of Oppenord, Meissonier, and Caffieri, by which these designs were inspired, were not adapted for use in England until the following decade, and it is probable that comparatively few of those for the more ornamental pieces were in fact executed.

English designs derived from the French made use of varied *motifs*: rocks and shells, flowers and foliage, birds, the *cabochon*, and scroll work. Designs were composed of a series of broken and associated curves; balance was preserved even with the adoption of asymmetry.

'The French taste' was most fully and successfully exploited in carvers' work – in chimney-pieces with overmantels, in brackets, wall-lights, *torchères*, and console tables, which might well be of fantastic form yet not at all impracticable for use. Lock was himself a carver of merit. Mirror frames were among the pieces to be affected by this reaction against the straight line and measured design. In chairs and tables and in other pieces of basically rectangular structure, in the work of the chair- and cabinet-maker, the French *rocaille* was confined to surface ornament. In 1752, Lock first collaborated with the designer, H. Copland, in a *New Book of Ornaments.* The plates, which were of an elaborate nature, displayed an harmonious and successful blending of French and Chinese *motifs* when applied to ornamental pieces intended for gilding. Rococo was at that date becoming discredited in France.* Oppenord, Meissonier, and Caffieri were dead.

The severe architectural manner of the preceding period was continued in case furniture of the fifth decade of the

* In 1754, Cochin attacked the style in the *Mercure de France*: 'We will not ask for the suppression of the palm trees which are cultivated so profusely in apartments, on chimney-pieces, around mirrors and along

century. Well-proportioned bookcases with projecting centre and two recessed wings are found with moulded cornice, surmounted by a broken pediment; the pilasters frequently bear an applied decoration of pendant fruit and flowers carved in high relief. This latter form of ornament, which is associated with the style of Kent, is exemplified in a bookcase, of somewhat earlier date, constructed of painted pine with gilt enrichments, in the Victoria and Albert Museum (W.2 – 1923). The heavy character of these pieces became modified by about 1750, in part by the substitution of graceful lattice work for glazing bars. Some bookcases were designed with a light scrolled cresting in open carving, or with a straight cornice.

The mahogany display cabinet illustrated in plate 35 was formerly at Blenheim, and dates from about 1740. The upper stage is divided vertically into three sections; the centre main section which is surmounted by a broken pediment decorated with key pattern ornament and flanked by corbelled brackets, is in slight projection. The arched doors are glazed, and composed in the 'Venetian' manner, reminiscent of the style of Kent. The cabinet is, however, supported on an open stand of six legs, with palmated frieze and open carved shell ornament, which is of later date. Cabinets designed by Kent were invariably constructed with solid bases.

Plate 37 illustrates a remarkable cabinet on a base of drawers, formerly at Kirtlington Park, Oxfordshire, and now in the Lady Lever Gallery at Port Sunlight. The design has been attributed to William Kent and the cabinet dated about 1730. Kirtlington Park, built for Sir James Dashwood, was, however, not completed until about 1746; and the cabinet may have been made in that year. The doors are veneered with the figured Honduras mahogany, not often used until the mid-century; and the character of the apron piece of the lower stage, carved in open scrolled

walls; that would be to deprive our decorators of their dearest resource. But may we not at least hope that, when a thing is square without offence, they will leave it so and not torment it into an absurd design?'[4]

acanthus with a central escallop shell, supports the assumption of a later date. The cabinet is richly ornamented: a plain frieze, inlaid with brass, is surmounted by a swan-necked pediment, elaborately carved and parcel gilt, and supported at back and front by composite pilasters with similar enrichments. The base is contained within heavy, sculptural terminal figures of Cuban mahogany, representing the poet Homer, and parcel gilt, which terminate in vigorously carved paw feet. Stylistically, this cabinet may perhaps be associated with known productions from the workshop of Benjamin Goodison. The design is bold, and enriched by heavy carving and gilding. Use has been made of brass mouldings and inlay. The *motif* of opposed acanthus scrolls centering in a shell (which forms the apron piece) occurs on the long stools and day beds which make up part of a set of seating furniture at Longford Castle, Wiltshire, and which together with a pair of parcel gilt mahogany pedestals or terms, headed with a bust of Hercules supporting an Ionic capital, were supplied to Lord Folkestone *c.* 1740. The figure carving of the latter pieces is most distinctive and resembles closely that of the terminal supports of the cabinet at Port Sunlight. The furniture at Longford Castle has been assigned to Goodison on documentary evidence afforded by accounts. Goodison was without doubt among the principal early Georgian cabinet-makers; he supplied furniture over a long period to the Royal Palaces, to Holkham and elsewhere; and Frederick, Prince of Wales, the Fourth Earl of Cardigan, and Sarah, Duchess of Marlborough, were among his patrons at this time.

The mahogany bureau in two stages retained a classical character until mid century, when the Chinese style in its most advanced form was sometimes adapted to this piece. The finest bureau-cabinets of the second quarter of the century had, however, dignity and great beauty of craftsmanship; and the interior fittings of pigeon-holes, drawers, compartments, and small central cupboard were executed with extreme care. The cornice was finely carved and surmounted by a broken or swan-necked pediment, which was on occasion of fretted or perforated form. The doors enclosing the upper stage were sometimes framed in fluted pilasters or were panelled, with a decorative moulding. Ogee bracket feet commonly supported the base of drawers.

Ornamental wall brackets, carved in a soft wood and gilded, were made throughout the eighteenth century. Mahogany was rarely employed for these pieces. The earliest examples, dating from about 1690, had served to display to good advantage vases of Oriental porcelain or of Delft ware, which were then collected by fashion. Many were based on contemporary French models in the style of Louis XIV and presumably were made by refugee Huguenot craftsmen domiciled in England. Porcelain was also placed on tiered shelves above the chimney-piece or in the angles of rooms, or arranged in cabinets of Oriental and English lacquer. A pair of large brackets in the Lady Lever Collection at Port Sunlight which have been attributed to this period are of unusual character, with the quality of sculpture. They are boldly carved in a soft wood, originally gilt; the small carved flowers are intermingled with winged cherubs' heads. Later, larger, monumental brackets were used by the Palladians in decorative schemes, and bronze or marble statuary (such as a series of the heads of Roman Emperors) was supported on massive console brackets, of architectural design.

French influence persisted during the first half of the century: leaf carving, with which the smaller brackets were frequently decorated, became less formalized, and from about 1740 carving was disposed in free and graceful curves (Fig. 51). The adoption, by the middle of the century, of the rococo (and a closely related use of Chinese *motifs*) was foreshadowed in the development of wall brackets – objects well suited to that taste.

The furniture of the eighteenth-century French makers was rarely anonymous. The *maîtres ébénistes* of the Paris Guild were comparatively few in number; further, they were compelled by statute (after 1741) to stamp work with their names or individual marks. By contrast, cabinet-makers in England were not closely organized. With few exceptions, a printed label, at most, bearing a name and an address, was affixed to some pieces as a form of advertisement by apparently a proportion of firms. In some cases the labels have survived, but the custom cannot have been universal.*

The status of the cabinet-maker improved progressively throughout the course of the eighteenth century. Masters of workshops came to abandon the designation 'joiner', and for the most part called themselves 'cabinet-makers and upholders (upholsterers)'. In the immediate post-Restoration period, carpenters, joiners, and turners had been organized in distinct and separate London Companies. Their skill, however, was then relatively undeveloped and much of the finer new cabinet work of the baroque period in England is doubtless to be attributed to immigrant craftsmen. Subsequently the trades of joiner and chair-maker, upholsterer, and cabinet-maker became more or less distinct; tables and stands fell within the province of the joiner; bureaux, bookcases, and chests of drawers were made by the cabinet-maker; and beds, curtains, carpets, upholstered chairs, and settees were supplied by the upholsterer. By the middle of the eighteenth century the organization of a large London workshop was more complex. Specialized journeymen were employed – carvers, joiners, chairmakers, gilders, japanners, metal-workers, upholsterers, looking-glass makers, and ornamentalists. The work undertaken by the leading firms became more and more comprehensive; they were active too in interior decoration. Many of the shops were situated in Soho or in the neighbourhood of St Martin's Lane. St Paul's Churchyard was also a centre, mainly for the middle classes.

Conditions in the country were, of course, very different. In the words of Adam Smith: 'A country carpenter deals in

* See *The London Furniture Makers, 1660–1840*, by Sir Ambrose Heal, with a chapter by R. W. Symonds, F.S.A., 1953.

every sort of work that is made of wood. . . . [He] is not only a carpenter, but a joiner, a cabinet-maker, and even a carver in wood. . . .'[5]

Chair-making remained a distinct trade in the eighteenth century. The cabinet- and chair-maker Robert Manwaring produced in 1766, in addition to his other trade publications, a separate work entitled *The Chair-Maker's Guide*. And later, in 1803, Sheraton wrote: 'Chair-making is a branch generally confined to itself; as those who professedly work at it seldom engage to make cabinet furniture. In the country manufactories it is otherwise; yet even these pay some regard to keeping their workmen constantly at the chair, or to the cabinet-work.'[6]

As a rule changes of style found their most immediate and varied expression in the design of chairs. Between 1735–55 successive excursions into the French, Gothic, and Chinese tastes were reflected in the ingenious *motifs* which were applied as ornament to the chair frame. The form of the frame itself was during this period comparatively constant. In the early years of the century the typical chair veneered with walnut had been of rounded shape; and the hooped back, the S-curved side uprights, and shaped seat-rail were components which were necessarily of substantial construction. From about 1745, a lighter style inspired by the French taste was increasingly apparent. The chair frame, although at this time disposed in subtle and undulating curves, was basically rectangular in form. The hooped back was replaced by an open rectangular back with graceful undulating or cupid's bow top rail. The solid vase-shaped splat became pierced and was often enriched with sensitively executed carving in low relief. The central splat was usually retained as a basis of the design of the chair back, but free interlacing strapwork was an occasional alternative. The boldly shaped seat rail became straight fronted or serpentine. The refined cabriole leg, with a tendency to an excessive thinness at the junction with the foot, was frequently decorated at the knee with French *cabochon* and leaf ornament (Figs. 39 and 48). In fashionable pieces this *motif* was prominent during the years 1745–55. It is found used in conjunction with the paw, and also with the earlier claw-and-ball foot. *C.* 1745, the curl-over leaf and the scroll foot were introduced (Fig. 40B).

Armchairs were not very numerous. 'To tell the plain truth,' wrote Madame du Boccage in 1750, 'though there is great luxury in *England*, it does not come up to ours, which the people of this country imitate nevertheless, as all the nations of *Europe* do, to their destruction. There are scarce any armchairs in their apartments; they are satisfied with common chairs. The women who use no paint and are always laced, (as was formerly the custom in *France*), are fond of these seats: in their court dresses they resemble the pictures of our great grandmothers; but they are extremely affable and obliging in their behaviour.'[7]

Craftsmen of the Buckinghamshire villages continued to make chairs of 'Windsor' or spindle back pattern throughout the whole of the Georgian period; many went to furnish the cottages and farmhouses of Southern England. In design and construction these chairs were of a traditional nature, being affected only to a small degree by the fashions of the town. The industry was centred in Chepping (High) Wycombe, although chairs and seats of stick back construction were made in many widely separated districts of England – in London, in Somerset, in Lancashire. 'Bogers', working in clearings in beech woods in the Chilterns, prepared turned spindles in readiness for village makers. A variety of native woods was used: beech or ash furnished the spindles and legs, the frame was of yew, and the seat of elm. *C.* 1740 the cresting bar, a characteristic feature of earlier chairs, tended to be replaced by a rounded band (*cf.* Figs. 46 and 47); the back contained a central pierced splat, often decorated with a star. Legs, by concession to an established style, were sometimes of cabriole form; often at this period stretchers were curved. A number of these comfortable chairs were adapted to the Gothic taste about 1760. Examples, somewhat incongruously supported on cabriole legs, are found with splats pierced with Gothic tracery

(Fig. 47). Later in the eighteenth century, the popular Prince of Wales' feathers *motif* was for a time incorporated into conventional patterns.

The upholstered settee and that of double or triple chair-back form were both comparatively expensive pieces. The

Figure 46 – Arm chair of Windsor type, of stick back construction, with cresting bar and pierced central splat; made of various native woods

evolution of the latter type matched that of the contemporary chair: the splat was opened up and in subsequent development became more elaborate and of lighter appearance. The greater strength of mahogany was utilized by makers. Occasionally the design of the openwork back was independent of the chair form; and somewhat rarely the double chair-back was divided by a single upright only.

Upholstered settees were variously shaped. They are found with padded, C-scrolled arms or with open arm rests of wood. Settees in the French taste, with high arms which merge into an undulating back outlined by carved framing, were produced in emulation of Louis XV *canapés* and, after the middle years of the century, were sometimes covered

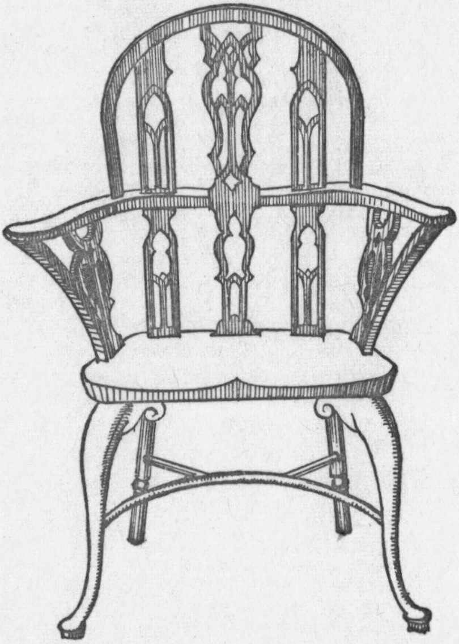

Figure 47 – Windsor chair, of native woods of Gothic design supported on cabriole legs tied by curved stretchers

with French tapestry or with work from the Fulham and Soho manufactories. There was some uniformity in the height of the back of the upholstered settee which however tended to become lower with the passing of the years. Squab cushions were not at this time in fashion.

It is probable that few day beds were made during the second quarter of the century. The *chaise longue* or 'single-headed couch' which was included in published drawings for furniture from the early years of George III was, however, evolved from the day bed of an earlier period, with chair back and long frame supported on legs of cabriole form, awkwardly tied by turned stretchers.

The furniture of the dining-room was augmented by 1740 by the provision of the dumb waiter, an English invention and a piece which was not adopted in France and elsewhere until some thirty years later. Use was made of the dumb waiter at dessert. Its value on informal occasions must have been considerable in some households. Dumb waiters were placed at the corners of the dining-table, and, as Miss Mary Hamilton recorded in her *Diary*, 'conversation was not under any restraint by ye Servants being in ye room'.[8] The form of the dumb waiter was not much altered until the closing years of the century. Circular trays ('waiters'), usually three in number and larger towards the base, and edged with a carved moulding, revolved on a central carved stem; the stands were invariably of tripod form. Dumb waiters were between 4 and 5 feet high; the trays were comfortably placed within the reach of a seated person.

The mahogany tea-table illustrated in plate 33 is in the collection of the Lady Lever Art Gallery at Port Sunlight. Its wavy edged, circular top is fitted with a carved and perforated gallery; and the shaft, fluted and with a vase-shaped base, is supported on a tripod finishing in paw-and-ball feet. Considerable ornamentation was characteristic of the more expensive tables of this type. Tea-tables, in the Chinese taste, with perforated lattice work decoration of fragile appearance, were frequently of a rectangular form, supported on four legs at the corners. The latter type of table existed contemporaneously with that having a tripod support.

Card tables with square projecting corners, which had been introduced about 1730, retained popularity throughout the mid Georgian period (Fig. 48); plain, square tables were also common. A shaped serpentine frieze is sometimes found on tables of this date, and was used in conjunction with the cabriole leg on claw-and-ball or paw foot. Decoration was frequently in the French taste. The frame was enriched with rococo mouldings and carved with *coquillage* and acanthus scrolls. Until *c.* 1750–55, when the rage for 'Chinese' and 'Gothic' furniture was exploited by cabinet-makers, the cabriole leg was in almost exclusive use; its

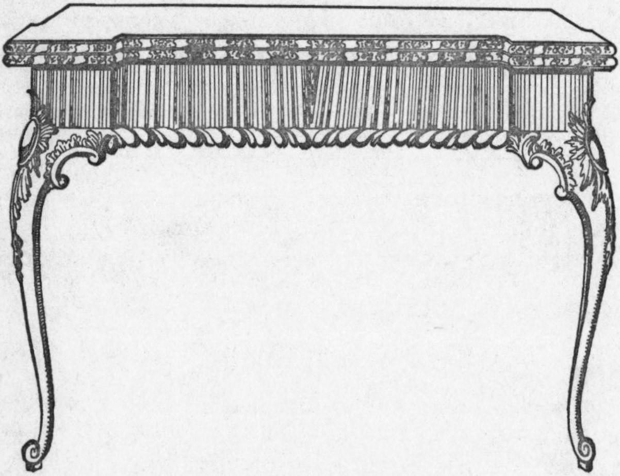

Figure 48 – Card table of mahogany; the double top with square projecting corners; the cabriole legs hipped on to the frieze and carved on the knee with *cabochon* and leaf ornament

form was elegant, but had now become less robust. The carved ornament of the knee sprang from and was dependent on the attached ear-pieces, bordered by scrolled mouldings (Fig. 49). The leg frequently terminated in a 'French' or scrolled foot (Figs. 40B and 48). Some tripod tables with triangular or polygonal tops, made specifically for card playing, date also from this period.

Considerable attention was given to the equipment and refinements of library writing tables. These massive pieces, based on low plinths, were usually of open pedestal form, or were designed with a central recessed cupboard; they were occasionally made with drawers or cupboards or both at front and back. Ingenuity was shown in the disposition of numerous drawers, partitioned cupboards, and 'rising desks', which were intended to receive large prints, estate maps, and folio volumes.

Figure 49 – Side table of mahogany, with marble top and plain frieze; the cabriole legs carved on the knees with scrolls and acanthus

For a brief period after 1740, until the rococo prevailed, mahogany side tables with marble tops displayed a reticent taste (Fig. 49). The apron piece was now dispensed with or was of modest dimensions, except in Irish tables. The cabriole form was retained after 1750 when the straight leg was re-introduced, for those specimens in the French manner.

Some modification to the design of state beds had been made during the reign of Anne with the introduction of boldly shaped and moulded cornices. The cornice contributed to the ornamental appearance of the deep valances necessary in the case of these tall and excessively costly pieces. After about 1720, the posts were made of mahogany and were left exposed; the cornice, which was still covered with the fabric of the curtains, was normally of carved deal. Ordinarily, beds were smaller and plainly curtained in needlework, linen, or chintz, and a cornice was not thought essential to their composition. Mention of a small four-poster bed, 'one of the new-fashioned low-beds without a cornice', occurs in the correspondence of the Purefoy family. Provision had to be made for a considerable quantity of covering material, and Mrs Elizabeth Purefoy wrote in January 1735 to a Mr Baxter at the Naked Boy in Henrietta Street, Covent Garden: 'I desire you will send mee by Webster the Buckingham carrier ... some patterns of Quilting you mention together wth. the lowest prices of each pattern.' The stuff was selected and the order placed for 'five & forty yards of it at ten shillings & sixpence a yard'. The 'bed' (i.e. the material) was not to be made up in town, as Baxter suggested, but in the house; and Henry Purefoy showed attention to detail when he wrote: 'pray see that the two cloaths of each side the Quilting be as good as the pattern & the work as good. You must also send the pattern itself whereon is wrote H. Purefoy ... & send with it 4 yards of fine thick plain white Dimmothy or I think it is called Vomilion, it has a little nap on it on one side, tis to make mee night caps' – an afterthought which was to cost him eight shillings. The bedstead was of lesser importance and was described as 'a wainscoat one with 4 posts turned pillows [pillars] brasse ferrells & castors to be taken too peices or put together by any servant & to draw about the room upon wheells'.[9]

The so-called 'Indian' needlework was an expensive fabric. Floral patterns, worked in silk on a white ground, imitated those of materials imported originally from China. The 'Indian' embroidery on white satin of the Queen's Chamber of State, at Windsor (where the Royal apartments were in part rebuilt and refurnished during the reign of

Charles II), was much admired by visitors. The embroidery was the gift of the East India Company and was therefore of Oriental origin. It may well have contributed to the later fashion for the English imitations.

Towards the middle of the eighteenth century the cornice of the bedstead was made of carved mahogany; and both it and the footposts were left uncovered, being exhibited as decorative features. The footposts were often of cluster column form, based either on short cabriole legs with claw-and-ball feet or on square pedestals. The cornice, frequently decorated with lobings, tended, as the rococo style became established in England, to open carving and to increasingly free forms. By about 1755 the cornice was sometimes of serpentine shape, and gilded. Beds were lower and appeared squarer.

Tables designed for dressing were at this period usually of knee-hole form, with a long top drawer fitted with boxes, compartments, and a hinged toilet mirror. Alternatively the top was constructed so as to lift up (Fig. 50). The central cupboard was flanked by short and deep drawers on either side. Specimens were sometimes japanned; and that they were intended to be used for occasional writing is suggested by the provision on some of a baize-covered top. They develop directly from dressing-tables of this type, made in walnut, which were in use at the beginning of the century (Fig. 44).

Mahogany was introduced noticeably late into the bedroom. Most chests of drawers were of relatively undistinguished appearance and stood on plain bracket feet. In mahogany specimens the drawer fronts were usually edged by a small cock beading (from about 1730 throughout the century). One type of chest, however, constructed with three long drawers and supported on legs of cabriole form, carved with acanthus and finishing in paw or claw-and-ball feet, would seem to have been made about 1750 by certain fashionable makers. There were made also, about the same time, a limited number of elaborate commode chests of drawers with veneered serpentine fronts and with carved corners. These pieces were usually based on bracket feet of ogee form or on shaped plinths, and enriched by carved mouldings. From the middle of the century Chinese lattice work was a common form of ornament, which harmonized with the serpentine lines of the fronts of the

Figure 50 – Kneehole dressing table of mahogany; the top lifts up to disclose a fitted interior

commodes and with their richly chased lock plates and handles of rococo design. Tallboys, which were usually straight fronted, and which were constructed by necessity with a regular disposition of drawers, were of comparatively severe appearance. The ornament, applied to cornice, frieze, and canted corners, sometimes took the form of lattice work decoration (Pl. 34). The lock plates were occasionally designed in a similar style. Tallboys of the more usual architectural character differed only in details of carving: fluted columns with Corinthian capitals were set at the corners of the upper portion of the tallboy and were commonly surmounted by a plain frieze and dentil cornice. 'Chests of drawers' are infrequently mentioned in the catalogues of the trade. Compilers, presumably by reason of the ascendance of French taste, almost universally preferred to show designs for 'commode chests of drawers' or 'dressing commodes'.

'The French commode', a side table with long drawers, was a piece directly inspired by the work of the French *ébénistes*. It was distinct from the 'dressing commode' and mainly ornamental. In Paris, Oeben, Jacques and Jean-Jacques Caffieri, Cressent, and others were producing elaborate furniture of unprecedented technical accomplishment; the furniture was ingeniously decorated with a marquetry of exotic woods and enriched by chased gilt-bronze mounts. English cabinet-makers did not attempt to reproduce the appearance of these pieces. They worked at first in mahogany, and gilding was not usually employed. Subsequently japanned, marquetry, and painted specimens became fashionable. French interiors were not congenial to our taste. Horace Walpole, while finding himself 'wonderfully disposed to like' [10] France and the French, was struck the most by 'the total difference of manners between them and us, from the greatest object to the least'.[11] In a letter of 1765 to the Countess of Suffolk, he wrote from Paris: 'Yesterday I dined at La Borde's, the great banker of the Court. Lord! Madam, how little and poor all your houses in London will look after his! In the first place, you must have a garden half as long as the Mall, and then you must have fourteen windows, each as long as the other half, looking into it, and each window must consist of only eight panes of looking-glass. You must have a first and second ante-chamber, and they must have nothing in them but dirty servants. Next must be the grand cabinet, hung with red damask ... immense *armoires* of tortoise-shells and ormolu, inlaid with medals. And then you may go into the petit-cabinet, and then into the great *salle*, and the gallery, and the billiard-room, and the eating-room; and all these must be hung with crystal lustres and looking-glass from top to bottom, and then you must stuff them fuller than they will hold with granite tables and porphyry urns, and bronzes, and statues, and vases, and the L—d or the devil knows what.' [12]

The early commodes introduced into fashionable drawing rooms about 1740 were sober versions of French models. The *bombé* shape was rarely adopted, and in most cases the exuberant curves of French pieces were reduced to a gentle serpentine. Carved decoration was effectively placed at the corners of pieces, sometimes taking the form of lion-headed terminals, festoons of flowers, or acanthus ornament; and scrolling outlined apron pieces or bases.

The interest in the Chinese and in their productions (in particular their lacquer and porcelain) which had been active since the time of the Restoration crystallized towards the middle of the eighteenth century into a vogue for 'the Chinese taste'. J. B. du Halde's *Description géographique, historique, etc. de l'empire de la Chine, et de la Tartarie Chinoise*, which was translated from French into English in 1741, aroused some curiosity. By 1750, the Vauxhall Pleasure Gardens could claim 'Chinese Pavillions and Boxes'. In a letter of the preceding year, Mrs Montagu had written: 'Thus has it happened in furniture ... we must all seek the barbarous gaudy *goût* of the Chinese; and fat-headed Pagods and shaking Mandarins bear the prize from the finest works of antiquity; and Apollo and Venus must give way to a fat idol with a sconce on his head.' [13] But, Mrs Montagu, too, succumbed to the fashion and a room was soon afterwards decorated for her in this taste. Chinese ornament was found beneficial by makers of furniture. The pagoda roof, bamboo framing, and the many frets were pleasing forms of ornament, and, as such, were easy of application in design. The Chinese was a rather later adoption than the Gothic style and was at the height of popu-

Interior of a room in the early fifteenth century

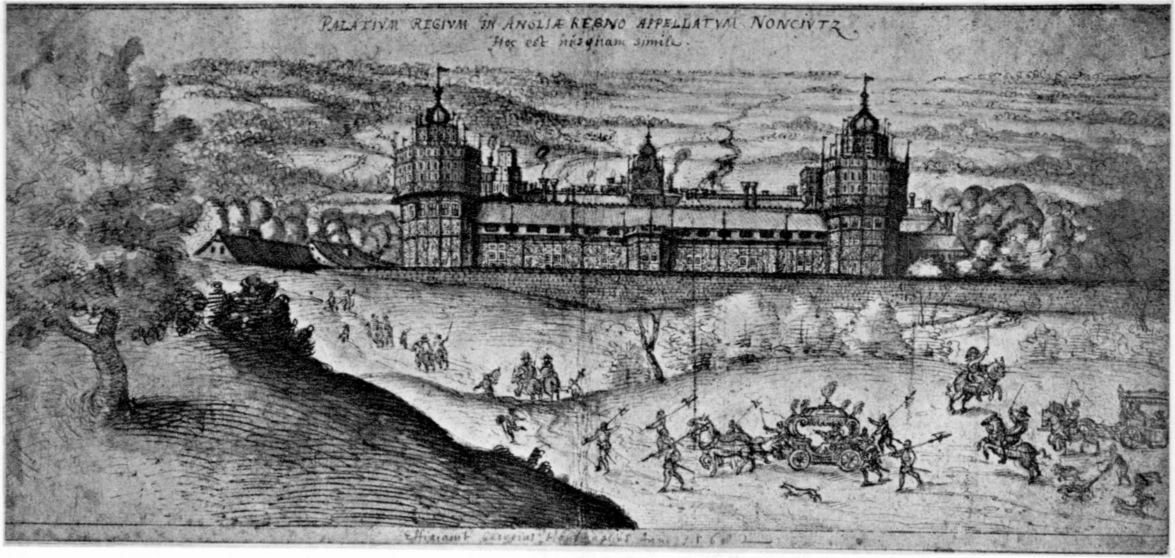

Nonesuch Palace, 1568

Writing desk, inlaid with various woods. Second half of the sixteenth century

(A) Turned chair of yew. Sixteenth century

(B) Arm chair, with carved and inlaid decoration. About 1600

(C) Arm chair, carved with conventional foliage and scrolls. About 1660

Chest. Early sixteenth century

Chest of oak. Early seventeenth century

Chest of elm. Dated 1639

Court cupboard of walnut. About 1600

(A) Stool of oak. Early sixteenth century

(B) 'Joint' stool of oak. About 1600

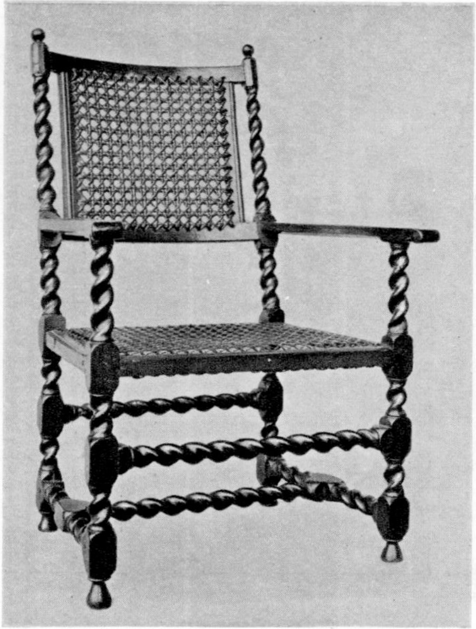

(A) Arm chair of walnut, with caned seat and back. About 1665

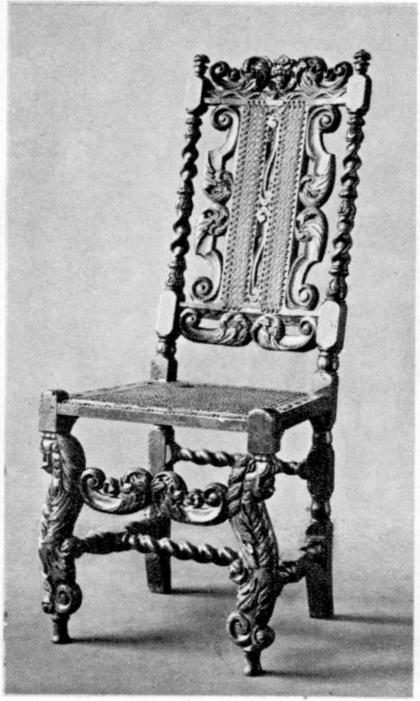

(B) Chair of walnut, with caned seat and back. About 1670–5

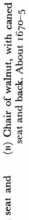

(C) Beechwood chair, carved and painted black. About 1690

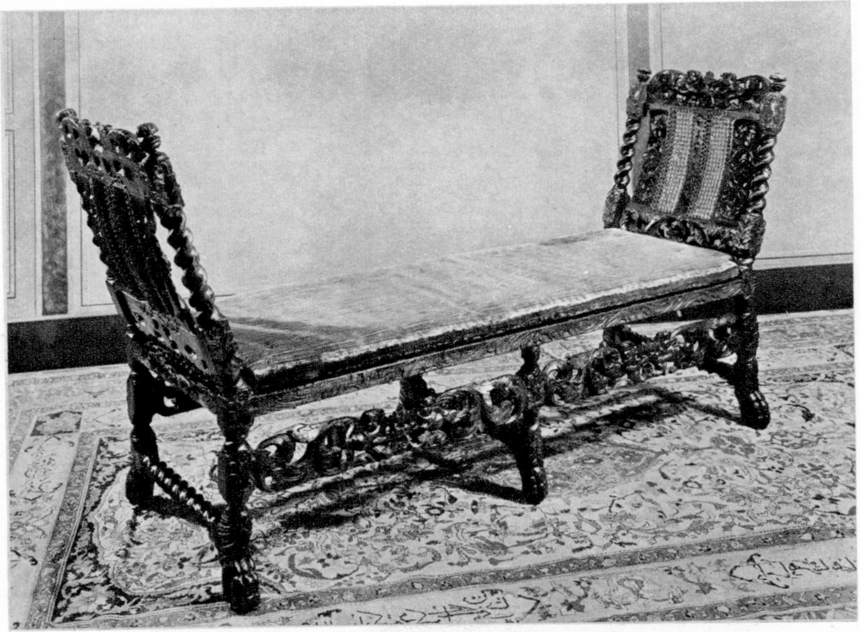

Day bed of walnut. End of third quarter of the seventeenth century

Table of walnut, with marquetry decoration. Late seventeenth century

Top of walnut table (Plate 12), with floral marquetry

Walnut chest of drawers. Late seventeenth century

Bookcase of oak, made for Samuel Pepys

Box, veneered with walnut and floral marquetry of various woods. Late seventeenth century

Interior of a bedroom. From a French painting of the late seventeenth century

Frame of carved pinewood, attributed to Grinling Gibbons.
About 1680

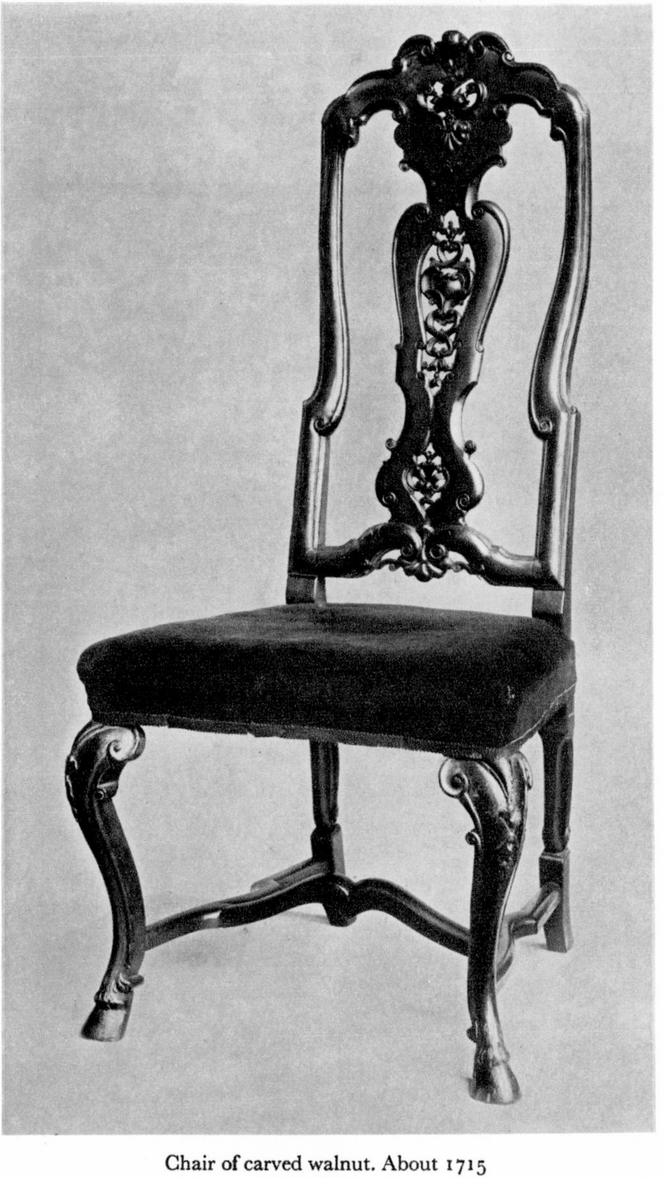

Chair of carved walnut. About 1715

Day bed, painted black and gilded. About 1695

Settee of walnut. About 1710

Writing cabinet of walnut. Beginning of the eighteenth century

Small walnut bureau on stand. About 1700

Plate from the *Treatise* (1688) by Stalker and Parker

(A) Chest, lacquered in black and gold. Late seventeenth century

(B) 'Ebony Table garnish'd with silver'. About 1670

One of a pair of hanging cupboards. First quarter of the eighteenth century

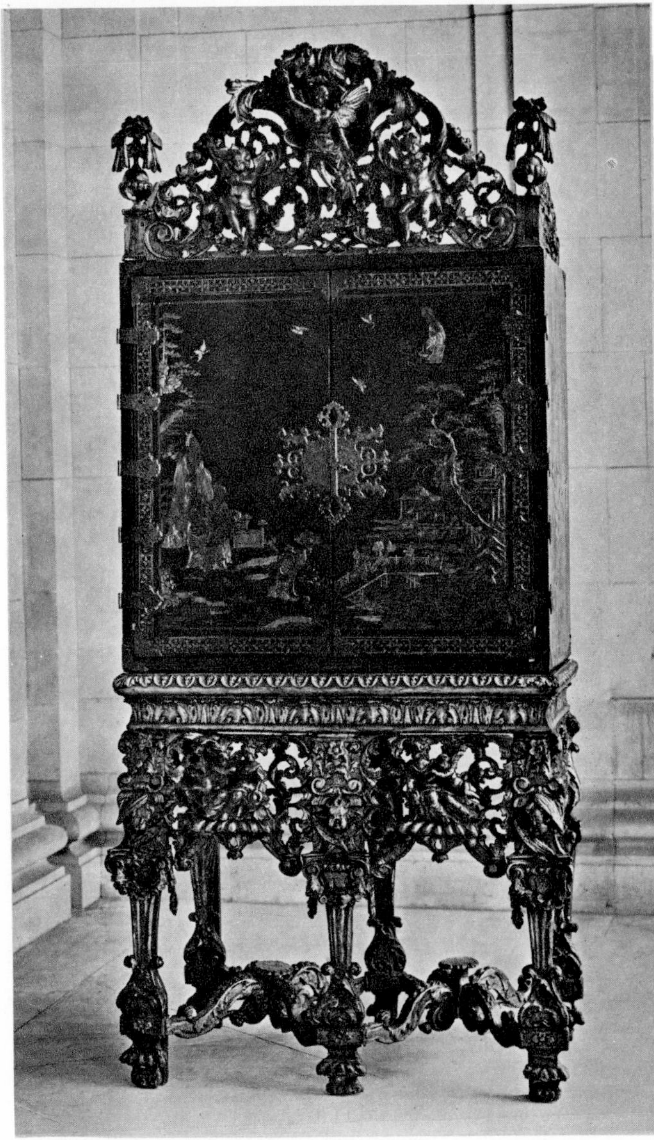

Cabinet, japanned in black and gold. End of the seventeenth century

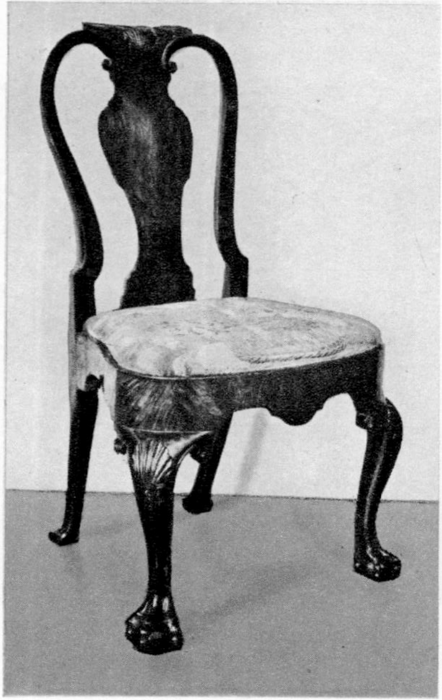

(A) Chair of walnut. Early 18th century

(B) Chair of mahogany. About 1740–50

Mr and Mrs William Atherton by Arthur Devis. Painted in second quarter of the eighteenth century

Side table, of carved and gilt pinewood. Designed by Henry Flitcroft. 1726

Side table of mahogany. About 1730

Card table of mahogany, of 'concertina' type. About 1740

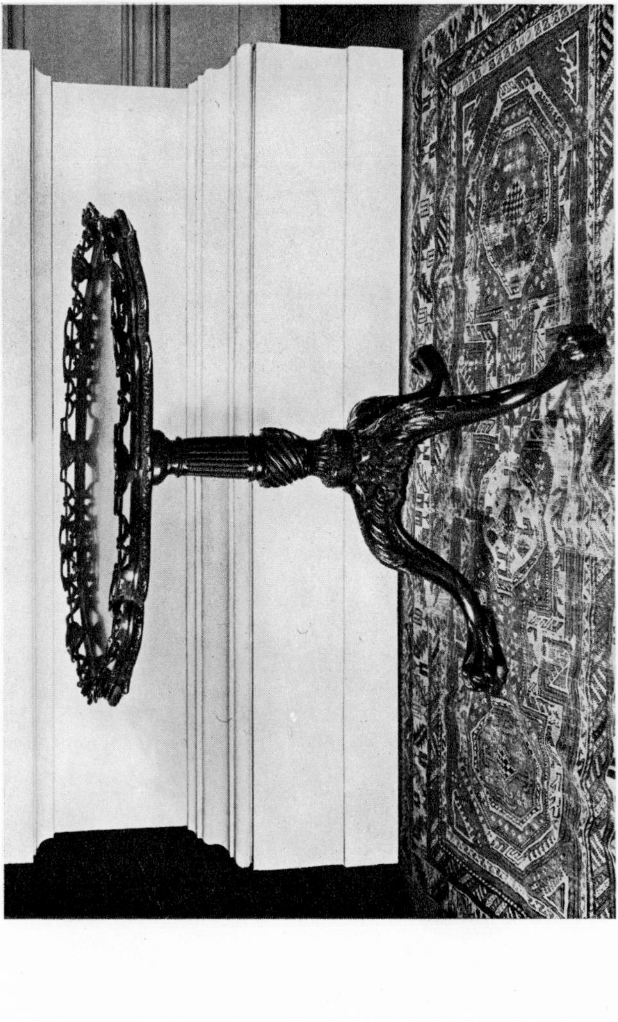

Mahogany tripod table. Mid eighteenth century

Mahogany tallboy. Mid eighteenth century

Mahogany cabinet with glazed doors. About 1740

China stand, decorated in black, gold, and red lacquer. Probably made by Thomas Chippendale. About 1750–5

Mahogany cabinet. About 1745

Cabinet on stand. Beginning of the third quarter of the eighteenth century

Gentleman at a Reading Desk by Arthur Devis. Painted 1761

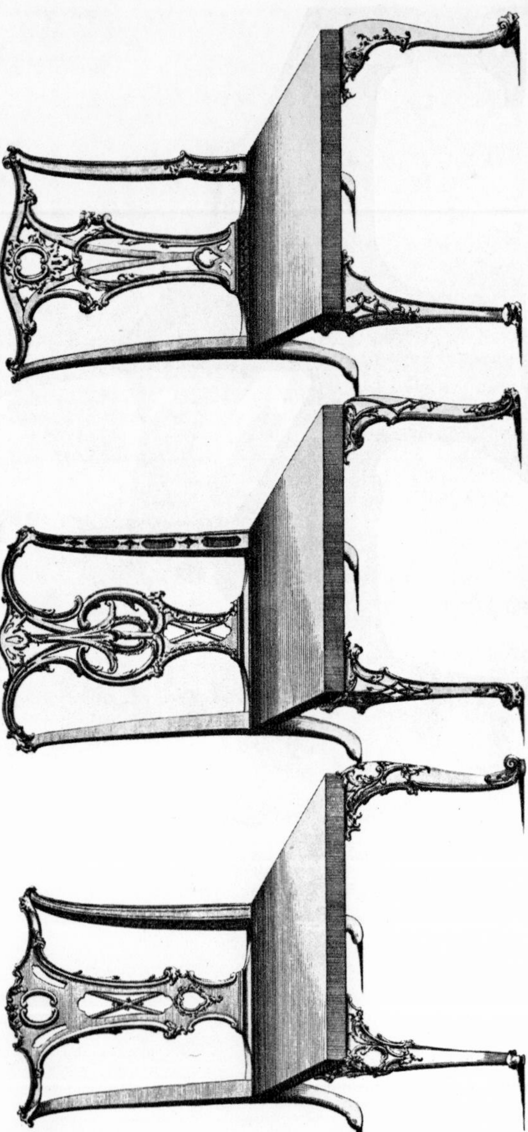

Three 'new-pattern Chairs' from the 1754 *Director*

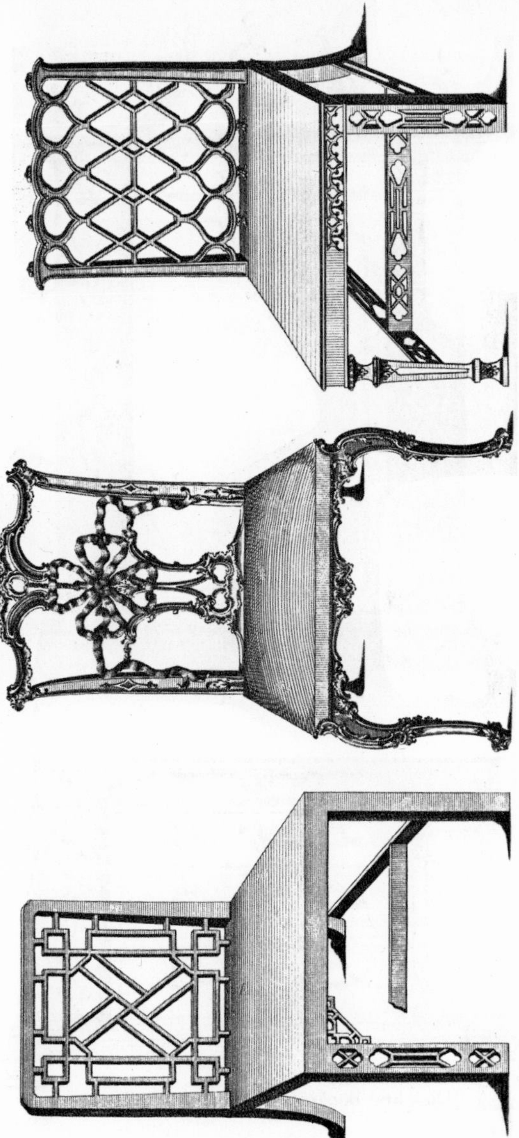

'Chinese Chair', 'Ribband Back Chair', and 'Gothick Chair' from the 1754 *Director*

'Desk and Bookcase' from the 1754 *Director*

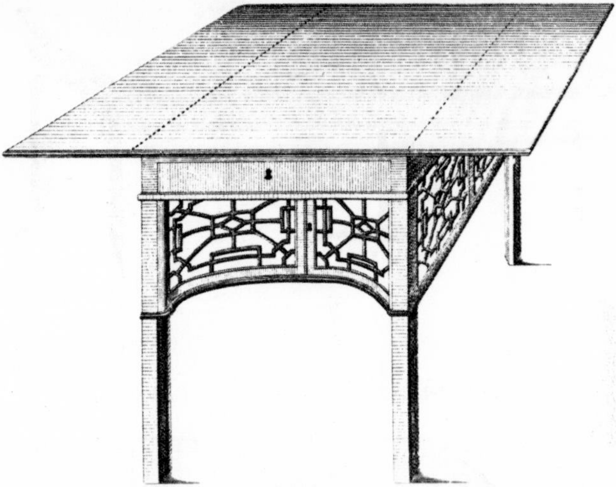

(A) 'Breakfast Table' from the 1754 *Director*

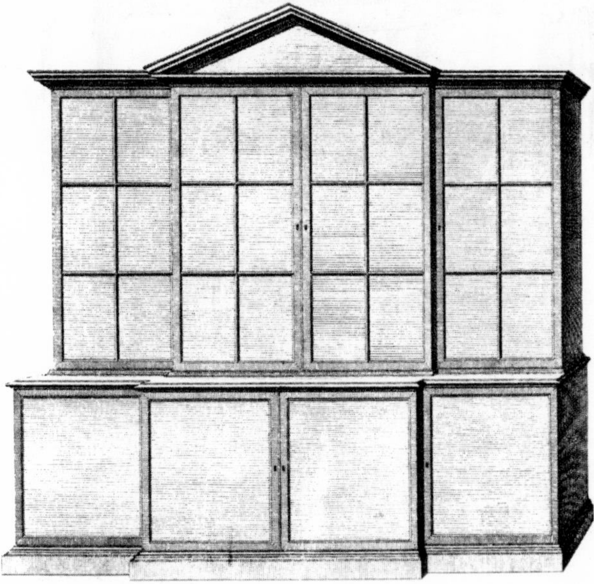

(B) 'Library Bookcase' from the 1754 *Director*

(A) 'Sideboard Table' from the 1754 *Director*

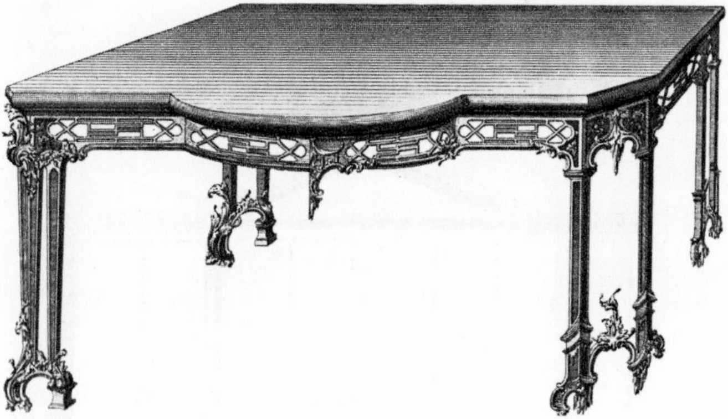

(B) 'Sideboard Table', with two different sorts of feet, from the 1754 *Director*

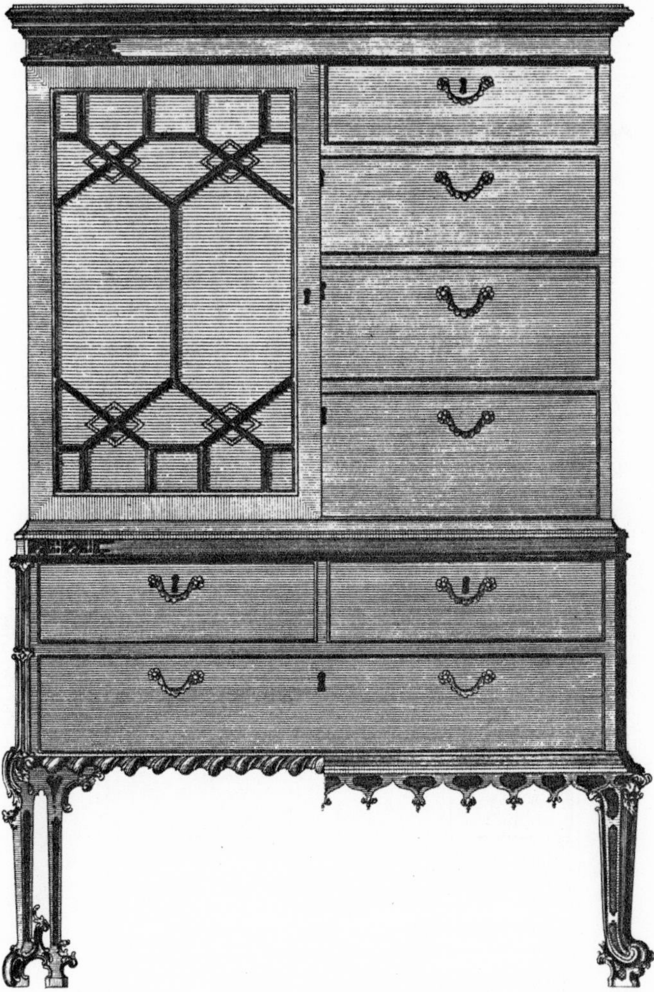

'Chest of Drawers upon a Frame, of two different designs' from the 1754 *Director*

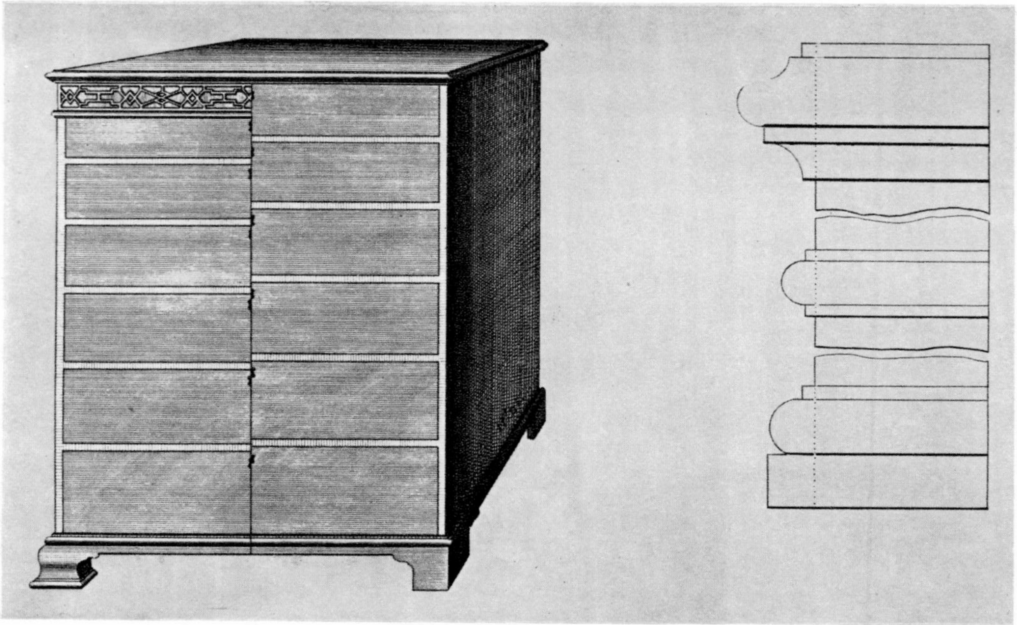

'Chest of Drawers' from the 1754 *Director*

(A) Arm chair of beechwood. Probably by Samuel Norman, after a design by Robert Adam dated 1764

(B) Design for arm chair by Robert Adam. About 1777

Designs for furniture at Kenwood. From R. & J. Adam's *Works in Architecture*, 1774

(A) Design for 'Table and Frame' by Robert Adam

(B) Design by Robert Adam for top of table (above)

(A) Design by Robert Adam for State bed of satinwood

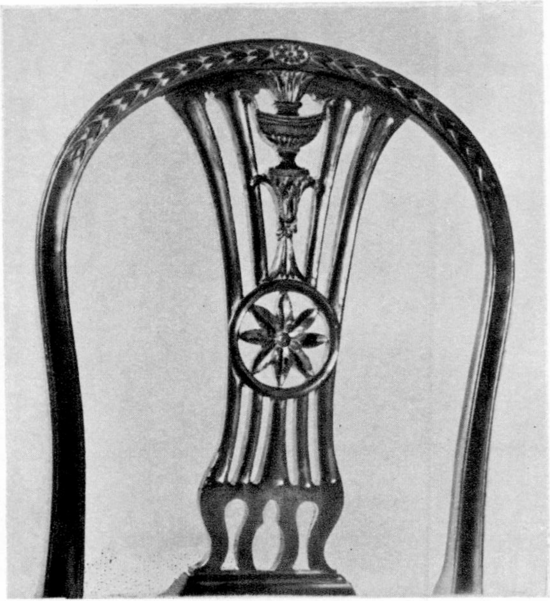

(B) Detail of mahogany chair. Third quarter of the eighteenth century

Plan for the Drawing Room of a town house from Thomas Sheraton's *Drawing Book*, 1791–4

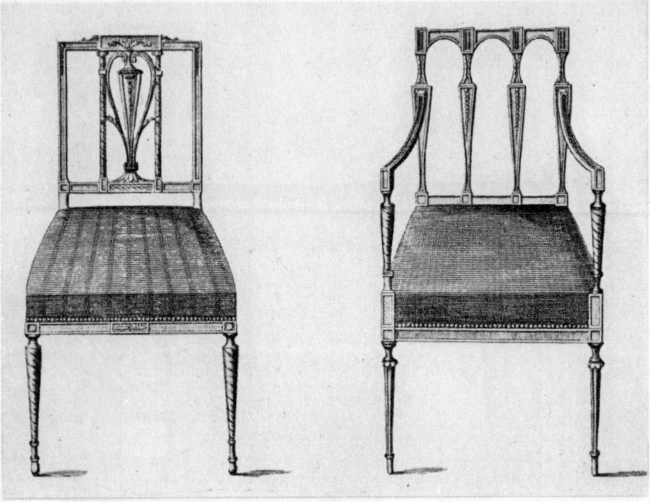

(A) Two 'Parlour Chairs' from Thomas Sheraton's *Drawing Book*, 1791–4

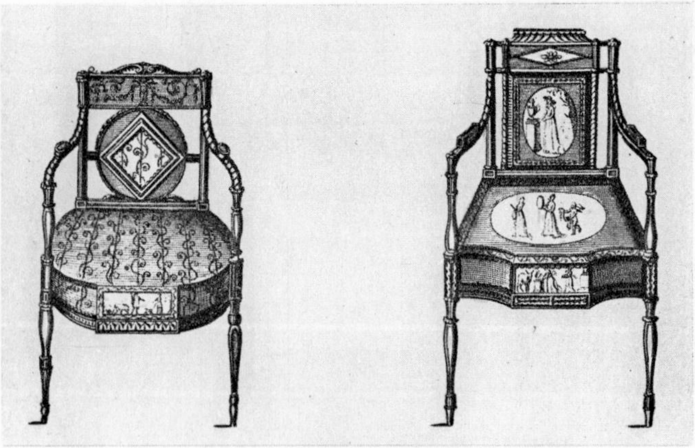

(B) Two 'Drawing Room Chairs' from Thomas Sheraton's *Drawing Book*, 1791–4

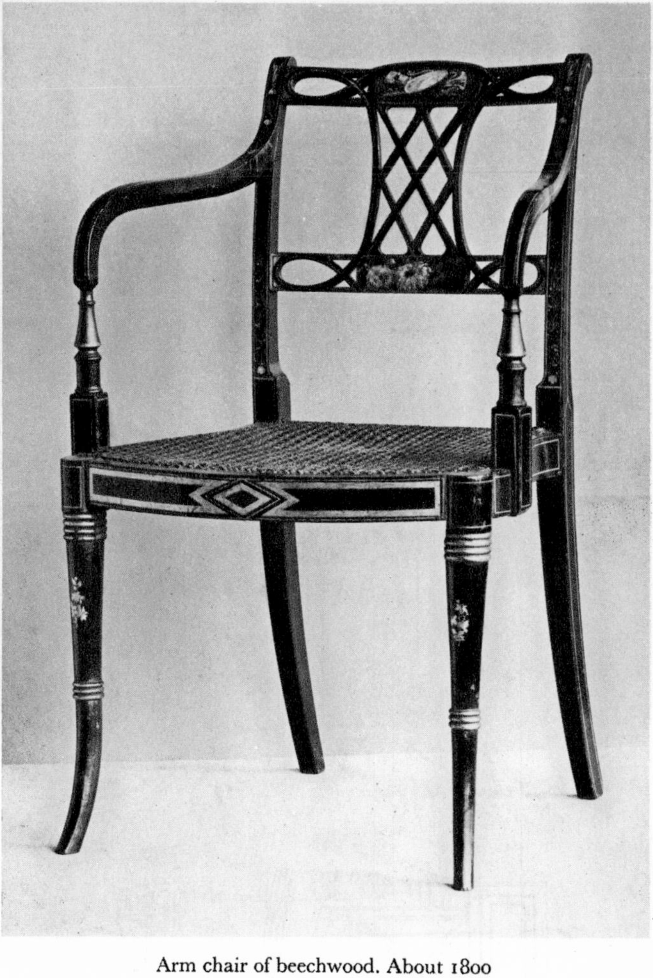

Arm chair of beechwood. About 1800

Front and side of an arm chair and side of a chair from Thomas Hope's *Household Furniture and Decoration*, 1807

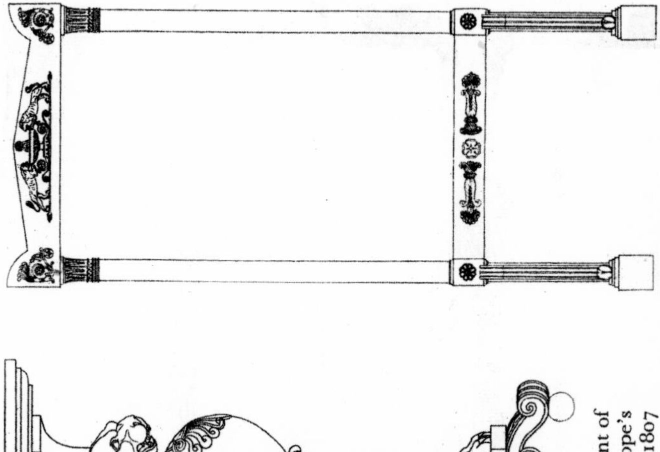

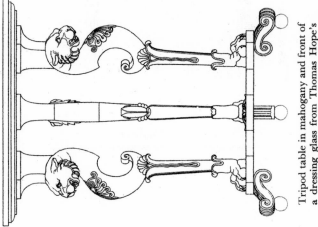

Tripod table in mahogany and front of a dressing glass from Thomas Hope's *Household Furniture and Decoration*, 1807

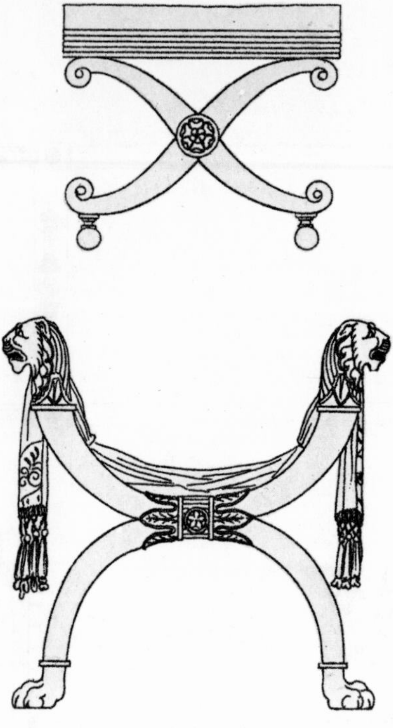

Two stools from Thomas Hope's
Household Furniture and Decoration, 1807

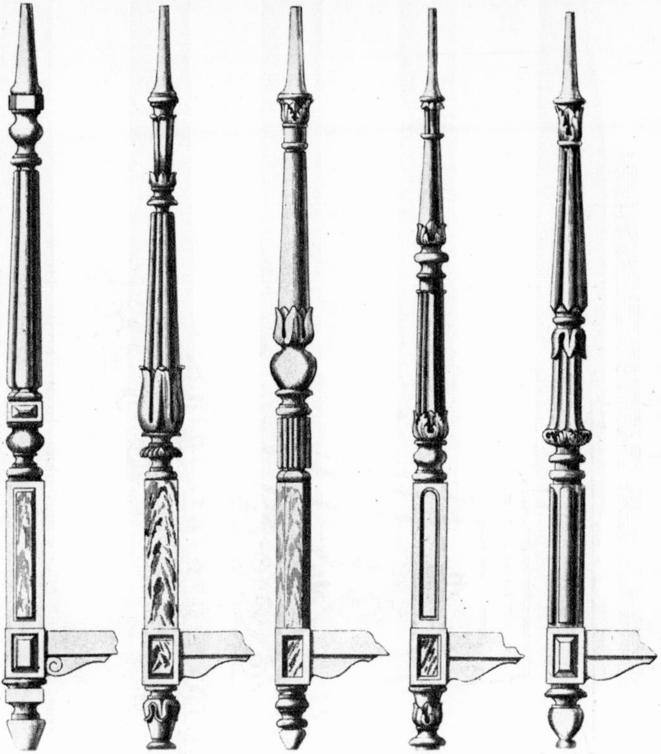

Designs for bed pillars from George Smith's *Cabinet-maker and Upholsterer's Guide*, 1826

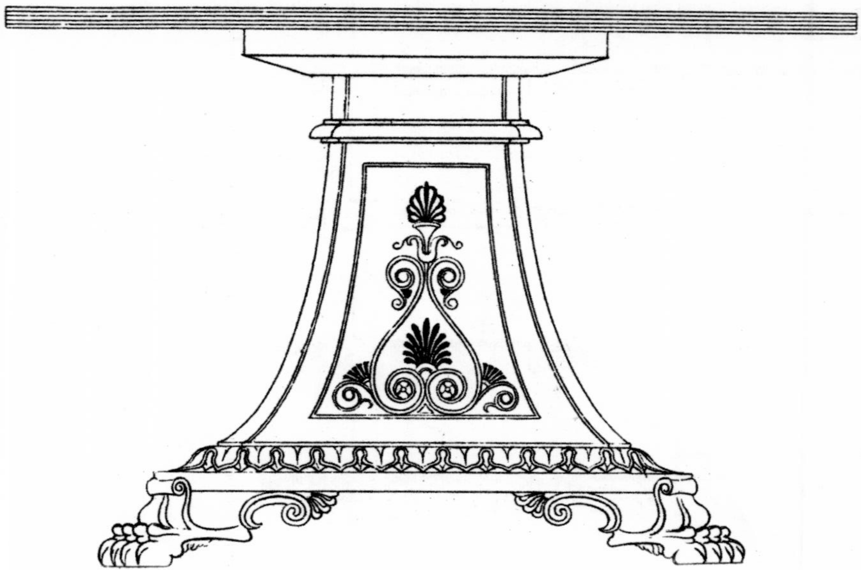

Elevation of a round table, inlaid in ebony and silver, from Thomas Hope's *Household Furniture and Decoration*, 1807

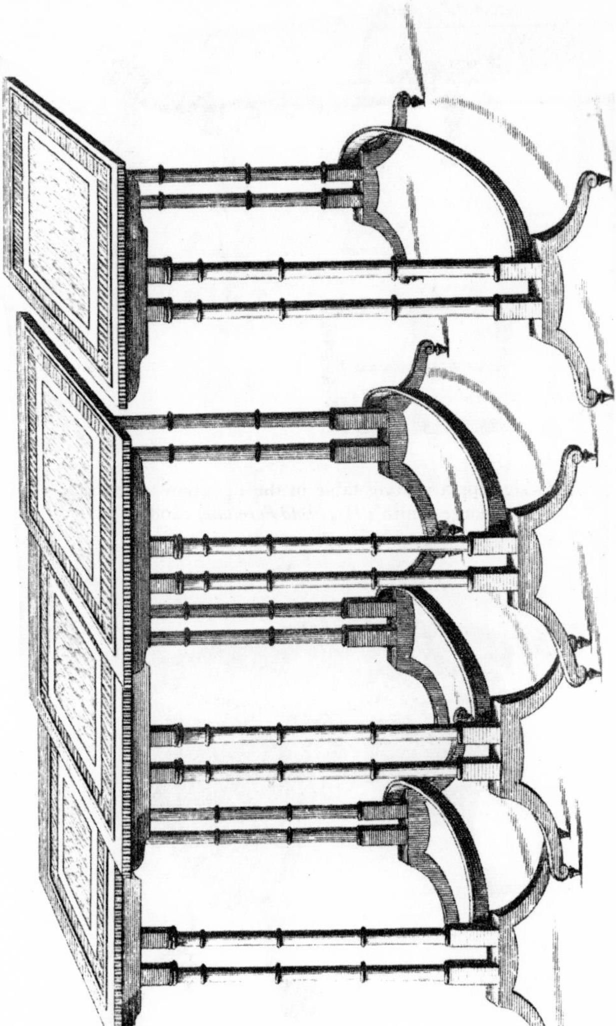

Set of tables from T. Sheraton's *Cabinet Dictionary*, 1803

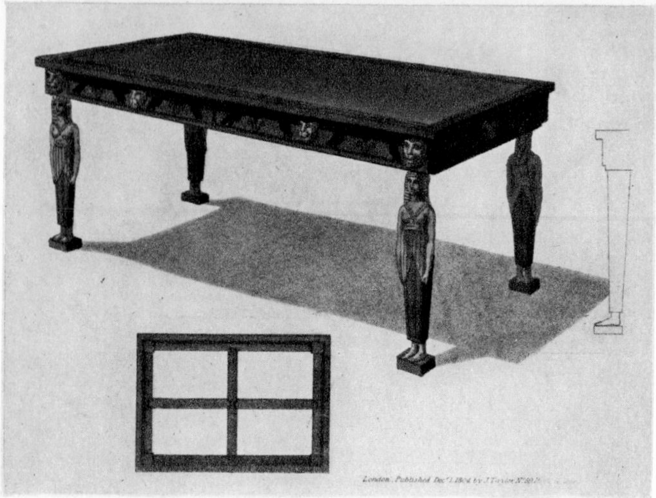

(A) Design for a writing table in the Egyptian taste from George Smith's *Household Furniture*, 1808

(B) Dressing table, with end pedestals, from George Smith's *Household Furniture*, 1808

Secretaire of mahogany, veneered with zebra wood. About 1810

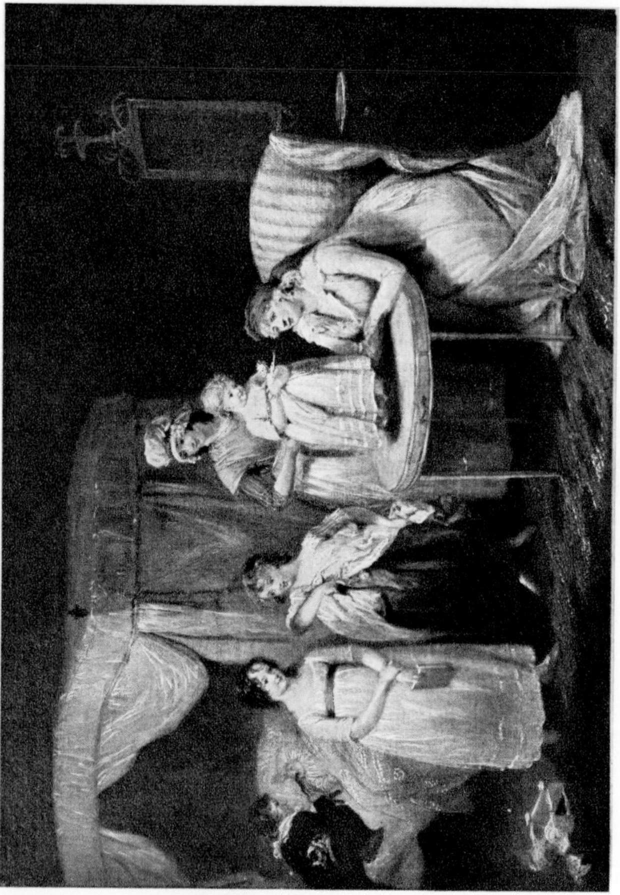

The Clean Face Rewarded by James Ward, R.A.

'The Octagonal Tent Room' from George Smith's *Cabinet-maker and Upholsterer's Guide*, 1826

(A) *Interior*, from Henry Moses' *Designs of Modern Costume*, 1823

(B) *Interior*, from Henry Moses' *Designs of Modern Costume*, 1823

larity in 1753. 'According to the present prevailing whim, everything is Chinese, or in the Chinese taste; or, as it is sometimes more modestly expressed, *partly after the Chinese manner*. Chairs, tables, chimney-pieces, frames for looking-glasses, and even our most vulgar utensils are all reduced to this new-fangled standard; and without doors so universally has it spread, that every gate to a cow-yard is in T's and Z's, and every hovel for the cows has bells hanging at the corners. The good people in the city are, I perceive, struck with this novelty; and though some of them still retain the last fashion, the Gothic, yet others have begun to ornament the doors and windows of their shops with the more modern improvements.'[14]

The vogue, which was exploited most thoroughly in a single room – a bedroom or perhaps a tea-room – was interpreted by such trade publications as a *New Book of Chinese Designs Calculated to Improve the Present Taste*, a work by Edwards and Darly which appeared in 1754. Matthew Darly, the leading partner, was a print-seller, publisher, and engraver; he was not a craftsman with experience of furniture.

The furniture of the well-known Chinese bedroom at Badminton was probably supplied to Charles Noel, fourth Duke of Beaufort, by the elder Thomas Chippendale about the year 1750. The room is known to have been 'finished and furnished' by 1754.[15] The Duke of Beaufort was in any event a subscriber to the first edition of the *Director*, which contained a number of Chinese designs. The furniture, which included a bedstead of large dimensions, chairs with latticed backs, a commode, kneehole dressing-table, and a set of four open china stands, was japanned in black and gold; the walls were covered with a painted Chinese wall paper.

The bedstead, now in the Victoria and Albert Museum, is of the square form in favour at the time and is surmounted by a deep pagoda roof set at the angles of the cornice with dragons of gilt and carved wood and enriched with pendent icicle ornament. The head-board, which extends to the height of the posts, is constructed in open lattice work.

The china stands or *ètagéres* (two of the original set of four are now in the Lady Lever Art Gallery at Port Sunlight) belonging to the suite were similarly decorated. The specimen illustrated in Plate 36 is japanned in black, gold, and red. The pagoda-shaped top is hung at the corners with small bells and supported on thin twisted columns; the three open shelves are enclosed by latticed sides.

William Hallett was one of the leading exponents of the style. Hallett was an extremely successful cabinet-maker and astute man of business. He is familiarly noted by Horace Walpole: 'Latimers belongs to Mrs Cavendish ... and the house has undergone Batty Langley discipline: half the ornaments are of his bastard Gothic, and half of Hallet's mongrel Chinese. I want to write over the doors of most modern edifices, "Repaired and beautified; Langley and Hallet churchwardens." '[16]

Sir William Chambers, 1726–96, was the first English architect to visit China. His *Designs for Chinese Buildings, Furniture, Dresses etc.* was published in 1757, and was unusual in that it, at least, was based on personal experience of China and compiled from drawings made in that country. Chambers was of the same mind as Horace Walpole and, not wishing to venture his reputation on what he rightly considered to be a passing craze, protested against the prevailing rage for 'extravagant fancies that daily appear under the name of Chinese'. As architect to George III, he was responsible for the improvements to the gardens at Kew. The Pagoda is, however, his only surviving contribution there in the Chinese taste.

NOTES TO CHAPTER 6

1. R. Campbell, *The London Tradesman*, 1747. Quoted by Helen Comstock, the *Connoisseur*, March 1951, p. 50.
2. *The Letters of Philip Dormer Stanhope, 4th Earl of Chesterfield*, ed. by Bonamy Dobrée, 1932, vol. IV, p. 1211. No. 1586; to Madame la Marquise de Monconseil, from London, dated 5th Sept., 1748.
3. *London Magazine, or, Gentleman's weekly intelligencer*, Nov. 1738. Quoted by Percy Macquoid and Ralph Edwards, *The Dictionary of*

English Furniture, 1924–7, vol. I, p. 231; revised edit. by Ralph Edwards, 1954, vol. I, p. 276.

4. See Trenchard Cox, *A General Guide to the Wallace Collection*, 1938, p. 78.
5. Adam Smith, *An Inquiry into the Nature and Causes of the Wealth of Nations* (1776), 1869 edit., by J. E. T. Rogers, vol. I, p. 19.
6. Thomas Sheraton, *Cabinet Dictionary*, 1803, p. 145.
7. Marie Anne Fiquet du Boccage, *Letters concerning England, Holland and Italy*; trans. from the French; 2 vols., London, 1770.
8. Mary Hamilton, *Diary* (1784). Quoted by Macquoid and Edwards, *op. cit.*, vol. II, p. 232; Edwards, *op. cit.*, vol. II, p. 227.
9. *Purefoy Letters, 1735–53*, ed. by G. Eland, 1931, vol. I, pp. 99–101.
10. *Letters of Horace Walpole*, ed. by Peter Cunningham, 1861–6, vol. IV, p. 404. To Lady Hervey, from Paris, Sept. 14th, 1765.
11. Cunningham, *op. cit.*, vol. IV, p. 414. To John Chute, from Paris, Oct. 3rd, 1765.
12. Cunningham, *op. cit.*, vol. IX, p. 490. To the Countess of Suffolk, from Paris, Dec. 5th, 1765.
13. Quoted by Percy Macquoid, *English Furniture, etc.*, Lady Lever Art Gallery Collections III, 1928, p. 72 (item 285).
14. *The World*, March 22nd, 1753. Quoted by R. W. Symonds, *Furniture in the French, Chinese and Gothic Tastes*, in the *Connoisseur*, May 1941.
15. *The Travels through England of Dr Richard Pococke*, published by Camden Society, 1888–9.
16. Cunningham, *op. cit.*, vol. II, p. 447. To Richard Bentley, from Strawberry Hill, July 5th, 1755.

Figure 51 – Ornamental wall bracket of rococo design; of pine, carved and gilded

CHAPTER SEVEN

THE POST-'DIRECTOR' PERIOD

THE elder Thomas Chippendale was born at Otley, in Yorkshire, in 1718. He was the son of a joiner there, and probably as a youth helped to make a quantity of plain, country furniture of oak and other native woods. His grandfather, John Chippendale, had been also a joiner, or carpenter, of Otley.

Chippendale established himself in London, at Long Acre, before the middle of the century, and subsequently removed nearby to St Martin's Lane, perhaps the most fashionable quarter for the trade at that period. His status, therefore, was quite considerable, but not exceptional. Among his rivals were such men as William Vile, cabinet-maker to the Crown under George III, and his partner, John Cobb (who, until Vile's retirement in 1765, attended largely to the upholstery side of the business); William Ince and John Mayhew; the 'great and eminent' William Hallett; Giles Grendy, later a Master of the Company of Joiners; Robert Manwaring, and others. Chippendale counted as their competitor in trade.

Chippendale had no pretensions to rising above his occupation. (He placed his son in his own firm, then Chippendale and Haig, which in later years became much expanded.) His workshop, 'wherein were the chests of 22 workmen' (and which was destroyed by fire)[1] was at first comparatively small, although very possibly not his main premises. His name does not appear in the Royal furnishing accounts and, so far as is known, on no occasion did he receive the patronage of the Crown. Cobb,* however, is

* Cobb was described by J. T. Smith, writing in 1828, as 'one of the proudest men in England'. 'The corner house of Long Acre,' stated

recorded to have expressed the wish to found a family of 'private gentlemen'; both he and Hallett were extremely successful men and left large fortunes.

Vile and Cobb produced furniture of the finest sort. In 1761, for example, the firm supplied Queen Charlotte with 'a very handsome jewel cabinet', listed in the last quarter's account for that year as being 'of many different kinds of fine wood, on a mahogany frame, richly carved, the fronts, ends and top inlaid with ivory in compartments neatly engraved, the top to lift up and two drawers, the drawers all lined with black velvet'.[3] Executed at the outset of the reign, it must have been one of the first commissions given to Vile and Cobb in their capacity of cabinet-makers in chief to George III.* The piece is about 42 inches high, made of mahogany veneered with padouk, amboyna, tulip, olive, and rosewood, and inlaid with ivory. The back and

Smith, 'now No. 72 [St Martin's Lane], formed a small part of the extensive premises formerly occupied by that singularly haughty character, Cobb, the Upholsterer ... [who] always appeared in full dress of the most superb and costly kind, in which state he would strut through his workshops, giving orders to his men. ... The late King frequently employed him, and often smiled at his pomposity. One day, when Mr Cobb was in his Majesty's library at Buckingham-house, giving orders to a workman, whose ladder was placed before a book which the King wanted, his Majesty desired Cobb to hand him the work, which instead of obeying, he called to his man, "Fellow, give me that book!" The King, with his usual condescension, arose, and asked Cobb, what his man's name was. "Jenkins," answered the astonished Upholsterer. "Then," observed the King, "Jenkins, you shall hand me the book." '[2]

* George II had given little heed to furniture. It would seem that he was indifferent to the furnishing of his private apartments: at St James's 'The King lies on the ground floor, in a room looking into the Garden; it was formerly Lady Suffolk's apartment. Behind the head of his bed are the backstairs up to his closet, & a passage opening into a court, in which passage two beefeaters sit at night. He dines in a wretched low room next to his bedchamber, which is no better. ... He rises at six o'clock & lights his own fire, with wood always ready piled by the chimney. There is nothing but a green Damask bed, a buroe & two or three chairs, & a green couch & some chairs, in these two rooms which are not even hung. He has never suffered the Queen's room to be touched since She died – I saw the wood lying on the hearth in this year 1758, which had been laid for her fire the day she died in 1737.'[4]

front are serpentine; the sides are concave. The cabinet doors enclose eight half-drawers, with one long drawer below. The cabinet is supported on four elaborately carved cabriole legs with whorl feet. A charge of £138. 10*s*. was made for this article – an unusually high price at that time for a piece of small dimensions.

Some of Chippendale's work, especially in later years, was of the finest quality. He supplied furniture to Nostell Priory, in his native Yorkshire, between 1766–70, and to Harewood House in the same county a few years later. (Authorship of the furniture is in each case confirmed by existing accounts.) He was patronized by Sir Edward Knatchbull at Mersham-le-Hatch, in Kent, and in all probability pieces at, for instance, Badminton (Gloucestershire), Renishaw Hall (Derbyshire), and Alnwick (Northumberland) were also from his workshop.* Technically, Chippendale's finest work was done in the 1770s, under the guidance of Robert Adam, and consisted of inlaid furniture in the neo-classical style, when, to anticipate the later judgement of Sheraton, the designs of the *Director* were 'wholly antiquated and laid aside, though possessed of great merit, according to the times in which they were executed'.[5] This later furniture was not of the character which has since become associated with his name. His posthumous reputation is to some degree unmerited, resting, as it does, on the publication in 1754 of *The Gentleman and Cabinet-Maker's Director*, a volume containing 160 plates and brief descriptive notes. This trade catalogue, although conceived primarily as an advertisement, was issued at the then comparatively large sum of £2. 8*s*. and was certainly contributory to Chippendale's growing business. It was prefaced with the hope that 'the novelty, as well as the usefulness of the performance', would 'make some atonement for its faults and imperfections'; it was indeed the first complete and comprehensive pattern book for furniture to

* See *Georgian Cabinet-Makers*, by Ralph Edwards and Margaret Jourdain, 1945, wherein extensive researches on the part of the authors on leading makers of this period are concisely set out.

appear. Although it has been established of late years that the designs were largely the inventions of Matthias Lock and H. Copland, who were at that date in Chippendale's employ, the *Director* provides evidence of their master's acumen and sound organizing ability.[6] By the early nineteenth century, the *Director* had earned Chippendale a quite disproportionate renown. J. T. Smith wrote of him as: '... the most famous Upholsterer and Cabinet-maker of his day, to whose folio work on household-furniture the trade formerly made constant reference. It contains, in many instances, specimens of the style of furniture so much in vogue in France in the reign of Louis XIV, but which, for many years past, has been discontinued in England. However, ... I should not wonder ... if we were to see the unmeaning scroll and shell-work, with which the furniture of Louis's reign was so profusely incumbered, revive; when Chippendale's book will again be sought after with redoubled avidity, and, as many of the copies must have been sold as waste paper, the few remaining will probably bear rather a high price'.[7]

The *Director* was reprinted in 1755 – in itself an indication of some immediate success. In 1762 a third and enlarged edition was in production. Many of the old plates were then withdrawn and additional designs for chimney-pieces, window cornices, garden seats, and hall chairs were introduced. The French influence was still very marked and references to gilding were prominent. As in the earlier editions, many pieces were intended to be gilded, and japanning or painting was thought very suitable for those designs in the Chinese taste – which in a much modified form persisted into the nineteenth century.

Chippendale was employed from 1771–2 in the decoration and furnishing of Garrick's new house in Adelphi Terrace, at a cost of nearly £1,000. The furniture was in part drawn from Garrick's villa at Hampton, and this sum included numerous small renovations. Garrick was a vain man and he no doubt wished to ensure that a good show should be made. In later years 'his table, his equipage, and manner of living' became most expensive; he lived 'rather as a *prince* than as an actor'.[8] A set of twelve chairs for the dining parlour, covered in red leather, the seat rails studded with brass nails (a method of upholstering which, it is to be believed, Chippendale favoured in preference to others), and a heavy pedestal sideboard were made of mahogany. But in the papered drawing-room (decorated with *chinoiseries* by Pillement) gilt mirrors and pairs of Pembroke tables and commodes, 'curiously inlaid with fine woods' in the style of Adam, were accompanied by sofa and chairs, painted green and yellow. The Victoria and Albert Museum possesses furniture formerly at Garrick's villa at Hampton, in a bedroom which had a Chinese wallpaper. Pieces of this set are japanned in green and yellow, mainly in the Chinese style, and include a number of bamboo chairs with rush seats, wardrobes (two of which are painted with Chinese landscapes), a washstand, towel horse, and bedstead. The bedstead is hung with the East India Company 'chintzes' from Masulipatam presented to Mrs Garrick by some merchants of Calcutta. The Indian cotton fabric is painted in colours with 'Tree of Life' patterns. The bedstead has a coved canopy which is supported on reeded columns and bases painted with classical ornament. It was probably executed by Chippendale, Haig & Co. Cotton fabrics were popular in the third quarter of the century. Dr Johnson, for one, accounted them 'elegant'.*

The extreme Chinese vogue was abandoned during the 1760s. The 'elegant and useful designs' in that taste, which had been particularized in the first edition of the *Director*, were outmoded by the date of the third (1762). For example,

* 'The house and the furniture are not always nicely suited,' he wrote in connexion with an incident which occurred during his tour of the Hebrides with James Boswell in 1773. 'We were driven once, by missing a passage, to the hut [i.e. a dwelling of one storey] of a gentleman, where, after a very liberal supper, when I was conducted to my chamber, I found an elegant bed of Indian cotton, spread with fine sheets. The accommodation was flattering; I undressed myself, and felt my feet in the mire. The bed stood upon the bare earth, which a long course of rain had softened to a puddle.'[9]

in practice the pagoda roof form, which had frequently been adapted to the design of the bedstead or cabinet, was now more rarely made, along with the elaborate frets and railing which had been used to fill the chair back. Japanned pieces tended to be absorbed in a class of painted furniture with revived classical ornament.

Chippendale was associated with the bankruptcy proceedings of 1772 against Mrs Cornelys, the singer, by which it would appear that his firm may well have supplied furniture to her house in Soho Square in 1767, when extensive decorations were being undertaken. Much of the furniture at Carlisle House was in the Chinese taste.*

* Teresa Cornelys, like Garrick, was a public figure. She was the daughter of an actor, of German extraction, and had been born in Venice in 1723, where she contracted a youthful friendship with Jacques Casanova, who later re-visited her in London. He has made mention of Mrs Cornelys in the *Memoirs*. The public entertainments given by her at Carlisle House were notorious.[10] Horace Walpole on one occasion remarked: 'We wore out the wind and the weather, the Opera and the Play, Mrs Cornelys's and Almack's, and every topic that would do in a formal circle.' [11]

Fanny Burney went to Mrs Cornelys's with her father. She had imagined that an evening so passed 'would have been the most charming in the world'. She allowed 'the magnificence of the rooms, splendour of the illuminations and embellishments, and the brilliant appearance of company exceeded any thing' she had ever before seen, but added 'I must own this evening's entertainment more disappointed my expectations than any I ever spent. ...' [12] This excursion was made in 1770, a year or two after the additions with which Chippendale was probably concerned.

Samuel Curwen, an American citizen in England, has left, too, an account of a visit of 1780 to a Sunday evening promenade at Carlisle House. The entertainment was not then exclusive. As Curwen phrased it: 'among the wheat will be tares'. The company were employed in 'walking through the rooms; being allowed tea, coffee, chocolate, lemonade, orgeat, negus, milk, etc.', and 'ladies were rigged out in gaudy attire, attended by bucks, bloods, and maccaronies ...'. The place was 'also resorted to by persons of irreproachable character'. The former scheme of decoration was apparently retained, two of the rooms being 'covered with carpets, and furnished with wooden chairs and seats in the Chinese taste', a style considered suitable for houses of this nature; these perhaps approximated to common 'rout chairs', which were hired out by cabinet-makers to public rooms, and were here small painted chairs

Craftsmen figured prominently among those subscribing to the first edition of the *Director*. Certainly a half (about 150) of these individuals were cabinet-makers, joiners, upholders or otherwise of the 'profession'. It was for their benefit that the proportions of pieces were stressed and that careful and detailed measurements were given, particularly as to correct mouldings.* Nevertheless, furniture executed from these designs, both by Chippendale himself and by other makers, above all in the provinces, was generally altered and much simplified, and bore a superficial resemblance only to the published designs.

The *Director* was duly followed by a number of other works of a similar nature, of which perhaps the most important was the *Universal System of Household Furniture*, by William Ince and John Mayhew, which was issued 1759–63. The firm of Ince and Mayhew was established in Broad Street, Soho, and evidently enjoyed a good position in the trade. Both partners had served their time under eminent masters. 'William Ince, cabinet-maker' had subscribed to the first edition of the *Director*. The *Universal System* contained more than 300 designs, some being for varieties of furniture disregarded in the *Director*. Explanatory notes were printed in both English and French. English furniture had a good reputation for workmanship at the time, and to some extent was exported to the Continent. Ince and Mayhew palpably wished to capture the French market. They are known to have had dealings abroad and to have imported

with rush-bottomed seats. The narrow gallery was 'fronted near three feet high with an open Chinese fence or railing'. The long room, also carpeted, was 'lighted with glass chandeliers and branches fixed to side walls, against which stand sofas covered with silk' and each of the tea rooms contained 'tables for forty sets of parties'.[13]

* 'Upon the whole,' stated Chippendale, 'I have here given no design but what may be executed with advantage by the hands of a skillful workman, tho' some of the profession have been diligent enough to represent them (especially those after the Gothic and Chinese manner) as so many specious drawings, impossible to be work'd off by any mechanic whatsoever. I will not scruple to attribute this to malice, ignorance and inability. ...'

furniture from Paris. There was in England a limited demand for French furniture. In 1769, Lady Mary Coke referred to chairs 'bespoke at Paris': 'I have got my chairs [away] from Paris without being beholden to any body, but I don't intend to have them covered with the damask or have the frames gilt till after I return from abroad.' [14] The *Universal System* was supplied with a metal-work section, which suggests that the activities of the partners were widespread. Very few pieces of furniture can now be assigned to their workshop, but there is little doubt that output was considerable and of high quality.

Robert Manwaring is chiefly remembered by reason of his publications. In 1765, he published *The Cabinet and Chair-Maker's Real Friend and Companion*, with 40 plates, a work which consisted of 100 and more designs, mostly for chairs; they were said to be original conceptions, invented and drawn by the author. Certain curious 'rural' chairs and seats for summer houses, gardens, and parks were stated to be 'the only ones that ever were published' and certainly were novel. They were intended to be executed with 'the Limbs of Yew, Apple, or Pear Trees', and painted. Manwaring remarked: 'I have made it my particular Study to invent such Designs, as may be easily executed by the Hands of a tolerable skilful Workman ... there are two Things to be principally considered, first, the Merit of the Design itself, and secondly, the Facility of putting it into Execution.' He was familiar with the *Director*, and apparently referred here to some of Chippendale's more extravagant inventions. The merit of all Manwaring's designs was obscured by extremely clumsy drawing; many were certainly bad as designs, but others were competent enough. Manwaring had 'the Boldness to assert, that should the ornamental Parts be left out, there will still remain Grandeur and Magnificence behind'. Most of the contemporary chair-makers who used the designs no doubt made simplifications on them.

Both an attenuated cabriole leg with curl-over foot, sometimes enriched with *cabochon* and leaf carving on the knee, and a straight leg, ornamented or plain, were employed by Manwaring in his designs for parlour chairs. Rococo scroll work was still in evidence at this date. Manwaring favoured also a characteristic interlacing of splats. The square-backed chairs in the Chinese and Gothic styles were remarkably like, and were for the most part heavily ornamented. It may be noted in this connexion that one 'Gothic Garden Seat' was designed with legs of cabriole form, composed of two opposing C-scrolls. The cabriole was used with more reason for 'French elbow chairs' and for single chairs with upholstered backs and seats.

Sheraton despised the *Cabinet and Chair-Maker's Real Friend and Companion.* 'This publication,' he stated, 'professes to shew the method of striking out all kinds of bevel-work, by which, as the author says, the most ignorant person will be immediately acquainted with what many artists have served seven years to know. But this assertion both exceeds the bounds of modesty and truth, since there is no thing in his directions for bevel-work, which he parades so much about, but what an apprentice boy may be taught by seven hours' proper instructions.'[15] In 1766, Manwaring published the *Chair-Makers' Guide*, wherein the designs, although by no means in the height of fashion, showed an independent and interesting, if unequal, invention.

In the 1754 *Director*, Chippendale gave fourteen plates to chairs, illustrating thirty-eight new designs. A section of twelve 'new-pattern Chairs' was the most extensive. These chairs, of the type with which his name is popularly associated, were usually made of mahogany and are found in a variety of pattern and ornamentation (Pl. 40). Chippendale stated in the notes that much of the ornament could be 'omitted at pleasure'; and he observed that the 'fore feet' in these designs were 'all different for your better choice'. These chairs were in the rococo taste: frequently a modified cabriole leg, carved with leaf ornament (Fig. 52), was terminated by a scroll or curl-over foot. The established claw-and-ball foot, which to judge from extant chairs, was typical of the period, was disregarded, presumably as being unlikely to catch the public eye. A central open-work splat, enriched by delicate carved ornament, was surmounted by a top rail of undulating, serpentine, or cupid's bow form. The hooped back also was adapted for use with the straight or slightly curved uprights. The 'proper dimensions' of the chairs were stated to be 'one foot ten inches in the front, one foot five inches ½ behind, and one foot five inches from the front of the back foot to the front rail; the back, one foot ten inches ½ high; the seat one foot five high; but ... made lower according as the seat is to be stuffed'. The proportions were noticeably rigid, and calculated. The lighter and more

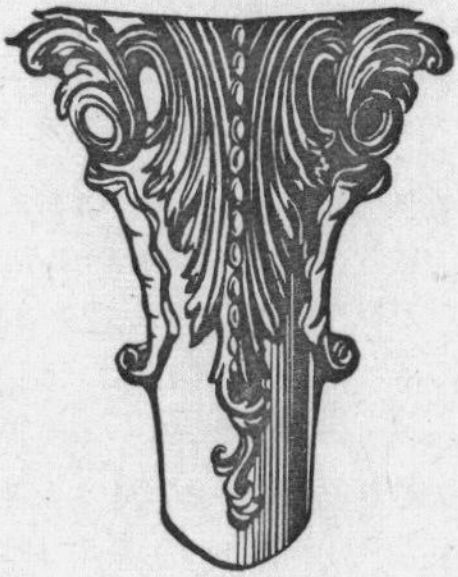

Figure 52 – Detail of the knee of a cabriole leg carved with acanthus foliage

graceful style deriving from France, which first became apparent about 1735, was probably looked on, in general, with satisfaction.*

* Caroline Girle (Mrs Philip Lybbe Powys) noted in 1757 that she went 'to see a house of the Duke of Devonshire's, called Hardwick'. She wrote: 'It was built in 1578 by Elizabeth, Countess of Shrewsbury. Of course it is antique, and render'd extremely curious to the present age, as all the furniture is coeval with the edifice. Our ancestors' taste for substantialness in every piece makes *us* now smile; they too would, could they see our delicateness in the same articles, smile at us, and I'm certain, if any one was to compare three or four hundred years hence a chair from the drawing-room of Queen Elizabeth's days and of the light French ones of George II, it would never be possible to suppose them to belong to the same race of people, as the one is altogether gigantic and the other quite lilliputian.' [16]

Concerning the following three designs for 'Ribband-back' chairs, Chippendale wrote: '[These], if I may speak without vanity, are the best I have ever seen (or perhaps have ever been made).' One design apparently had already been successfully executed by the date of publication. Chippendale had good reason for satisfaction. The riband-back chair (Pl. 41) notably expressed the style of his *Director* period. The knotted and interlaced ribbon sometimes accompanied by a tassel and cord, which was incorporated in the design, emphasized the rococo character of this popular variety of chair, and blended happily with the employment of C- and S-scrolled forms and with other details of carved decoration. The *motif* was not new, but had originated in France earlier in the century. The graceful cabriole legs, often connected by a shallow carved apron piece ornamented with acanthus, were also 'French'.

The number of plates allotted to specimen chairs in the Gothic and Chinese tastes (two and three plates respectively, each with three designs) provides a suggestion as to their relative popularity at that time. The Chinese taste, as Chippendale wrote, admitted 'of the greatest variety' and was indeed 'the most useful'. Gothic designs were seldom carried out, and more often than not such Gothic detail as was introduced scarcely affected the structure of pieces: the chair back was rectangular and filled by an openwork pattern in which such forms as the cusped arch were used. Gothic ornament appeared, however, in Chippendale's 'new pattern' chairs, when the central splat was sometimes pierced in imitation of Gothic tracery. Then, chairs of the same basic form were constructed with 'French' or with 'Gothic' splats and were equally pleasing in appearance. Both types were essentially novelties and the disparity between them was often not great (Pl. 40). Sometimes the 'Gothic' and 'Chinese' were unobtrusively blended; and either is to be found in pleasing combination with the rococo.

Upholstered elbow chairs, of rather larger dimensions and with open arms, which Chippendale designated as

'French', provide an instance of this want of order: the stuffed backs were variously shaped; legs were straight and connected by fretted stretchers, or were of a decorated cabriole form; and ornament was diversely in all styles.

There survive a number of 'Chinese' chairs of intricate and eccentric design; the top rail is often carved with a pagoda *motif*. These show the style 'in its most advanced degree'. In general, the back was filled with a relatively simple design composed of Chinese railing or lattice work. The structure was lightened to a considerable extent by this means. The chair was supported on straight legs united by stretchers. In some instances legs and stretchers were quite plain, but this revived form lent itself equally to an elaborate perforation or to enrichment by means of applied frets.

The straight leg returned to fashion about 1750, the cabriole having then enjoyed almost exclusive use over nearly fifty years. At first regarded as an alternative form characteristic of the Chinese and Gothic tastes, or as one particularly suited for those pieces intended for the dining-room, it readily became adopted by all makers. Most extant versions of the simplified 'Chippendale' chair produced by the provincial maker have a plain square leg.

During the seventh decade of the century, in particular, single chairs showed a very great variety of invention. Many types were quite unrelated to those illustrated in the *Director*. The fan-shaped filling to the back which is found on specimens of this date, and earlier, is associated with Ince and Mayhew. Certain rather clumsy designs in which use was made of looped and interlacing bands were favoured by Manwaring. One example approximates to types illustrated by him in the *Cabinet and Chair-Maker's Real Friend and Companion*. The popular 'ladder-back' chair, composed of serpentine horizontal rails, frequently pierced, was made in great numbers and in all likelihood produced in most workshops.

A quite substantial part of the *Director* was devoted to the illustration of furniture proper to the library, and some prominence was given to the library breakfront bookcase. Exact measurements were attached to designs and, for the most part, the profiles of mouldings were shown 'at large' on separate plates, engraved with great attention to detail. Concerning the first three bookcases (1754 edition) Chippendale remarked: 'If you have occasion to alter their sizes, it would be well to keep as nigh the same proportion as possible; otherwise the upper doors may have but an ill appearance. It would be needless to say any thing more about them, as their forms are so easy.' The regard paid to good proportion was characteristic, and was particularly appropriate in the case of the first design (Pl. 43B) which is of an unusually severe character. The centre compartment was surmounted by a plain triangular pediment and flanked by recessed wings; the cornice was straight; the glazing bars were straight and, like the enclosing doors of the base, without ornament. Bookcases varied considerably in size, some larger specimens attaining a width of 15 feet and being constructed with five compartments. The architectural form was always fitting, and Chippendale made indiscriminate use of the triangular, the broken, the swan-necked, and the segmental pediment. The base (corresponding to the pedestal of the Order) was solid or enclosed by solid doors, and was not glazed.

Gothic bookcases figured in all editions of the *Director* and were evidently 'fancy' pieces which were not in fact executed without drastic modification.* 'This book-case, made by an ingenious workman,' wrote Chippendale of one design, 'will have the desired effect'; and he stated of yet another, 'one of the best of its kind', that it would give him 'great pleasure to see it executed, as I doubt not of its making an exceeding genteel and grand appearance ...'.

* Horace Walpole's library at Strawberry Hill was altogether exceptional. The house was neo-Gothic; it was a source of interest and amusement to Walpole, to which at this time he was striving to impart a 'whimsical air of novelty'. 'My present occupation,' he observed to Richard Bentley in 1754, 'is putting up my books; and thanks to arches, and pinnacles, and pierced columns, I shall not appear scantily provided.' [17] This interest was retained throughout his life. As late as 1781, he expressed the pleasure he had felt on having converted a friend

The Gothic taste of the middle eighteenth century was removed in spirit from the medieval. Its charm lay in picturesque associations with the past.* Like the rococo, it was a delicate style and a romantic reaction against the discipline of Palladianism. In furniture Gothic was reflected only in ornamental detail; Gothic forms are found, for example, in endless variety in patterning of the glazing bars of bookcases.

The cabinet with wings often resembled in form the contemporary bookcase. A fine cabinet in the collection of Viscount Leverhulme is illustrated in plate 38. This piece is designed in the Chinese taste. The central compartment is surmounted by a pagoda roof to which are affixed an upright, carved escutcheon, and a pair of bracket candlesticks, hung with small ivory bells. The wings, which are lower, carry an open-fretted balustrading. The tall doors of the cabinet are veneered with a golden amboyna wood and

'Dickey Bateman', 'from a Chinese to a Goth'.[18] The latter was the subject of the following lines also:

> ' "See Betty, see who's there."
> "'Tis Mr Bateman, Ma'am, in his new chair."
> "Dicky's new chair! the charming'st thing in town,
> Whose poles are lacker'd and whose lining's brown." '
> (*Isabella or The Morning*, by Sir C. H. Williams.)

* Mrs Delany was a devotee of the Gothic. Her admiration was not infrequently expressed in letters to her sister, Mrs Dewes. Staying at Lucan in 1754, she pronounced St Catherine's, Dr Sam Cook's house on the River Liffey, to be 'as formal as a bad taste could make it ... from the house to a chapel there was a fine gothic gallery with bow windows, which the present owner *pulled down*, and has put up a palisade in the stead of it. 'Tis provoking to see such beauties *thrown away upon Vandals*'.[19] Her attitude is clear from a letter dated from Welbeck, 7 September, 1756. She then wrote with pleasure: '[Lady Oxford's] apartment is the prettiest thing I ever saw, consisting of a skylight antechamber or vestibule, adorned in the Gothic way. The rooms that encompass it are a library, a dressing-room, a room fitted up with china and japan of the rarest kinds, and a Gothic room full of charming pictures, and embellished with everything that can make it look gay and pleasant: it is lighted by a window something of the Venetian kind, but prettier, and the whole breadth of one side of the room. It is indeed an enchanting pretty room, but never was made use of. ...'[20]

are bordered in rosewood, relieved by an inlay of ebony and holly. The cabinet is supported on an open stand of seven legs, enriched by card-cut lattice work. The insides of the doors are veneered in rosewood. The interior of the cabinet contains approximately ninety small drawers; each is fronted with a different and, in many cases, a rare wood.

The Chinese style was favoured for china cabinets, and a number of smaller cabinets or 'cases' of this character, but without wings, have survived. An open-work frieze provided an alternative to the pagoda roof; the upper portion was glazed, the doors being ornamented with a fret pattern. The stand was constructed with four straight legs.

The bureau in two stages was in practice often made with the upper portion enclosed by solid wooden doors, although Chippendale's designs for this composite piece, which he referred to as the 'Desk and Bookcase' and which was extremely rich, show that, in the fine specimen at least, he intended the doors to be glazed with looking-glass. This was in the early Georgian tradition. Plain wooden doors ensured a saving in the cost of manufacture and would have been quite generally adopted by those makers following the designs. One example (Pl. 42), rather wider (3 feet 10 inches) than was usual, was shown with a centre in slight projection, enclosed by a single door. This centre portion, which was surmounted by a swan-necked pediment, was glazed, while the recessed flanking doors were decorated with carved floral pendants in the French taste. Narrow upright cupboards in both the upper stage and the base formed an integral part of the design and were of practical use in housing the larger books.

The 'Desk and Bookcase' was illustrated in the *Director* in all current styles of ornament and in a variety of forms. The desk or bureau is found usually as a base of three long and two short drawers on bracket feet, or alternatively as a 'frame' supported on modified cabriole legs. The kneehole desk was also employed as a base often, seemingly, for a piece of furniture called the 'Dressing Chest and Bookcase', purposed for use in the dressing-room, where letters were written and the morning's business despatched.

Some small bureaux designed for the bedroom were fitted with a light superstructure of open shelves for the display of china.

It is a curious fact that the dining-table was disregarded by compilers of the trade catalogues of the period. The dining-table was not illustrated in the first edition of the *Director*, although as many as six designs were shown both for open pedestal library tables of an ingenious and expensive nature and for French commode tables, and attention was given to other varieties, notably to writing, breakfast, and china tables. The dining-table was usually composed of two, three, or more separate tables or parts which were constructed so as to fit together, as needed, as one extended table, and would appear in consequence to have been usually of a somewhat clumsy and workaday character, allowing small scope to the talents of the designer; the basic cost of a plain dining-table was indeed to be estimated at about a shilling per foot. If in the form of a pair of tables, each was normally provided with one falling flap and was supported on five legs, one leg being hinged to the frame and swinging out on the inner side so as to support the flap when raised. The table when extended thus provided adequate foot room only at its middle portion; four outside legs were closely grouped at each of the ends. Garrick possessed 'a set of Mahogany Dining Tables with Circular Ends to Joyn together complete' for which he was charged the comparatively small sum of ten guineas by Chippendale and Haig. The dining-table was also frequently composed of three units – a centre with rectangular extension flaps and a pair of semi-circular ends. The latter were detachable and had independent use as wall or side tables. The type persisted throughout the whole of the latter half of the eighteenth century, figuring in the bills of those years.*

* In a letter dated 'Mount Panther, 21 Aug. 1758', Mrs Delany described the arrangements that were made to seat company. She wrote to her sister of the ball which had been held in this Irish house: 'Tea from

Gate-legged tables were out of fashion by the reign of George II, and by mid century were produced only in outlying and country districts. Towards about 1760, however, a light, small table of mahogany, constructed on the gate principle, was evolved. It was of rectangular form, with two flaps, or occasionally a single flap. The fragile appearance of this variety of table imparted by the extremely slender turned legs and stretchers led to its being appropriately described, at an early date, as 'spider-legged'.

According to Sheraton, the 'Pembroke', another small table with extending top, was named after that 'lady who first gave orders for one of them, and who probably gave the first idea of such a table to the workmen'.[22] Pembroke tables, which were introduced shortly after the middle of the century and soon became very popular, were made with two flaps, each upheld by hinged wooden brackets. At first, these tables were usually of rectangular form, with straight legs united by X-stretchers. Some were very decorative; they are found with chamfered legs on guttae feet connected by shaped and perforated stretchers, or with cluster column legs in the Chinese taste. They resemble the breakfast tables illustrated by Chippendale, and sometimes served the same purpose.

Breakfast tables were often fitted below the table top with a shelf. The shelf was sometimes enclosed on three sides by open lattice work and cut away in front so as to give knee room to the user. In a specimen, figured in the 1754 *Director* (Pl. 43A), the shelf was enclosed by fretwork on all four sides, and the front 'cut out for a recess for the knees and two folding doors to open'. Frets were cut from a single

seven to ten: it was made in the hall, and Smith presided. When any of the dancers had a mind to rest themselves they sat in the little parlour, and tea was brought to them. They began *at six* and ended *at ten*: then went to a cold supper in the drawing-room made of 7 dishes down the middle of different cold meats, and plates of all sorts of fruit and sweet things that could be had here, in the middle jellies: in all 21 dishes and plates. The table held twenty people; the rest had a table of their own in the little parlour, but all the dancers were together, and I at the head to take care of them. . . .'[21]

board, or alternatively were built up in successive layers. In other versions of the breakfast table the flaps were shaped or the shelf was dispensed with, its place being taken by cross stretchers. Normally, these tables were supplied with one long drawer beneath the top.

J. T. Smith related that Cobb, of Vile and Cobb, Chippendale's near neighbours, brought into fashion 'that very convenient table ... that draws out in front, with upper and inward rising desks, so healthy for those who stand to write, read, or draw ...'. Nathaniel Dance, the portrait painter, 'considered Cobb's tables so useful, that he easily prevailed upon the adonised Upholsterer, to allow him to paint his portrait for one; which picture, after it had remained in Cobb's show-room for some time, purposely to be serviceable, as he said, to the "*poor painter*", he conveyed, in his own carriage, to his seat at Highgate'.[23] The reference is to the type of artists' or reading table, with four straight legs and a drawer ingeniously fitted with numerous small compartments, which might be pulled out from the body of the piece and supported by the attached half-sections of the front legs. The pull-out front was not obligatory. The rising top was made adjustable by means of a ratchet (Pl. 39). The draughtsman might choose between a standing or seated position. A table, or 'desk', of this nature was purchased by the Purefoy family from 'Mr Belchier at the Sun the South side of St Pauls in St Pauls Churchyard London' and despatched to their home at Shalstone in the summer of 1749.* The purchase was made for the sum of £3. 10*s*. This table was plain but of good quality – as might be expected from a maker whose workshop was in that quarter of the town. It was of sturdy construction, with heavy straight chamfered legs, and was fitted with candle brackets and a lock. The piece had suffered apparently from the damp conditions encountered in transit to Buckinghamshire, for Henry Purefoy was obliged to write thus to Mr Belchier: 'I have received the Desk, but wee

* John Belchier died in 1753, and was succeeded at *Ye Sun* by one Thomas Atkinson.

can't open the Draw but do suppose it opens in the two Slitts down the Legs. I desire you will let mee have a letter from you next post how to open & manage it . . .'[24]

Alternatively tables of this type were made with a central pillar supported on a tripod base. A carved mahogany reading table made by William France for Lord Mansfield, and now in the Victoria and Albert Museum, is fitted with a square top (measuring 26 inches), with four drawers below. The top is hinged in the middle and may be raised so as to form a slope. France charged £6. 14*s*. for this 'large Mahogany Reading Stand on a stout Pillar and Claw with a screw Nutt worked very true, capable of screwing to rise

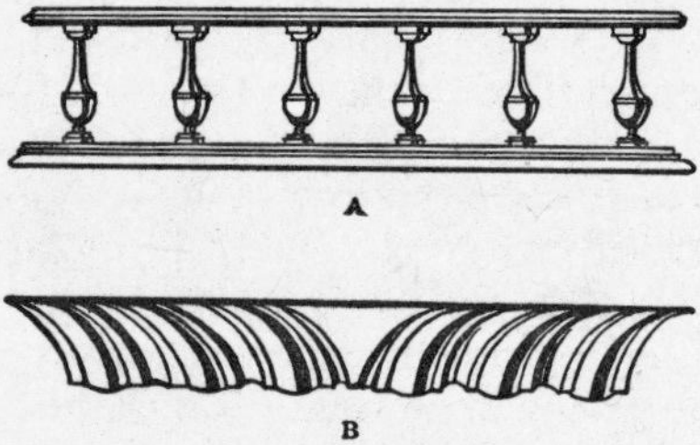

Figure 53 – Details of (A) a spindle gallery; (B) a gadrooned border

10 Inches if required, the whole of very Good Mahogany, and the pillar and Claw richly carved'.[25] The table was made for the library at Kenwood in 1770.

About 1760, the popular tripod tea table, with circular or shaped, tray top, was in more decorative specimens often fitted with a small spindle gallery, or with carved ornamental edges (Fig. 53), or was bordered by a fret.

Extreme simplicity distinguished the first of six of Chippendale's designs for the sideboard table (Pl. 44A). Fretted, C-shaped angle brackets, placed at the juncture of legs and frieze, offered a bare suggestion of the Chinese taste, and formed the only ornamental feature. The table was supported on four square legs with chamfered inner sides. The plate was engraved in 1753, and provides further evidence of the date by which the straight leg had become adopted for a plain but fashionable piece, as this table. The following dimensions were recommended as suitable: width, 5 feet; depth, 2 feet 6 inches (precisely half the width); and height, 2 feet 8 inches. The thickness of leg was put at 2¾ inches.

These proportions were varied for a rather larger and more ambitious table (Pl. 44B), designed with canted corners and a bow to the centre of the front. The depth was again 2 feet 6 inches, but the width was increased by 6 inches to 5 feet 6 inches and height by 2 inches to 2 feet 10 inches. The specimen shows a blending of the rococo and Chinese tastes.

The 'bureau dressing table', as the name implies, was intended primarily for use in the bedroom. It bore some resemblance in form to the open pedestal library table. Two specimens illustrated in the *Director* were to be constructed with a straight front and were of moderate size (3 feet 9 inches). A central kneehole, flanked on either side by three short, deep drawers, decreasing in height towards the table top, was closed by a shallow recessed cupboard. One long drawer was fitted above. These pieces stood on six bracket feet (two pairs in front), of square or ogee form. Fretwork ornament was a feature of a number of tables of this type, in some of which the top was made so as to lift up and disclose an array of small compartments and a hinged mirror.

Chippendale illustrated three larger and more elaborate specimens, one of which was designed with a bold serpentine front, shaped sides, and prominent rounded corners. Its execution would have necessitated a very high degree of skill. In another design, a single door front, decorated with applied leaf carving, was suggested as the alternative to the usual three short drawers; and consoles, carved with acanthus pendants, were placed at the angles of the straight front.

One design for a plain chest of drawers (Pl. 46) would appear somewhat unusual in that it provided for as many as six long drawers and was in consequence of increased height (4 feet 8 inches) – other dimensions being: width, 3 feet 6 inches; and depth, 1 foot 11 inches. This chest was to be supplied with plain, or alternatively, shaped bracket feet. A 3-inch frieze of applied fretwork was recommended as a suitable accompaniment to the latter, more ornamental foot. In case furniture of this nature, such enrichments were confined generally to frieze, plinth, canted corners or feet. Inlay was not considered appropriate to ornamentation in the Chinese manner. The designation 'chest of drawers' was used also in the two immediately succeeding plates both for an ordinary double chest or tallboy and for a chest on stand or 'frame'. The latter (Pl. 45) was more ambitious, one of the two alternative designs making provision for an upper stage enclosed by glazed doors.

A number of designs were given for clothes presses – pieces which were evolved from the ubiquitous chests of earlier periods and 'which need no description ... the use of them [being] well known'. Specimens did not in general greatly exceed a width of 4 feet and were rather squat, the more elaborate being often supported on a low stand and richly decorated on the front with applied ornament.

The character of most early Georgian mirror frames was straightforward; they were designed to conform closely to an architectural setting. Mirror frames were unaffected by the rococo taste until the comparatively late date of about 1745–50, when the change of style was pronounced. The straight-sided rectangular frame, surmounted by a formal entablature and pediment, was replaced by one in which straight lines became curved, being composed of a series of associated C-scrolls. At first, a basically rectangular and solid frame was retained, and floral pendants were attached to the sides. Next, the frame was perforated and lighter, and the pediment was dissolved into a freely designed heading (Fig. 54). By the middle of the century designs in openwork carving were various and extremely ornamental, and free use was made of the scroll, *coquillage*, bulrushes, and curling leaf forms. Borders were sometimes in the form of framed panels of glass. Many mirror frames were derived from plates in the *Director* and *Universal System*, and from the

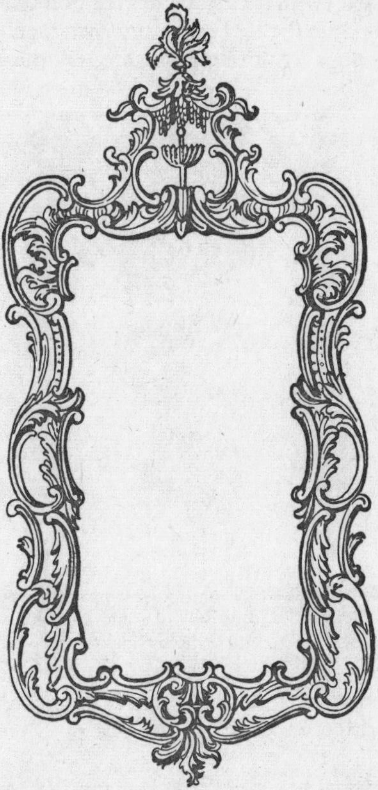

Figure 54 – Mirror in pierced frame of gilt wood, carved with symmetrical scroll-work and acanthus

pattern books issued by Matthias Lock and Thomas Johnson. The latter's claims to be regarded as an 'anti-gallic spirit' were not supported by the rococo character of the plates in his publications.* The designs were in general of such a fantastic nature as to be scarcely practicable of realization in wood. They were intended for the carver and were executed (with a varying degree of modification) only in a soft wood, and gilt. Mahogany specimens, on the other hand, were almost entirely unaffected by these extravagant

Figure 55 – Bracket, carved and gilded – the decoration in mixed Chinese and rococo styles, consisting of a human head, scrolled acanthus and dripping icicles

fashions and were small and plain, being evolved from the modest, walnut frames of the reigns of Queen Anne and George I.

The wayward nature of many designs for overmantels is accountable in part by the fact that the overmantel and the mantelpiece were by preference regarded as a single decorative unit of a room. Temples, ruins, bridges, mandarins, and small exotic figures, trophies or long-tailed birds were

* *Twelve Girandoles*, 1755; *One Hundred and Fifty New Designs*, 1758; *A New Book of Ornaments*, 1760.

motifs which could easily be incorporated in the design of such a feature. Overmantels were divided into compartments. Some were fitted with brackets for the display of china, or with candlebranches. However, as with mirrors, the majority of those now surviving show restraint of taste.

The rococo would seem best to have been realized in wall brackets or in small, ornamental gilt girandoles or candle brackets. These wall pieces were made in sets or in pairs. Four examples of the latter were figured by Chippendale. The form of all was asymmetrical, and candlebranches were attached at haphazard intervals. Some specimens were backed by looking-glass, while others offered an open-carved representation of a picturesque scene or incident. A selection was made from such *motifs* as: Chinese figures of men and women, ruined columns, trees and foliage, pagodas, Gothic tracery, icicles, dripping water, and spiky acanthus sprays (Fig. 55). The resulting medley composition, dominated by the repeated C-scroll, was always dainty.

NOTES TO CHAPTER 7

1. *Gentleman's Magazine*, 'Historicle Chronicle, April 1755', entry for Sat. 5th.
2. J. T. Smith, *Nollekens and his Times*, 1828, vol. II, pp. 243–4.
3. See article by H. Clifford Smith, 'Some mid-Georgian furniture from the Royal collections', *Apollo*, May 1935.
4. *Horace Walpole's Journals of Visits to Country Seats etc.*, ed. by Paget Toynbee, *Walpole Society*, vol. XVI, 1927–8, 'St James's 1758', p. 16.
5. Thomas Sheraton, *Drawing Book*, 1791–4, preface – 'To Cabinet-makers and Upholsterers in general'.
6. *Metropolitan Museum Studies*, May and November 1929, 'The Creators of the Chippendale style', by Fiske Kimball and Edna Donnell.
7. Smith, *op. cit.*, vol. II, p. 238.
8. Quoted by Oliver Brackett, *Thomas Chippendale* (1925).
9. *Johnson's Journey to the Western Islands of Scotland* and *Boswell's Journal of a Tour to the Hebrides with Samuel Johnson, LL.D.*, ed. by R. W. Chapman, Oxford Univ. Press, 1930, p. 91. (Johnson.)
10. See Brackett, *op. cit.*, chapter VII.

11. *Letters of Horace Walpole*, ed. by Peter Cunningham, 1861–6, vol. IV, p. 342. To the Earl of Hertford, from Strawberry Hill, April 7th, 1765.
12. *The Early Diary of Frances Burney, 1768–1778*, ed. by Annie Raine Ellis, 1889, vol. I, p. 83.
13. *Journals and Letters of the late Samuel Curwen from 1775–84*, ed. by G. A. Ward, New York, 1842, pp. 289–90.
14. See Austin Dobson, *Eighteenth Century Vignettes*, 1892–6, 2nd Series.
15. Sheraton, *loc. cit.*
16. *Passages from the Diaries of Mrs Philip Lybbe Powys of Hardwick House, Oxon., 1756–1808*, ed. by Emily J. Climenson, 1899.
17. Cunningham, *op. cit.*, vol. II, p. 415. To Richard Bentley, from Strawberry Hill, Dec. 24th, 1754.
18. Cunningham, *op. cit.*, vol. VIII, p. 51. To the Earl of Strafford, from Strawberry Hill, June 13th, 1781.
19. *The Autobiography and Correspondence of Mary Granville, Mrs Delany*, ed. by Lady Llanover, 1st series, 1861, vol. III, pp. 281–2.
20. Llanover, *op. cit.*, p. 437.
21. Llanover, *op. cit.*, p. 505.
22. Thomas Sheraton, *Cabinet Dictionary*, 1803, p. 284.
23. Smith, *op. cit.*, vol. II, pp. 243–4.
24. *Purefoy Letters, 1735–53*, ed. by G. Eland, 1931, vol. I, p. 111.
25. Illustrated in *Victoria & Albert Museum, Catalogue of English Furniture & Woodwork*, vol. IV by Ralph Edwards, 1931, Pl. 42. W.202 – 1923.

CHAPTER EIGHT

ROBERT ADAM – THE CLASSICAL REVIVAL

THE style of most fashionable varieties of furniture made during the last quarter of the eighteenth century formed a distinct contrast with that of the earlier rococo period – when the Chinese, Gothic, and French manners were in reality variations on one theme. Shortly after the accession of George III, a new simplicity and severity of *form* was sought. In general, curved outlines became straight (although the oval form was popular, particularly for the mirror and the chair back (Pls. 47B and 48), and some tables and cabinets were designed with swelling fronts), ornament was abundant and sometimes intricate, but of a less robust character, and was usually painted, inlaid, or applied in low relief; often chased metal mounts of fine quality added to the richness of the decoration – a feature exemplified in certain ornate library tables of the period. At Matthew Boulton's Soho works near Birmingham, ormolu mounts, part of an enormous range of plate, metal, and stone wares, were produced on an extensive scale from 1762.[1] This reversal of taste was paralleled in France, where the style of Louis XVI, becoming effective as early as 1760–5, was established well before his accession to the throne. The change arose from the interest in classical remains and had been inspired by the excavations at Herculaneum and Pompeii earlier in the century. The main exponent of the neo-classical movement in England was Robert Adam (1728–92). He broke, in the phrase of Sir John Soane, both 'the talismanic charm' of the rococo, and the outworn style of the Palladians. His furniture, in the rather frigidly expressed manner of the classical revival, was first made for a few great houses in the 1760s; thereafter the style was more generally adopted, and by lesser men, sometimes to the detriment of his reputation. Adam designed for a cultured oligarchy; his furniture is, in this respect, comparable with the exquisite productions of Riesener, Oeben, or Carlin. In 1778, in the *Works in Architecture*, Adam remarked '... we have not only met with the approbation of our employers, but even with the imitation of other artists, to such a degree, as in some measure to have brought about, in this country, a kind of revolution ... the skilful ... will easily perceive, within these few years ... in the decoration of the inside, an almost total change'.[2]

Robert Adam was the second son of the Edinburgh architect, William Adam (d. 1748). He attended Edinburgh University and later received in his father's office the instruction which prepared him for a period of study in Italy (1754–8). (He and his brothers John, James, and William were all trained as architects.) He met Charles-Louis Clérisseau on his outward journey in France; he knew Giambattista Piranesi in Rome, where he was elected member of the Academy (1757); and, throughout his travels he made the acquaintance of men whose work and interests lay in the arts. His *Ruins of the Emperor Diocletian's Palace at Spalatro*, a survey published in 1763, after his return to London, resulted from an expedition to what was formerly Venetian Dalmatia. Clérisseau and the painter Zucchi accompanied him to the site; the party set sail from Venice in July 1757. This work, with Winckelmann's *History of Ancient Art*, which appeared in the same year but was unfortunately based on inferior Graeco-Roman remains and on copies executed often in a different material to the originals, Stuart and Revett's *Antiquities of Athens* (1st vol., 1762), and the earlier *Ruines de Grèce* by Le Roi, was instrumental in forming the taste of the 'enlightened' public.

Little is known of Adam's activities immediately after his return from Italy in 1758, but lightness and variety which soon became characteristic of his style were not apparent in the early work at Hatchlands, near Guildford, the property of Admiral Boscawen (1759). By good fortune, Adam enjoyed the patronage of Lord Bute (to become Prime Minister); he built the Admiralty Screen in 1760, and in the course of the next few years received various commissions for large country houses or for the extension and modification of existing houses. His brothers James (who returned from Italy in 1763 where, acting as agent for George III, he had purchased a collection of drawings and prints) and, in a business capacity, William were associated with him; John, the eldest, who inherited Blair Adam, spent most of his life in Scotland. Adam was engaged at Kedleston, Osterley, Syon, Luton Hoo, Moor Park, Nostell, and elsewhere, in work which was classical in character. His work on town houses (more decorative in style) in the 1770s left something to be desired; later, he appears to have made use of indifferent materials, or substitutes. Stucco work, for instance, was often cast in moulds.

Adam was primarily an architect. He and Sir William Chambers held the appointment of 'Joint Architects to His Majesty's Works'. But the desire for complete harmony in the interiors of his buildings necessitated supervision of all details of household equipment. The conventions on which Adam based his domestic architecture were new; this fact led to the creation of new forms for furniture. 'We have not trod in the path of others,' he declared, 'nor derived aid from their labours.' [3] He was not, however, the only architect of the time specifically to design furniture for the interiors of his buildings. James Paine, 'Athenian' Stuart, James Wyatt, and Chambers, his rivals, regarded this branch of interior decoration with a degree of interest – as had Vanbrugh, William Jones, William Kent, and others of earlier generations.

Horace Walpole's disparagement of Adam was unamiable. In a letter to Sir Horace Mann of April 1775 he wrote: 'We have ... very good architects; but as Vanbrugh dealt in quarries, and Kent in lumber, Adam, our most admired, is all gingerbread, filigraine, and fan-painting. Wyatt, less fashionable, has as much taste, is grander, and more pure. We have private houses that cost more than the Palace Pitti. Will you never come and see your fine country before it is undone?'[4] Wyatt had been called in at Fawley Court, Bucks, a house which had been improved at heavy expense a few years previously, and one with which Mrs Lybbe Powys, who was a frequent visitor, was well acquainted: 'Mr Freeman has laid out £8,000, I believe, in inside decorations, besides having the celebrated Mr Brown to plan the grounds. ... Every room is of a good house size, being fitted in an elegant, and each in a different style. The hall is a very noble one; round it statues on pedestals, some fine ones large as life. It's stucco'd of a French grey. The saloon answerable to the hall, with light blue and gold cord ... the drawing-room, fitted up with every possible elegance of the present taste, hung with crimson strip'd damask, on which are to be pictures; a most beautiful ceiling painted by Wyatt; the doors curiously inlaid, the window-shutters painted in festoons, a sweet chimney-piece, a grate of Tutenar's [tutenag – an imported alloy of copper, zinc, and nickel], cost 100 guineas; two exceedingly large pier glasses, the chairs and confidant sofa in the French taste ... the breakfast-parlour, a sweet apartment, pea-green stucco, gold border, elegant chimney-piece, green marble with gilt ornaments; the sofa and chairs, Mrs Freeman's work, a French pattern, pink, green, and grey; curtains, peagreen lute-string.'[5]

Adam's interiors, although formal and conceived on a grand scale, were deliberately treated with lightness and grace – and called to mind, according to Chambers, 'filigrane toy-work'. 'The massive entablature, the ponderous compartment ceiling, the tabernacle frame, almost the only species of ornament formerly known, in this country, are now,' wrote Adam, 'universally exploded, and in their place, we have adopted a beautiful variety of light mouldings, gracefully formed, delicately enriched and arranged with propriety and skill. We have introduced a great diversity of ceilings, freezes, and decorated pilasters, and have added grace and beauty to the whole, by a mixture of grotesque stucco, and painted ornaments.'[6]

Adam's new 'Grecian' treatment was eclectic; he was not a pedant and his taste was catholic. The visit to Italy had provided him with fruitful sources of inspiration. He had examined the ruins of the palace at Spalato (constructed *c.* A.D. 300 and extending over nearly ten acres) which contained abundant, rich ornamental details; he had studied both the grotesques of the Villa Madama, Rome, painted at the beginning of the sixteenth century by Raphael and his pupils in imitation of the Græco-Roman work of the catacombs, and those of the *Loggie* of the Vatican. When in England, he drew freely on recollections and drawings of these places: '... we flatter ourselves,' he afterwards wrote, 'we have been able to seize, with some degree of success, the beautiful spirit of antiquity, and to transfuse it, with novelty and variety, through all our numerous works.'[7] In those works he made continual use of *motifs* such as the vase, the urn, the terminal figure, the female sphinx, the goat's head, the ram's head, the griffin, the festoon of flowers or husks, the honeysuckle, the palm leaf, the oval patera, and medallion.

The interior architecture of his houses, the walls, furniture, and fittings followed a single style, consistently applied. Often similar patterns and ornament were employed in ceilings and carpets, overmantels, and over-doors. Curtain boxes, pier glasses, *girandoles*, commodes, tables, picture frames, even the handles and lockplates of doors and furniture were designed as the harmonious parts of one scheme. Such articles inevitably lose quality and character when detached from their proper surroundings. The drawings made in the 1770s for Sir Watkin Williams-Wynn's house at 20 St James's Square, now among the extensive collection of Adam drawings in the Soane Museum, London, provide an instance of his method. Sketches for ceilings, friezes, doors, grates, chimney-pieces, mirrors, sideboards, silver plate, locks, even a sedan chair, were included in those submitted to this client.

Adam's manner was presently taken up by the trade. 'The light and elegant Ornaments, the varied compartments in the Ceilings of Mr Adam, imitated from the Ancient Works in the Baths and Villas of the Romans, were,' pronounced Sir John Soane in a lecture to the students of the Royal Academy, 'soon applied in designs for Chairs, Tables, Carpets, and in every other species of Furniture. To Mr Adam's taste in the Ornament of his Buildings, and Furniture, we stand indebted, inasmuch as Manufacturers of every kind felt, as it were, the electric power of this Revolution in Art.' [8]

The revival of marquetry decoration for furniture was due to the example of Adam. Arabesque ornament, derived from the grotesques he had studied in Rome, and executed in stucco on ceilings and wall panels, was best translated to furniture in the form of a delicate veneer of coloured woods. The practice called for a very high degree of skill. The fashion was new enough to arouse comment in 1771, when Mrs Lybbe Powys, visiting Sir Walter Blount's seat at Mawley in Shropshire, remarked: 'In what is call'd the little drawing-room, the wainscot, floor, and furniture are inlaid with festoons of flowers in the most curious manner with woods of different colours.' [9] Two side tables made, with accompanying pier glasses, for the Music Room at Harewood House, where, in all probability, much of the furniture was supplied by Chippendale to Adam's designs, illustrate the refined character of the technique. The framework and legs of these tables are gilt, the tops are of rosewood enriched by a design of acanthus spirals, and are inlaid in satinwood, tulip, and other woods, dyed and in places engraved. The ornament of the table tops bears a close resemblance to that executed in plaster on the walls.

Satinwood, a medium suited to the designs of the Adam brothers, was used both as a veneer and in the solid. Many pieces were enriched by painted instead of inlaid decoration. On occasion furniture was painted to tone with the interior, and intended to remain *in situ*. Library bookcases, fitted to a recess, were sometimes of pine or deal and painted, although large mahogany and satinwood specimens, designed with a triangular central pediment and invariably of good proportions, were more usual. Colour was used to considerable effect in the Adam interior, where ceilings and plasterwork were tinted to conform with a general scheme; light pinks and greens, in particular, were fashionable. At Syon, Adam used brilliant and contrasting colours with remarkable success. In some cases alternative colour schemes were submitted on the firm's drawings. The compartments of ceilings and walls were painted with classical subjects, when the painted medallions which formed part of the decoration frequently coincided in style with those on the furniture (Pl. 49). Adam employed, among others, Joseph Rose for stucco work, and Angelica Kauffmann, Zucchi (her husband), Pergolesi, Cipriani, and Bonomi as painters. Furniture was supplied to Adam's designs by various makers – Samuel Norman, for instance, was employed at Moor Park (*c.* 1764) (Pl. 47A), and work of the firm of France and Beckwith, and of Thomas Chippendale survived at Kenwood (*c.* 1770) until the dispersal of the contents of the house in 1922.

In 1768, Adam was completing the furnishing of Lansdowne House (now demolished); in that year Lady Shelburne recorded in her *Diary*: 'My Lord being to carry us to Cipriani's, Zucchi's, and some other people employed for our house in town, called my Lord with whom we first went to Zucchi's, where we saw some ornaments for our ceilings, and a large architecture picture painting for the antichamber, with which however my Lord is not particularly pleased. From there to Mayhew and Inch where is some beautiful cabinet work, and two pretty glass cases for one of the rooms in my apartment, and which, though they are only deal, and to be painted white, he charges £50 for. From thence to Cipriani's where we saw some most beautiful drawings and where Lord Shelburne bespoke some to be copied for me, to compleat my dressing room, which I wish should be furnished with drawings, and crayon pictures. From thence to Zuccarelli's where we also saw some pictures doing for us and from thence home it being half an hour past four.' [10]

During the thirty years preceding the war with France in 1793, many Englishmen travelled on the Continent. They brought home a large number of works of art. Greek and Roman antiquities were admired by collectors, and much copied. An Etruscan style was adopted by Wedgwood who made vases and plaques (sometimes inset in furniture) at his new factory at 'Etruria'. Adam designed in this taste a room at Osterley Park, causing Horace Walpole to comment unfavourably – '... The last chamber after these two proud rooms, chills you: it is called the Etruscan, and is painted all over like Wedgwood's ware, with black and yellow small grotesques. Even the chairs are of painted wood. It would be a pretty waiting-room in a garden. I never saw such a profound tumble into the Bathos. It is going out of a palace into a potter's field. ...' [11] Walpole also disliked the new 'green velvet bed-chamber'. This room contained an ornate state bedstead [12] of satinwood, with columns inlaid with green upright laurelling; the bases and capitals of the columns were enriched with chased metal and the cupola, decorated with finials and festoons of flowers, was carved and gilt. A drawing for the bedstead is preserved at the Soane Museum (Pl. 50A). It was 'too theatric, and too like a modern head-dress, for,' wrote Walpole, 'round the outside of the dome are festoons of artificial flowers. What would Vitruvius think of a dome decorated by a milliner?' [13] Walpole was not seemingly on good terms with Adam, whose work he had at first been disposed to admire. Osterley was a 'palace of palaces! – and yet a palace *sans crown, sans coronet*', with 'hall, library, breakfast-room, eating-room, all *chefs-d'œuvre* of Adam'. '... Such expense! such taste! such profusion!' had he exclaimed, and in conclusion observed: 'the Park is – the ugliest spot of ground in the universe – and so I returned comforted to Strawberry'.[14]

Mirrors, *girandoles*, and picture frames were designed, without difficulty, so as to conform with a chosen decorative scheme. Towards the end of the century composition frames began to supersede those of carved wood. In part composition was used also for *girandoles*. These articles were subordinated to the ornamental plasterwork of wall surfaces.

Pedestal stands and terms, which supported the vases, lights, antique busts, and statues of fashionable classical interiors, were frequently of tapered form and were supplied in a wood corresponding to that of the other furniture of the room, or were painted to match the walls. The average height of the pedestal was about 4 feet; a lower, broader type (about 2 feet 6 inches in height) is also found.

A number of candle stands on tripod bases were illustrated in the *Works in Architecture*. Some specimens were made of bronze. Rams' heads, human masks, swags of flowers, and leaves were all favourite ornamentation. In some cases the stand was accompanied by a matching candelabrum. A similar type of stand, but wider and with dished top, served to hold flowers.

The tripod base was employed also for the many small circular tea-tables dating from these years. Those with a diameter of less than 2 feet were intended for individual use. The more elaborate specimens were decorated with carving or inlay, and sometimes constructed with a gallery edge.

Chairs, sofas, and settees dating from the early period of Adam's work were somewhat florid in style, with curving outlines, to be distinguished from those in his later manner, which follow the architectural principles based on a study of the antique (Pl. 47A and B). A greater austerity of form was then disguised by rich decoration in low relief. More often than not the wood itself was hidden by painting or by gilding. Supports were straight tapered and fluted, of either square or circular section. Frequently oval paterae were carved in a sunk panel at the level of the seat rail, or were applied. An oval back was very popular, in particular for those upholstered chairs based on French models, and constructed with oval or circular seats and fluted, tapered, cylindrical legs of Louis XVI type.

Mahogany settees were usually comparatively simple,

ornate examples being carved and gilt. Coverings were of French or English tapestry, damask, striped or figured silks, or in some cases of leather. There was some small fashion for satinwood specimens with caned seats and backs, despite their lack of comfort. Castors are usually found on settees made towards the end of this period.

Adam was responsible for changes in the character of the furnishing of the dining-room. His views were expressed in the following passage, which related to an explanation of the plan of the principal floor of Syon House: 'To understand thoroughly the art of living, it is necessary, perhaps, to have passed some time amongst the French. ... In one particular, however, our manners prevent us from imitating them. Their eating rooms seldom or never constitute a piece in their great apartments, but lie out of the suite, and in fitting them up, little attention is paid to beauty of decoration ... as soon as the entertainment is over, they immediately retire to the rooms of company. It is not so with us. Accustomed by habit, or induced by the nature of our climate, we indulge more largely in the enjoyment of the bottle. ... The eating rooms are considered as the apartments of conversation, in which we pass a great part of our time ... they are always finished with stucco, and adorned with statues and paintings, that they may not retain the smell of the victuals.'[15] The fashion of grouping sideboard table, two flanking pedestals (fitted as plate warmers, or used as cellarets), and surmounting urns was probably originated by Adam *c.* 1762 (Pl. 48). It was suited to large and formal apartments. The urns and pedestals were designed as the accompaniments to the table and were made, therefore, of similar wood and bore similar decoration. Pieces were often painted, sometimes with the addition of a mahogany top; a brass gallery was quite usual.

Adam made many drawings for side tables which were variously executed in mahogany, enriched by carving or by an inlay of woods, with swags of flowers, husks, ram-headed terminals, or were gilded or painted. In contrast to the Pembroke table which was in continuous domestic use, the console, side, and pier tables were primarily decorative objects. Many specimens were fitted with marble tops (imported at considerable expense from Italy), scagliola, and, on occasion, alabaster (Pl. 49). Adam ministered to 'the parade, the convenience, and social pleasures of life', which he claimed 'being better understood, are more strictly attended to in the arrangement and disposition of apartments'.[16] He was the originator of the neo-classical style in furniture adopted by the English cabinet-makers of the last quarter of the century, a style so modified in the interest of the general public that much of its character was lost. Adam designed furniture for individual patrons only, and for specific rooms, not for general production. Most 'Adam' furniture is in consequence the work of the rank and file of cabinet-makers of his and the next generation. Of these, George Hepplewhite is now perhaps the best known.

NOTES TO CHAPTER 8

1. See article by W. A. Seaby and R. J. Hetherington, *The Matthew Boulton Pattern Books*, in *Apollo*, February and March 1950.
2, 3. Robert and James Adam, *Works in Architecture*, 1773–9, 1822, preface to 1st No. of vol. I.
4. *Letters of Horace Walpole*, ed. by Peter Cunningham, 1861–6, vol. VI, p. 205. To Sir Horace Mann, from Arlington Street, April 22nd (1775).
5. *Passages from the Diaries of Mrs Philip Lybbe Powys of Hardwick House, Oxon., 1756–1808*, ed. by Emily J. Climenson, 1899.
6, 7. Adam, *op. cit.*, preface to 1st No. of vol. I.
8. *Lectures on Architecture, by Sir John Soane, as delivered to students of the R.A.*, ed. by Arthur T. Bolton, 1929, p. 180.
9. Climenson, *op. cit.*
10. Adam's work on Lansdowne House is discussed fully in Arthur T. Bolton's *Architecture of Robert and James Adam*, 1922.
11, 13. Cunningham, *op. cit.*, vol. VII, p. 95. To the Rev. William Mason, from Strawberry Hill, July 16th, 1778.
12. Illustrated by Percy Macquoid and Ralph Edwards, *The Dictionary of English Furniture*, 1924–7, vol. I, Beds, fig. 33; revised edit. by Ralph Edwards, 1954, vol. I, Beds, fig. 56.
14. Cunningham, *op. cit.*, vol. V, pp. 474–5. To the Countess of Ossory, from Arlington Street, June 21st, 1773.
15. Adam, *op. cit.*, vol. I, No. I, explan. of Pl. V.
16. Adam, *op. cit.*, preface to vth No. of vol. I.

CHAPTER NINE

HEPPLEWHITE:

THE CABINET-MAKER AND UPHOLSTERER'S GUIDE

THIRD EDITION, 1794

LITTLE is known about the life of George Hepplewhite, cabinet-maker and designer. An apprentice of Gillow, of Lancaster, he migrated to London, by 1760 being established in Redcross Street, St Giles's, Cripplegate. He died in 1786, when the business passed to his widow, Alice. At his death the firm of Hepplewhite did not enjoy an unusually high reputation. Two years later, however, 'A. Hepplewhite and Co.' published the *Cabinet-Maker and Upholsterer's Guide*, of which a second edition appeared the following year. This large-scale work (it was the most serviceable trade catalogue to be issued for more than twenty years, with illustrations of some 300 items) has since become famous. Shortly after publication it was referred to by Sheraton thus: 'if we compare some of the designs ... with the newest taste, we shall find that this work has already caught the decline, and perhaps, in a little time, will suddenly die in the disorder' [1] – an adverse judgement, which was not disinterested, although in some ways justified. In the preface to the *Guide*, 1794, the omission of 'articles, whose recommendation was mere novelty', was expressly remarked by the authors; such things were dismissed as being 'the production of whim at the instance of caprice, whose appetite must ever suffer disappointment if any similar thing had been previously thought of'. 'We hope for reward,' it was stated, 'in having combined near three hundred different patterns for furniture in so small a space.'

'Hepplewhite' is not an original style. The designs of the *Guide* followed the manner of Robert Adam, but were modified and strengthened to suit the requirements of working cabinet-makers, giving definitive expression to fashions which first had prevailed during the last years of the life of George Hepplewhite. In this respect the work was not singular. The *Cabinet-Makers' London Book of Prices,* first printed for the London Society of Cabinet-Makers in 1788, contained in the second edition (1793) a few designs by 'Hepplewhite'; these approximated in style to the other plates, most of which were contributed by Thomas Shearer. The third and revised edition of the *Guide* was published in 1794; its appearance at this comparatively late date indicates that many of the plates had been found to be useful. The volume was calculated to be of service to 'Countrymen and Artizans, whose distance from the metropolis makes even an imperfect knowledge of its improvements acquired with much trouble and expence'. Numerous surviving pieces of furniture in a simplified 'Hepplewhite' style, dating from the closing decade of the eighteenth century, or later, are often of country origin, owing their inspiration in widely varying degrees to this common source. Fine furniture of this period was extremely elegant, and lightly but strongly constructed. Much of it was made of satinwood, inlaid with various exotic woods.

The firm of Hepplewhite is commonly, but erroneously, credited with the invention of the shield-back chair, and a number of variants of this elegant form were illustrated in all editions. In most cases, the area enclosed by the shield was occupied by a central splat (Figs. 56A and 57B), designed with much elaboration and ingenuity, sometimes with interlaced members and usually incorporating such popular *motifs* as the classical urn, festoons of drapery, the Prince of Wales' feathers, the wheat-ear, the rosette, pendent husks, and the petals or calyces of flowers; occasionally the vertical bars, radiating from a semi-circular shoe-piece at the base of the shield, filled the whole of this space (Figs. 56B and 57A). In the majority of specimens, the base of

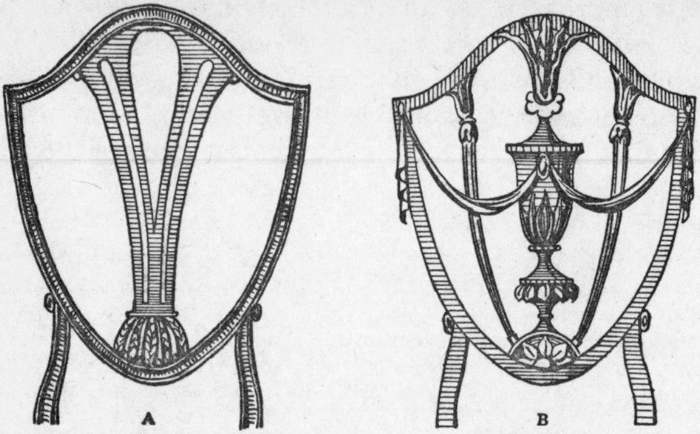

Figure 56 – Two chair backs; from the 3rd edition of *The Cabinet-Maker and Upholsterer's Guide*, 1794

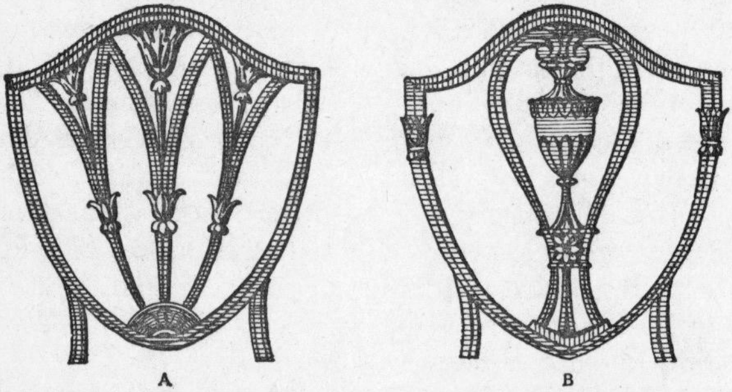

Figure 57 – Two chair backs; from the 3rd edition of the *Guide*

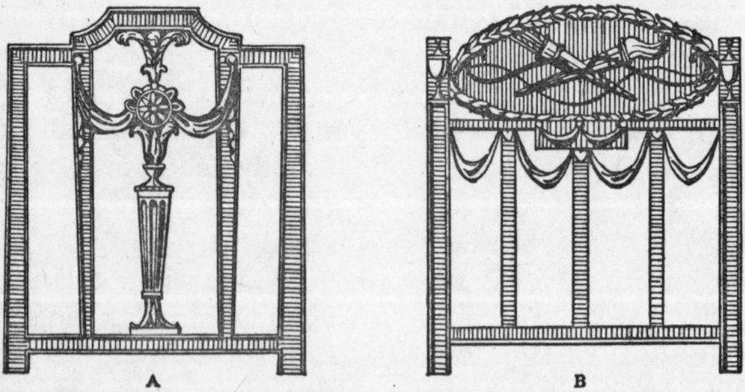

Figure 58 – Two chair backs; from the 3rd edition of the *Guide*

the shield was raised a few inches above the level of the seat (Fig. 56A and B); a lower positioning was relatively rare, although, where adopted, the design appears to greater effect (Fig. 57A and B). The stuffed or upholstered back of shield form was also recommended, and to judge from surviving examples, would appear to have been popular. Somewhat confusingly these chairs with stuffed backs were referred to in the *Guide*, and elsewhere, as 'Cabriole chairs'. (Sheraton defined the 'cabriole' as 'a French easy chair – from the name of the person who invented or introduced them'.)[2] Some revision in the 1794 edition may have been occasioned by Sheraton's gibe that the 'designs, particularly the chairs', were not in 'the newest taste'.[3] The square-back chair was there given adequate representation (Fig. 58A and B). The type was a more recent introduction and was extensively adopted in the last decade of the century, in particular by Sheraton. Those illustrated by 'Hepplewhite' are without much interest. The most satisfactory design may have been one which had appeared also in the original edition of the *Guide* (Fig. 58A). Chairs with rounded backs and carved open-work splats were common (Pl. 50B). Fine oval and heart-shaped back chairs were also among the productions of this period, and are frequently dubbed 'Hepplewhite' – but without reason. Legs were usually straight and tapered, and of either round or square section; an outward-turned foot was sometimes employed. Various alternative legs were shown (Fig. 59), most of these being ornamented by carving, often in the form of pendant husks, and by mouldings of unusual delicacy and refinement. The spade foot was a popular termination to the leg of square section (Fig. 59D). Stretcher bars and straining rails were absent in all examples save one – that for a 'grandfather' chair. In practice such a strengthening feature was often employed by the country maker who followed these designs. Hepplewhite and Co. recommended that chairs should conform to the following proportions: 'width in front 20 inches, depth of seat 17 inches, height of the seat frame 17 inches; total height about 3 feet 1 inch'; these are

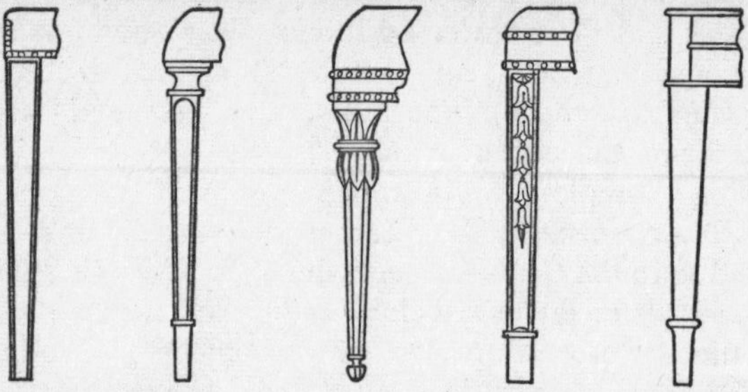

A B C D E

Figure 59 – Five chair legs; from the 3rd edition of the *Guide*

average measurements for a chair of the time, but other dimensions were 'frequently adapted according to the size of the room'. Chairs were generally of mahogany with 'seats of horsehair; plain, striped, checquered, &c. at pleasure'; caned specimens were supplied with cushions, which were covered with a material matching that of the curtains in the room. In fine mahogany chairs, the front surfaces of members comprising the framework and filling of the chair back were worked in decorative mouldings – the 'bars and frame in a hollow, or rising in a round projection, with a band or list on the inner and outer edges' (Pl. 50B). The seats were usually straight-fronted, bow or serpentine.

Painted or japanned furniture was approved as 'a new and very elegant fashion ... arisen within these few years'. Japanned chairs were of lighter construction, and were caned; a soft wood such as beech was commonly used and expense was much reduced. The material of the cushions was proposed to 'accord with the general hue of the chair'. (Fig. 58B shows a design suitable for mahogany or 'japan'.) Cheap rush-bottomed chairs were also made; properly the seats of these were primed with white lead, ground up in linseed oil and diluted with turpentine, and then coloured.

Medallions of printed or painted silk were sometimes introduced in designs for the chair back. The use of painted silk as a covering was not new. Arthur Young had noticed at Woburn Abbey (letter dated June 1768) that the chairs and sofas in 'the Duchess's dressing room' were covered in 'painted taffeta'.[4]

A less rational invention was applied to designs for ornamental hall chairs, which were made with solid backs and wooden seats; in one design, the back was conceived as a large vase with cover, the body being carved with festoons of drapery; legs were turned and tapered.

Mahogany or japanned stools were made *en suite* with chairs, and upholstered in matching materials. The *Guide* showed designs for stools of rectangular shape, supported at each corner by legs which were variously straight moulded, straight with outward curving feet, or cabriole with scroll feet (Fig. 60A, B, C). A narrowing cabriole leg (Fig. 60D) was suggested for use with a circular tripod music stool. In general, the seat rails of upholstered stools (straight fronted, bow, serpentine, or circular) were, like chairs, not exposed, but covered with material and ornamented by a double row of brass-headed nails.

In all, six window stools were illustrated in the edition of 1794. They were to be made to the size of the windows of the room, below which they were intended to stand. The height of the seats was not to exceed that of the chairs. The stools varied mainly in details of decoration. In the example

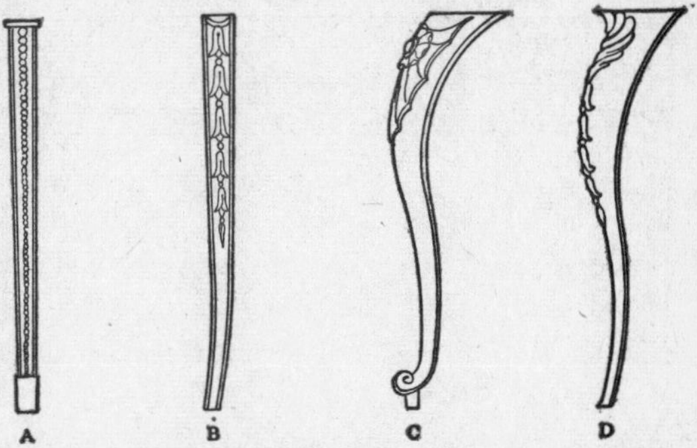

Figure 60 – Four stool legs; from the 3rd edition of the *Guide*

Figure 61 – A window stool; from the 3rd edition of the *Guide*

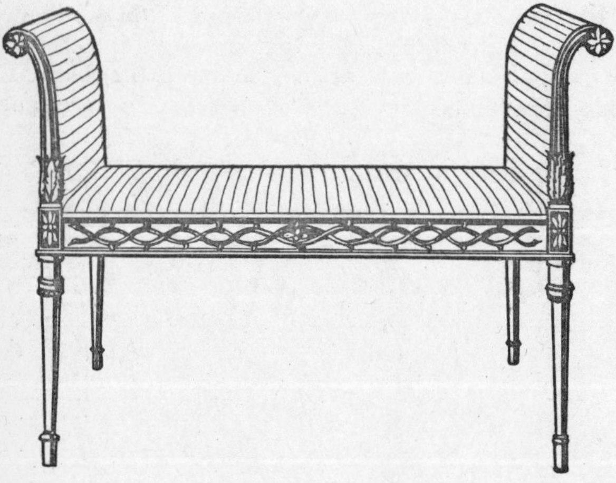

Figure 62 – A window stool; from the 3rd edition of the *Guide*

shown in figure 61 a valance, festooned and hung with tassels, is dependent from the seat rail; the S-scrolled ends terminate in rosettes; the seat and ends of the piece are upholstered, but the seat rail is uncovered and carved with fluting. Some examples were designed with vertical ends terminating in a graceful outward roll (Fig. 62).

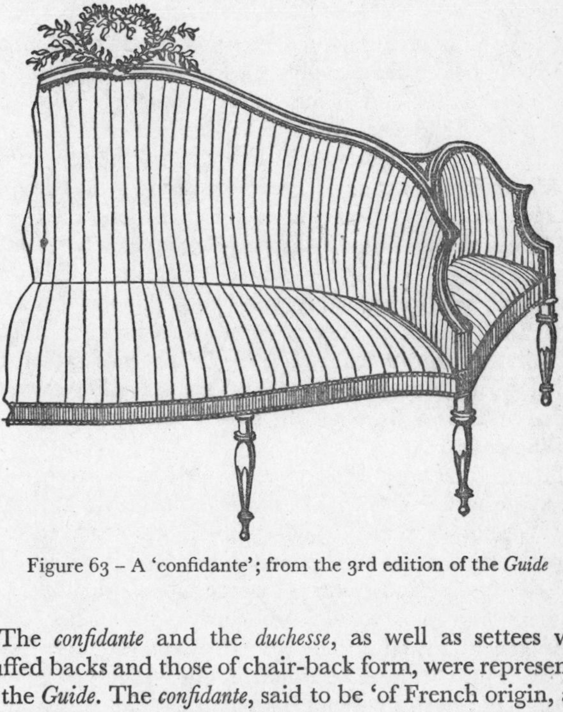

Figure 63 – A 'confidante'; from the 3rd edition of the *Guide*

The *confidante* and the *duchesse*, as well as settees with stuffed backs and those of chair-back form, were represented in the *Guide*. The *confidante*, said to be 'of French origin, and in pretty general request for large and spacious suits of apartments', consisted of a settee, to the ends of which 'Barjier' chairs were attached (Fig. 63). The chairs were set at an angle with the settee, and were sometimes detachable. Subscribers were informed that 'an elegant drawing-room with modern furniture' was 'scarce complete' without one of these pieces. The *duchesse*, intended for the ante-room, was also of a composite nature and was formed by two facing 'Barjier chairs of proper construction, with a stool in the middle'. The term '*duchesse*' was also applied to a kind of bed, constructed on a similar principle, but having short pillars; it was, according to Sheraton, 'intended for a single lady, and ... therefore not more than about 30 inches wide'.[5]

The habit of reclining on settees and couches, fashionable in France before the Revolution, was increasingly adopted here towards the end of the century, although indulged in with some diffidence. Mrs Delany has recorded that on a visit from the Princess Amelia in 1772, 'all the comfortable sophas and great chairs ... were banish'd for that day, and the blew damask chairs set in prim form around the room'.[6]

The centre part of the *confidante* (Fig. 63) closely resembles another design for a settee, which, given in all editions of the *Guide*, was presumably still quite popular by about 1790. Designed in a series of curves with high, undulating back and serpentine seat rail, the style is rococo rather than neo-classical; some departure from the prevailing taste was apparent also in the four chair-back settee with open in-curving ends.

Two distinct types of sideboard were popular throughout the last quarter of the eighteenth century – the sideboard table, usually without drawers, which was designed to be used in conjunction with pedestals and surmounting vases, and the smaller and more compact sideboard, fitted with drawers and containing cupboard space. The former arrangement, introduced by Robert Adam, was more formal and perhaps the more fashionable, but was less convenient for use in most households, being ill-adapted to small rooms; a very large sideboard of the latter type, however, with shaped front, deep side drawers, and six turned legs, was made in 1782 by William Gates for Windsor Castle.

Sideboard tables were often straight fronted and supported on four legs of square tapered form, while carved, inlaid, or painted enrichments were confined to the frieze and to the legs. Hepplewhite and Co. gave one design for a more elaborate variety of this type of table, with six legs (four in front) and with shaped front. The firm recommended that pedestals should be made 16 or 18 inches square, with a height corresponding to that of the table (28 to 32 inches). One pedestal served as 'a plate warmer, being provided with racks and a stand for a heater', and was lined with tin; the other was used as a 'pot cupboard'. Urns or vases were placed on the pedestals and held either water 'for the use of the butler, or iced water for drinking'; or alternatively, were fitted as knife cases. The height of the urns was to be about 27 inches. They were made, usually, of the same material as the pedestals, and were decorated in a similar style. These grouped pieces afforded considerable opportunity for display, and still were made variously in mahogany, rosewood, or satinwood (or painted wood), often with inlaid decoration of the most refined character. Among the numerous woods imported at the time and used also as an inlay were kingwood, thuyawood, amboyna, tulip, and zebra wood, as well as rosewood and satinwood. Birch was sometimes stained to imitate satinwood, for which also certain veneers of chestnut provided a substitute. Harewood, which is actually sycamore stained with an iron oxide, and sycamore itself were quite frequently employed.

Two examples of the rather more useful variety of sideboard shown in figure 64 were illustrated by the promoters of the *Guide*. The more elaborate of these was designed with a centre of serpentine, instead of bow, form and with canted inner legs, while the side drawers were considerably deeper. Table linen was to be kept in the long drawer; the side compartments were partitioned and fitted to provide receptacles for plate and for cloths, for a bottle rack and a container, lined with lead, which held the water used for rinsing glasses. Numerous small mahogany sideboards of this type have survived, but are usually of simpler construction, supported on four legs only and are commonly bow fronted. For some considerable time it had been customary for the washing of the silver and glass used during a meal to be done in the dining-room. Lady Grisell Baillie's written instructions to her servants had read: 'Never let the dirty knives, forks, and spoons go out of the dining room, but put them all in the box that stands for that use under

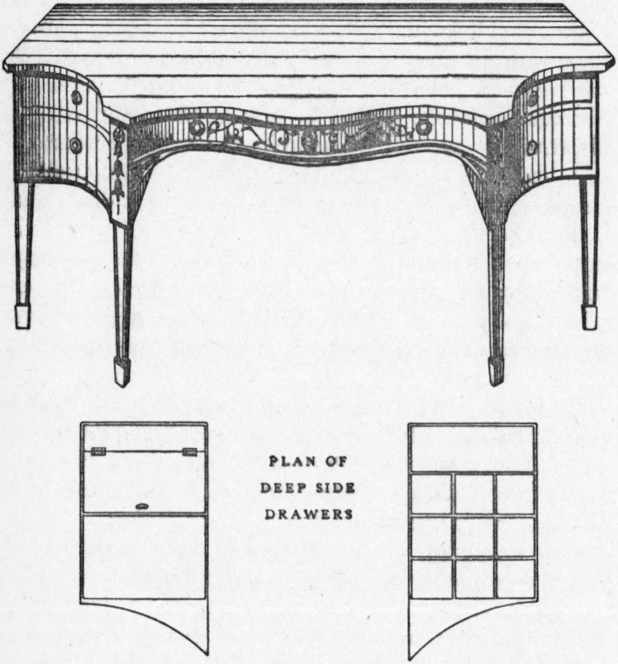

Figure 64 – A sideboard, with serpentine front and end compartments; from the 3rd edition of the *Guide*

the table. ... As soon as a glass is drunk out of, range it directly in the brass pail which you must have there with water for that purpose.'[7] These orders were given in 1743.

Several varieties of wine table were made during the latter part of the century. The *Cabinet-Makers' London Book of Prices* (second edition 1793) contained a design by 'Hepplewhite' for 'A Gentleman's Social Table', ingeniously constructed but of a quite unpretentious character, and moderately priced at 28*s*. These tables were intended for after-dinner drinking by the fireside; the larger specimens were, therefore, often of a convenient horseshoe shape. Sylas Neville, a guest at the great Holkham fête of 5 November, 1788, held to commemorate the centenary of the Glorious Revolution, recorded that 'a horseshoe table' was on this occasion put into service 'in the north dining room', with 'many other tables below in the Billiard room & audit room – in the style of the Pantheon Masque suppers'. It may have been a table of this kind. He thought that 'the ladies ought to have supped first for by the whole company attempting to sit together there was some confusion'.[8]

Pier tables were among the more decorative pieces of furniture produced during the 'Hepplewhite' period. They 'are become', stated the authors, 'an article of much fashion; and not being applied to such general use as other Tables, admit, with great propriety, of much elegance and ornament. ... The height of Pier Tables varies from the general rule [*i.e.* that the height of tables should not exceed 28 inches], as they are now universally made to fit the pier, and rise level with or above the dado of the room, nearly touching the ornaments of the glass. ...' Satinwood or mahogany specimens were often inlaid with great elaboration with a variety of woods, the designs being in a style inspired by Adam (Fig. 65). Decoration of similar character is found on the tops of the finer card, Pembroke, and commode tables of this time (Fig. 66). The Pembroke table (with two flaps) was usually of oval or rectangular shape (Fig. 67); the card table, when closed and standing against a wall, resembled the pier table in appearance, and exhibited a folded top of half-oval or modified rectangular form (Fig. 68). Most pier tables were, however, longer, with proportionately less depth. A number of these tables were japanned on a soft wood, the raised ornament being gilded and the tops having painted decoration.

Figure 65 – A pier table; from the 3rd edition of the *Guide*

By the generality of cabinet-makers, legs of identical basic design were adapted to the various types of table in production, and to a few other articles of furniture. The proportions of the leg were, however, altered to suit the requirements of the particular piece. The leg patterns shown in figure 69, which are characteristic of this time and are illustrated in the *Cabinet-Makers' London Book of Prices*

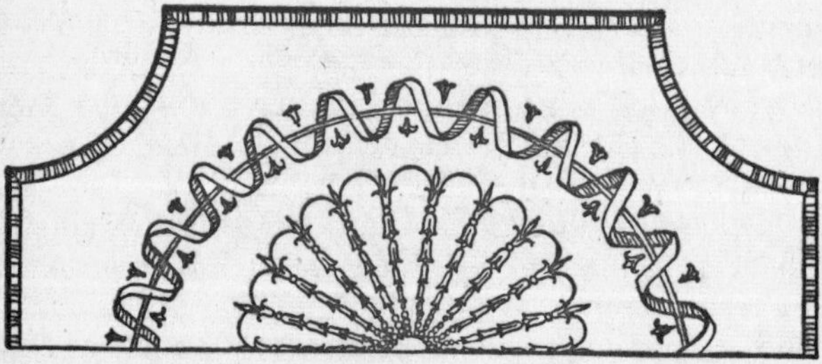

Figure 66 – Top for a card table; from the 3rd edition of the *Guide*

Figure 67 – A Pembroke table, supported on square tapered legs, with bow fronted drawer below the top; from the 3rd edition of the *Guide*

Figure 68 – Top for a Pembroke table; the style of the ornament inspired by Adam; from the third edition of the *Guide*

(second edition 1793), may be found variously in the cellaret, a low piece with comparatively short legs; in the card, the Pembroke, the 'chamber' or the work table; or again (another group) in the dining-table, the sideboard or the pier table. 'Therming in the neck' (A and B) was a refinement which increased the cost of the article and which was calculated to improve the appearance of the tapered leg of square section. Legs were of both square

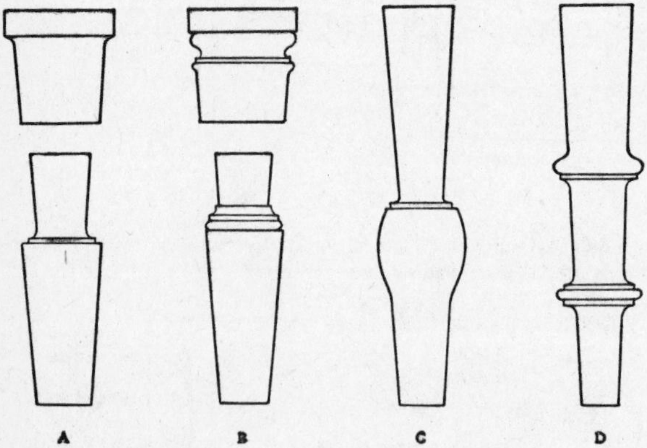

Figure 69 – Patterns for legs; from the 2nd edition of the *Cabinet-Makers' London Book of Prices*, 1793

(A and B) and round section (C and D); the latter form, however, was the more recently fashionable of the two and was destined to be in common use at the close of the century.

In general, mahogany was employed for the substantial furniture of the library. Library tables were comparatively plain. The knee-hole form, with end pedestals supported on a low plinth, retained popularity throughout the period. 'Hepplewhite and Co.' illustrated an example of this type (Fig. 70). The centre is recessed; each of the end cupboards is surmounted by a shallow drawer and is framed by pilasters which are carved with pendent husk ornament and capped by brackets. The table is otherwise undecorated. Four feet is recommended as its suitable length. Round tables and those of kidney-shape are also found.

Library bookcases were of considerable size, some larger examples attaining a length of more than 12 feet. The 'library case' resembled in form an enlarged secretaire bookcase, the centre portion (corresponding to the latter

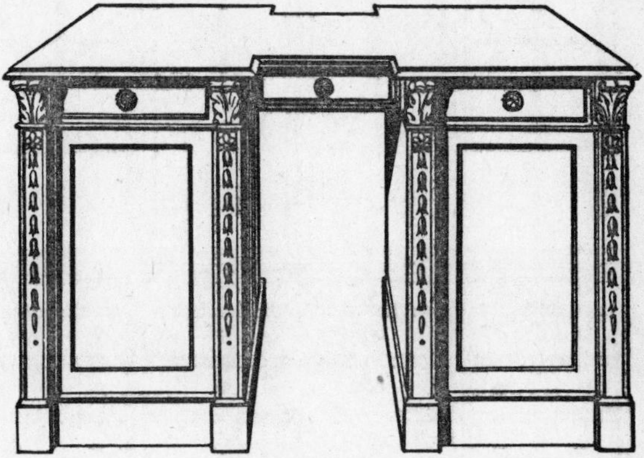

Figure 70 – A kneehole library table; from the 3rd edition of the *Guide*

piece) being extended on each side by a recessed wing or wings, which were sometimes the same height as the centre, and sometimes lower (Fig. 71). Usually the entire lower stage was supported on a low plinth and contained a secretaire drawer, cupboards, and drawers; the upper stage, which was set back from the base, providing a long but narrow shelf at a convenient level of 4 feet or less, was fitted with glazed doors varying in number according to the design and dimensions of the bookcase. Cornices were straight, although breaking back, and in practice were somewhat rarely surmounted by a central or end pediments, or by the ornamental urns, busts or foliate scrolls,

Figure 71 – A library bookcase; from the 3rd edition of the *Guide*

Figure 72 – A secretaire bookcase, with glazed doors to the upper stage, supported on a base of drawers; from the 3rd edition of the *Guide*

which were shown in the plates of contemporary pattern books. An almost limitless diversity of pattern was to be obtained by different arrangements of the glazing bars of the door fronts.

According to the *Guide*, the proportions of the bureau bookcase were: 'length 3 feet 6 inches, depth 22 inches, height of desk 3 feet 2 inches, including 10 inches for the inside of the desk; total height about 6 feet; depth of bookcase about 12 inches'. On the whole a tendency to increased height was general. The secretaire bookcase differed only from the bureau bookcase in 'not being sloped in front', but gained something of neatness in appearance (Fig. 72). Writing facilities were 'produced by the face of the upper drawer falling down by means of a spring and quadrant', affording 'the same usefulness as the flap to a desk'. Hepplewhite may perhaps have specialized in this class of furniture.

'Bedsteads,' observed the compilers of the *Guide*, 'may be executed of almost every stuff which the loom produces.' For state rooms they recommended plain or figured silks and satins, and fringed velvets; while the 'Manchester stuffs', printed cottons and linens and plain or corded white dimity, 'with a fringe with a gymp head', were said to be the most suitable for use in lesser rooms. The material of the hangings was of first importance. The several designs for bedsteads given by the firm were characterized mainly by a calculated disposition of curtains and valances. 'The Vallance,' it was said, 'should always be gathered full, which is called a Petticoat Vallance'; and bedposts (Fig. 73), often carved and decorated with reeding, were usually fashioned with a plain base, which was covered by the valance. The cornices, 'either of mahogany, carved and gilt, or painted and japanned', were in fact rarely of the elaborate nature which the plates suggest. No distinction was made between designs for 'Cornices or Pelmets for Beds or Windows' (Fig. 74), and it was quite usual for the windows to be curtained with the stuff of the bed 'furniture', and treated in a similar manner.

'Press beds' were not illustrated in the *Guide*, being perhaps insufficiently elegant to merit inclusion. These articles of furniture had been in use for many years. The firm 'purposely omitted' to provide examples, 'their general

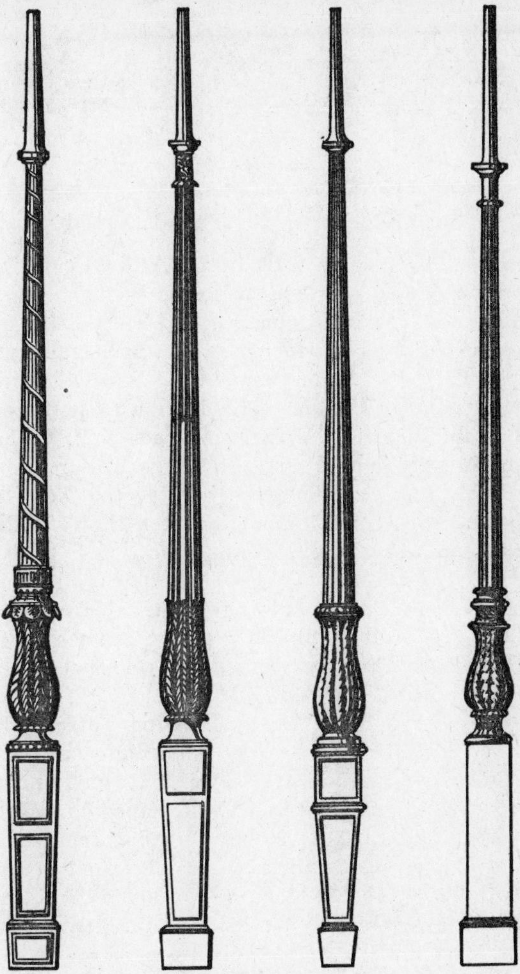

Figure 73 – Four bedposts; from the 3rd edition of the *Guide*

Figure 74 – A 'Cornice or Pelmet for Bed or Window'; from the 3rd edition of the *Guide*

appearance varying so little from wardrobes, which ... they are intended to represent' as to make the inclusion unnecessary. 'The wardrobe [Fig. 75] has all the appearance of a Press-Bed; in which case the upper drawers would be only sham, and formed part of the door which may be made to turn up all in one piece, and form a tester; or may open in the middle, and swing on each side; the under-drawers is useful to hold parts of the bed-furniture [fabrics].' Boswell slept in 'a little press bed' in the New Inn at Aberdeen, where accommodation was short: 'I had it wheeled out into the dining-room, and there I lay very well.'[9]

The fitted dressing-table was an extremely useful piece of furniture, and neat in appearance. A characteristic design by Thomas Shearer, dated 1788, for one such table was included in *The Cabinet-Makers' London Book of Prices*, and is here reproduced. This 'Lady's Dressing Table' (Fig. 76) was listed at three guineas. The glass frames at the ends, which were optional and which were provided only at an additional cost of a guinea and a half, turned on swivels and were raised by means of weights. Of the eleven drawers in front, five were sham. Shearer has illustrated a straight-fronted table, 33 inches long and 20 inches deep; but the tables which were in fact supplied from this design were not necessarily of this size and were variously straight, bow or serpentine fronted. Some tables were veneered at front and sides, some at the front only and others were plain. The charge for veneering was very small – a few shillings.

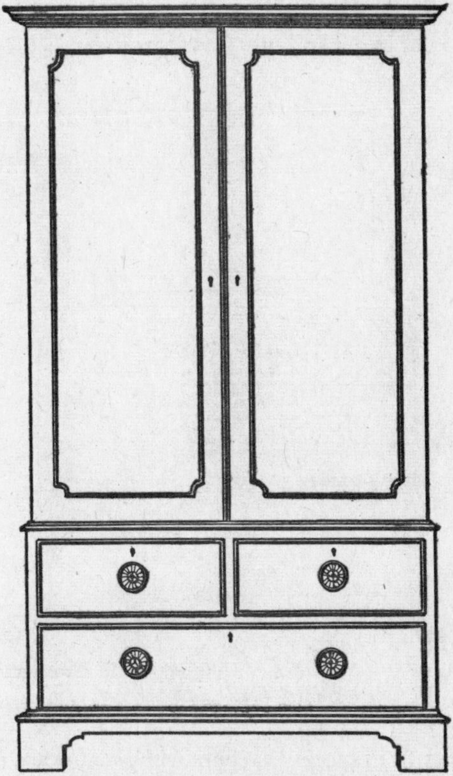

Figure 75 – A wardrobe, with 'all the appearance of a Press-Bed'; from the 3rd edition of the *Guide*

Wardrobes, or clothes presses, were more usually constructed with a base of two long and two short drawers – rather taller than the example shown in figure 75. The upper stage was fitted with solid doors which enclosed a series of horizontal 'press shelves'. At this date the 'hanging' wardrobe was not in general use, except in so far as the wings of

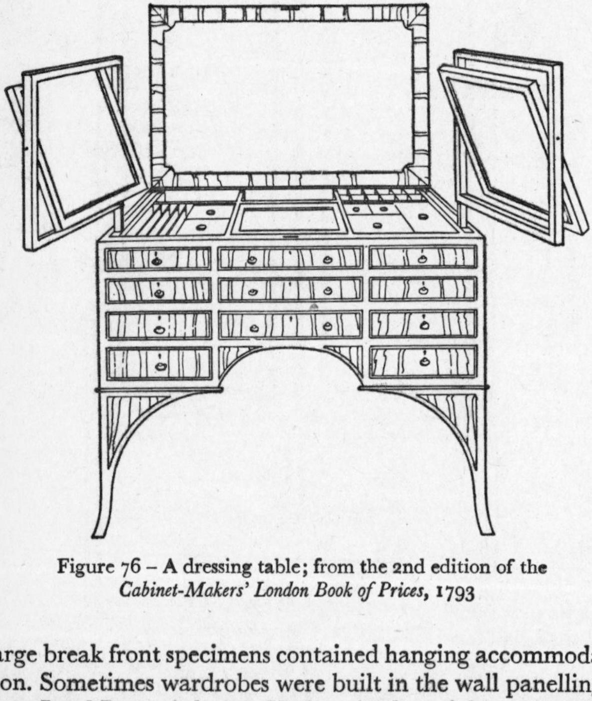

Figure 76 – A dressing table; from the 2nd edition of the *Cabinet-Makers' London Book of Prices*, 1793

large break front specimens contained hanging accommodation. Sometimes wardrobes were built in the wall panelling, as at Lord Boston's house, Hedsor, in the neighbourhood of Marlow, visited in 1780 by Mrs Lybbe Powys, who remarked: '... a new house, which tho' not to be styled large or magnificent, is altogether the most elegant one I've seen for a vast while. ... My lady's dressing-room octagon, the corners fitted up with the cleverest wardrobes in inlaid woods ... all over the house, a thousand elegant neatnesses and contrivances.'[10]

Tallboys continued to be made during the second half of the eighteenth century, although becoming progressively less fashionable towards its close, when wardrobes were preferred. To some extent their form was governed by tradition, and such modifications as were made were of a

Figure 77 – A chest of drawers, with serpentine front; from the 3rd edition of the *Guide*

minor nature. The deep cavetto moulding below the cornice found in early Georgian specimens was at first replaced by a flat frieze, sometimes decorated with an applied fret; later, the ornamentation of this feature was achieved by fluting or by an inlay of various woods.

During the Hepplewhite period chests of drawers were frequently bow or serpentine fronted and were supported on bracket feet which were taller than formerly and outward curving (Fig. 77). The feet were set on the chest, without any plinth moulding, so as to be aligned with its front and side surfaces; as a result there was an uninterrupted vertical line at the angles. A curved base line was produced by the addition of a shaped apron piece. A thin cock beading was applied to the edges of drawer fronts. This latter detail is usually found in chests of drawers dating from the second half of the century. Formerly, an overlapping moulded edge (a projecting lip moulding), of quite substantial width and worked on the drawer front itself, had been employed. Whereas in many specimens of the third quarter of the century drawer linings were constructed with the grain of the wood running from back to front, in those of a later period the drawer bottom was often divided by a central strut into two halves, each with the grain running across the panel.

Pier glasses, 'mostly of good carved work, gilt and burnished', were hung between the windows of reception rooms. They were made almost to 'fill the pier', nearly touching the tables beneath.The frames were consequently of tall proportions and (fundamentally) of plain rectangular shape, although in all designs given by Hepplewhite and Co. attached cresting pieces and bases were very prominent (Fig. 78). This open-work ornament of the frame, thin and spiny, was composed from a repertory of *motifs* popularized by Adam – the spread eagle, urns, wreaths, pendent husks, festoons of drapery, and spiky, foliate scrolls of characteristically rounded form (Pl. 62 and Fig. 78). Large glasses were still very expensive. Parson Woodforde, dining with Mr and Mrs Townshend at Honingham on 28 August, 1783, admired a looking-glass in the drawing-room, which, he wrote: 'was the finest and largest I ever saw, cost at secondhand 150.0.0. The Height of the Plate was seven feet and half, and the breadth of it was five feet and half, one single Plate of glass only. The frame and Ornaments to it, was carved and gilded and very handsome'.[11] The 'ornaments' of the frame were, in the new glasses of this date, usually modelled in composition on wire. Such imposing glasses were often, to save expense, made up of two plates, although Sheraton, obtaining his information from 'Mr Black, Glass Cutter, near the Seven Dials, Long Acre', stated (1803) that great glasses might be ordered to size (from 36 by 60 inches to 75 by 117 inches, which was the largest cast) from the British Factory, near Blackfriars

Figure 78 – A pier glass; from the 3rd edition of the *Guide*

Bridge.[12] A high proportion, approaching one-half, of the glass sold in England at the close of the eighteenth century was, however, imported from the Continent.

A formal arrangement of the furniture in the drawing-room was advised: 'on each side of the chimney piece there should be a sofa, and on the opposite side, instead of a sofa, . . . a confidante . . . an elegant commode [on the end wall]

... and the remaining [wall] space filled up with chairs'. There was usually a number of fire screens. A large pier glass was also quite properly placed over the *confidante*, and flanked by *girandoles*, which were often supplied in pairs or in sets of four or more. Additional lighting was sometimes obtained from glass lustres, raised on corner pedestals. Of these apparently expensive items Fanny Burney has noted 'one story extremely well worth recording'. On Sunday, 10 November, 1782: 'The Duke of Devonshire was standing near a very fine glass lustre in a corner of a room, at an assembly, and in a house of people who, Miss Monckton said, were by no means in a style of life to hold expense as immaterial; and, by carelessly lolling back, he threw the lustre down and it was broke. He showed not, however, the smallest concern or confusion at the accident, but coolly said, "I wonder how I did that!" He then removed to the opposite corner, and to show, I suppose, he had forgotten what he had done, leaned his head in the same manner, and down came the opposite lustre! He looked at it very calmly, and, with a philosophical dryness, merely said, "This is singular enough!" and walked to another part of the room, without either distress or apology.'[13]

Hepplewhite's was, probably, a small business, and the output of the shop may not have been very extensive. His name does not appear in the London directories. A proportion only of the furniture he supplied to clients will have corresponded with the designs publicized (posthumously) in the *Guide*, and they, while giving a good indication as to the nature of his best and most expensive pieces, were probably representative also of the work of several of his competitors. The largest and more important firms carried an enormous stock, of wide range and most varied quality. Seddon & Sons, of Aldersgate Street, as an instance, started the year 1790 with stock valued at a sum exceeding £100,000. George Seddon, the founder of the firm, described in 1768 as 'one of the most Eminent of cabinet-makers of London' (*Annual Register*), was a liveryman of the Joiners' Company in 1757 and master in 1795. The account of the workshop given in the diary of Sophie von la Roche, 16 September, 1786, is informative:

'... [Mr Seddon] employs four hundred apprentices on any work connected with the making of household furniture – joiners, carvers, gilders, mirror-workers, upholsterers, girdlers – who mould the bronze into graceful patterns – and locksmiths. All these are housed in a building with six wings. In the basement mirrors are cast and cut. Some other department contains nothing but chairs, sofas and stools of every description, some quite simple, others exquisitely carved and made of all varieties of wood, and one large room is full up with all the finished articles in this line, while others are occupied by writing-tables, cupboards, chests of drawers, charmingly fashioned desks, chests, both large and small, work- and toilet-tables in all manner of wood and patterns, from the simplest and cheapest to the most elegant and expensive. ...

'Charming dressing-tables are also to be seen, with vase-shaped mirrors, occupying very little space, and yet containing all that is necessary to the toilet of any reasonable person. Close-stools, too, made like a tiny chest of drawers, with a couple of drawers in, decorative enough for any room. Numerous articles made of straw-coloured service wood and charmingly finished with all the cabinet-maker's skill. Chintz, silk and wool materials for curtains and bed-covers; hangings in every possible material; carpets and stair-carpets to order; in short, anything one might desire to furnish a house; and all the workmen besides and a great many seamstresses; their own saw-house too, where as many blocks of fine foreign wood lie piled, as firs and oaks are seen at our saw-mills. The entire story of the wood, as used for both inexpensive and costly furniture and the method of treating it, can be traced in this establishment.

'Seddon, foster-father to four hundred employees, seemed to me a respectable man, a man of genius, too, with an understanding for the needs of the needy and the luxurious; knowing how to satisfy them from the products of nature and the artistry of manufacture; a man who has become intimate with the quality of woods from all parts of the earth, with the chemical knowledge of how to colour them or combine their own tints with taste, has appreciated the value of all his own people's labour and toil, and is for ever creating new forms.

'We were horrified to hear that three years ago the whole building was burned down with all its storage, and we were not a little surprised at seeing it working again on such a scale.

'Two wishes rose within me. Firstly, for time to examine all these works, and then to see the tools with which they are made, manufactured in Birmingham; for I handled some of them here, and regarded them as most valuable and beneficient inventions.'[14]

On the whole, furniture was not unduly expensive. *The Cabinet-Makers' London Book of Prices*, 1788, of which mention has been made in this chapter, gives a reliable indication of the basic cost of execution of various articles of furniture at that time – excluding timber and other materials, 'extras', and profits. The work went into a second edition in 1793; there were twenty-nine plates, in which were illustrated, in all, more than 200 designs for furniture. These were for pieces of good quality. None of the items was quoted at a sum exceeding £10, and many at a few shillings only, although a list of extras was in all cases of formidable length: dressing chests ranged from 8*s* to £4 10*s*; secretaries from £2 2*s* to £3 11*s*; double chests (tallboys) from £2 4*s* to £3 5*s*; clothes presses (wardrobes) from £1 14*s* to £3 15*s* – a large press with wings being £5 16*s*; library bookcases from £3 12*s* to £5 15*s*; cabinets from £3 8*s* to £4 16*s*; tambour writing-tables and desks from £1 10*s* 6*d* to £3 12*s*; knee-hole library tables from £2 8*s* to £5 2*s* – one of Carlton House type being £8; Pembroke tables from 10*s* 6*d* to £1 8*s*; card tables from 7*s* 6*d* to 15*s*; pier tables from 17*s* to £2 12*s*; sideboard tables and cellaret sideboards from 10*s* to £3 6*s*. Numerous small articles such as work tables, pole screens, dressing glasses or knife cases were all reckoned in shillings. It may be observed that satinwood was more costly than some varieties of mahogany by 2*s* 6*d* in the £, and tulipwood, rosewood, snakewood, zebrawood, yew, maple, etc., by as much as 4*s* in the £.

NOTES TO CHAPTER 9

1. Thomas Sheraton, *Drawing Book*, 1791–4, preface – 'To Cabinet-makers and Upholsterers in general'.
2. Thomas Sheraton, *Cabinet Dictionary*, 1803, p. 120.
3. *Drawing Book, loc. cit.*
4. Arthur Young, *A Six Months Tour through the North of England*, 2nd edition, 1771, vol. I, p. 34 (foot).
5. *Cabinet Dictionary*, p. 337.
6. *The Autobiography and Correspondence of Mary Granville, Mrs Delany*, ed. by Lady Llanover, 2nd series, 1862, vol. I, p. 455 (14th Sept., 1772).
7. Quoted by Percy Macquoid, *English Furniture, etc.*, Lady Lever Art Gallery Collections III, 1928, p. 49 (item 129).
8. *The Diary of Sylas Neville, 1767–1788*, ed. by Basil Cozens-Hardy, 1950, p. 331.
9. *Johnson's Journey to the Western Islands of Scotland* and *Boswell's Journal of a Tour to the Hebrides with Samuel Johnson, LL.D.*, ed. by R. W. Chapman, Oxford Univ. Press, 1930, p. 212. (Boswell, 21st Aug., 1773.)
10. *Passages from the Diaries of Mrs Philip Lybbe Powys of Hardwick House, Oxon., 1756–1808*, ed. by Emily J. Climenson, 1899.
11. *Diary of a Country Parson*, ed. by John Beresford, 1924–31, vol. II, p. 90.
12. *Cabinet Dictionary*, p. 236.
13. *Diary and Letters of Madame D'Arblay, 1778–1840*, ed. by her niece Charlotte Barrett, with preface and notes by Austin Dobson, 1904, vol. II, p. 124.
14. *Sophie in London, 1786*, trans. from the German by Clare Williams, 1933, pp. 173–5.

CHAPTER TEN

THOMAS SHERATON
(1751–1806)

THOMAS SHERATON was born at Stockton-on-Tees, Durham. About 1790 he came to London and set up as a drawing master. Among other activities he supplied designs to cabinet-makers. He was well qualified to do so, being an excellent draughtsman, and, having previously served for a number of years as journeyman cabinet-maker, possessed a practical knowledge of the trade and its technicalities. His trade card gives his address as 106 Wardour Street, Soho. It is most improbable that he owned a workshop or that he was concerned in the actual manufacture of any articles of furniture. He lived by 'his exertions as an author'. *The Cabinet-Maker and Upholsterer's Drawing Book*, which was his most important work, was published in four parts between 1791–4, containing in all 113 plates; it provides the most valuable indication of the fashions in furniture which obtained in England during the last decade of the eighteenth century. The *Drawing Book* was deservedly popular. The author, finding 'no one individual equally experienced in every job of work', had made it his business 'to apply to the best workmen in different shops'. Some firms specialized in certain pieces. Sheraton drew on his own experience and also on 'that of other good workmen'. The explanations to the designs were detailed and practical. He aimed to make the book 'permanently useful'. The names of some 600 makers, in London and far afield in the country, were included in the list of subscribers to the *Drawing Book*, and its material influence must have been great. Many 'Sheraton' pieces survive, clearly deriving from these patterns, but varying in quality and in detail.

The *Cabinet Dictionary, etc.*, of 1803, and the first volume of the *Encyclopaedia*, 1805, were less useful publications; some of the designs of the former, although ingenious, lacked just restraint and sense of proportion and the text is prosy. We glimpse something of the author's unsettled state in the following passage: '. . . though I am thus employed,' wrote Sheraton, 'in racking my invention to design fine and pleasing cabinet work, I can be well content to sit on a wooden bottom chair myself, provided I can but have common food and raiment wherewith to pass through life in peace.'[1] Sheraton was occupied with the *Encyclopaedia* in 1804. His mind was then disordered, and the work, if completed, would have been of a fantastic nature. In that year he employed Adam Black, the future publisher of the *Encyclopaedia Britannica*. Black, a young man newly come to London and 'seeking employment without success', has left the following account of their meeting: 'He [Sheraton] lived in an obscure street, his house half shop, half dwelling-house, and looked himself like a worn-out Methodist minister, with threadbare black coat. I took tea with them one afternoon. There were a cup and saucer for the host, and another for his wife, and a little porringer for their daughter. The wife's cup and saucer were given to me, and she had to put up with another little porringer. My host seemed a good man, with some talent. He had been a cabinetmaker, was now author and publisher, teacher of drawing, and, I believe, occasional preacher. I was with him for about a week, engaged in most wretched work, writing a few articles, and trying to put his shop in order, working among dirt and bugs, for which I was remunerated with half a guinea. Miserable as the pay was, I was half ashamed to take it from the poor man.'[2] Sheraton was worn out, and died two years later, leaving his family in distressed circumstances.

The designs for chair backs submitted by Sheraton to the public were numerous and elegant, distinguished by a consistent style. His invention was fluent, the patterns were diverse, with the appearance of having been produced with ease. Sheraton favoured the square back, which he usually divided, by means of an arrangement of uprights (in many cases grouped so as to form a central splat), into three vertical areas (Pl. 52A). Vertical emphasis to the filling is apparent even in the case of the shield back chair, of which there were two examples only. *Motifs* fashionable during the last quarter of the eighteenth century, such as the vase, the festoon of drapery, the lyre (Fig. 79A), the wheat-ear, the ostrich plume, and latticing were used with originality and reticence. In this connexion it is interesting to compare the

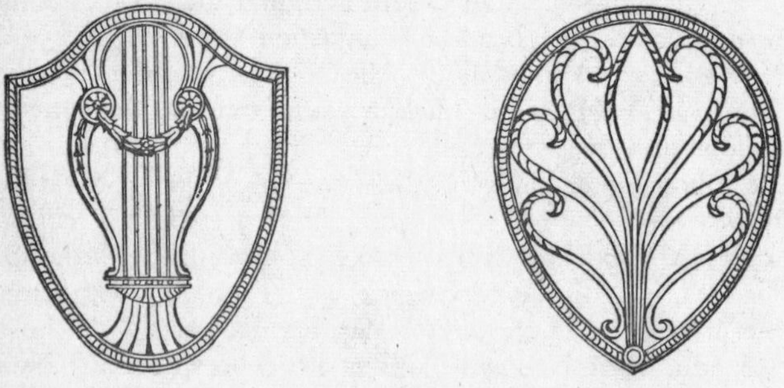

A B

Figure 79 – Two chair backs, incorporating (A) the lyre, and (B) the anthemion *motif*

two chair backs illustrated in figure 79. The bold treatment of the anthemion *motif*, which provides the whole filling of the back of the second (Fig. 79B), while characteristic of the style of a rather earlier period, is foreign to that of Sheraton.

The horizontal top and bottom rails of the chair back were usually narrow and quite straight. The member derived from the shoe piece, which occurs on a number of the specimens in this and the immediately preceding period, was attached, not to the chair seat as formerly (*cf.* Pl. 28B), but to the bottom rail of the back (Pl. 52A).

A lighter construction had been adopted for both parlour and drawing-room chairs by about 1790 (Pl. 52). Mahogany was employed in the manufacture of the former variety, for which Sheraton recommended a hard, straight-grained Cuban mahogany, stating that it would 'rub bright and keep cleaner than any Honduras wood'. The furniture of the dining-parlour was, without exception, to be made 'of mahogany, as being the most suitable for such apartments', and the room was to be furnished 'in substantial and useful things, avoiding trifling ornaments and unnecessary decorations'. In the *Cabinet Dictionary* Sheraton wrote thus: 'The large sideboard, inclosed or surrounded with Ionic pillars; the handsome and extensive dining-table; the respectable and substantial looking chairs; the large face glass; the family portraits; the marble fire-places; and the Wilton carpet; are the furniture that should supply the dining-room.' For the drawing-room, chairs with shaped or rounded seats would appear to have been fashionable. Sheraton drew a clear distinction between the two types. The parlour chair was straight-fronted.

Beech wood (and, in many places in the country, plane wood) chairs, japanned black or in colour, and gilt, many with caned seats, were produced with less expense after designs which differ only in detail from those of their mahogany counterparts. In the majority of cases legs were cylindrical, decorated with reeding, spiral reeding or cabling, and sometimes fluting, although the latter moulding was now becoming supplanted in public taste. Reeding, which was exceedingly popular in the last decade of the century, mostly as ornament for chair and table legs and also occurring on such features as the pilasters of cabinet fronts, was considered to be stronger than fluting or cabling; and it was esteemed more sightly than the former, perhaps by reason of novelty. Sheraton stated that the number of reeds employed to decorate a flat surface should always be odd; he further observed: 'if reeds be on a table leg, or bed pillar, &c. there should be one on the centre facing the eye.' (*Cabinet Dictionary*, 1803.)

'Conversation chairs', constructed with seats deeper than the usual and narrowing at the junction with the back, were used in drawing-room or library. Sheraton supplied the information that the 'parties who converse with each other sit with their legs across the seat, and rest their arms on the top rail, which, for this purpose, is made about three inches and a half wide, stuffed and covered'.

A set of mahogany chairs, 'made in the style of the French, with broad top rails hanging over each back foot', which were remarked in 1793 as being in the Prince of Wales's dining-parlour at Carlton House, were apparently of a newly-fashionable type – one not adopted in the first edition of the *Drawing Book*. They were described as having turned legs, and the seats covered with red leather.

Sheraton devoted little attention to settees in the *Drawing Book*, showing two upholstered specimens which in general appearance did not deviate greatly from contemporary French models. Their lines were straight and severe. His lack of invention here is curious. Settees were regarded as essential pieces in the drawing-room, 'in furnishing of which,' he said, 'workmen in every nation exert the utmost efforts of their genius'. These settees were to be constructed

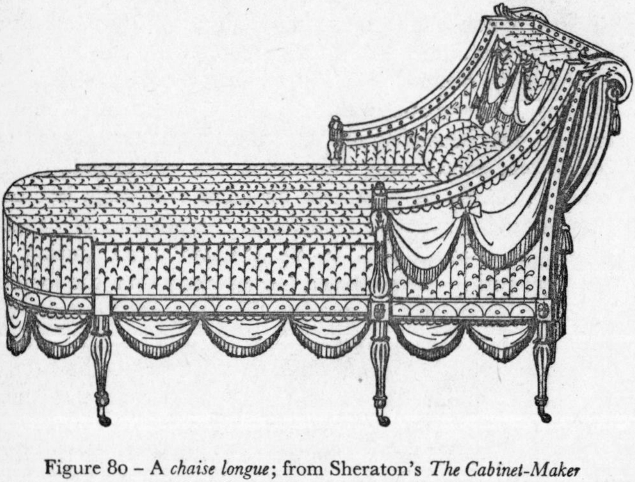

Figure 80 – A *chaise longue*; from Sheraton's *The Cabinet-Maker and Upholsterer's Drawing Book*, 1791–4

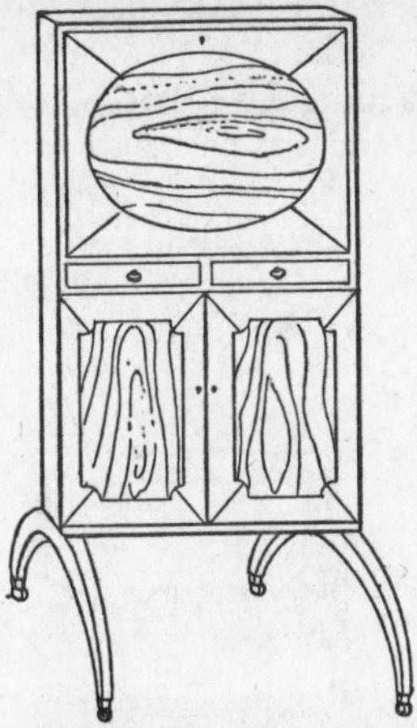

Figure 81 – A 'Lady's Writing Fire Screen'; from a design by Thomas Shearer in the *Cabinet-Makers' London Book of Prices*, 1788

with short cylindrical legs, and provided with stuffed seats and a squab cushion; the arms were filled in with upholstery, and the supports, forming a continuation of the outside front legs, rose vertically, without break or sweep, to meet horizontal padded elbow rests. In some examples the flat cresting centred in an unobtrusive oblong panel, in others a three-chair-back form was adopted. In the latter case, sofas were 'bordered off in three compartments, and covered with figured silk or satin', with 'cushions to fill their backs, together with bolsters at each end'. Caning was frequently employed, both for japanned and satinwood seats. Neither stools nor window seats were illustrated in the *Drawing Book*, although the author exhibited two designs for a *chaise longue*. These articles, he said, 'have their name from the French, which imports a long chair. Their use is to rest or loll upon after dinner . . .'. One of the pieces (Fig. 80), it was explained, 'is framed first in two parts. The end, or chair part, is made to receive the stool part within its sides; and the sides of the stool part screw in against the inside of the chair.' The other, designed with a low back, would 'serve for a sofa'.

The 'Lady's Writing Fire Screen' was a popular small piece at this time, and was perhaps found useful. A number of such screens have survived. A design for this article by Thomas Shearer was published in *The Cabinet-Makers' London Book of Prices* and is dated 1788 (Fig. 81). The screen was provided, as an extra, with two flat panelled doors

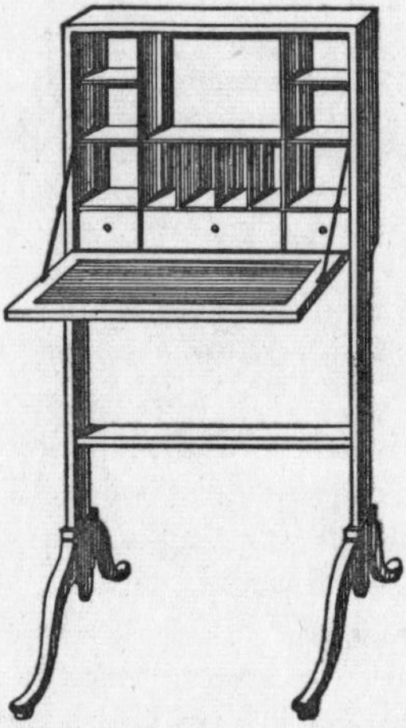

Figure 82 – A 'Lady's Screen Desk', with open base; end of the eighteenth century

below. Its dimensions were 18 inches long by 3 inches deep. A reading flap and book rest were contained in the upper part. With some refinements of execution, this piece was valued at rather less than a guinea and a half. Many such 'screen desks' were open at the base, being supported between standards, tied by a horizontal stretcher (Fig. 82). The interiors, although very much shallower, were arranged like those of writing cabinets, or were sometimes fitted for needlework.

According to Sheraton the usual height of cheval fire screens was about 3 feet 6 inches, with a breadth of 1 foot 6 inches. One specimen (Fig. 83), with carved and gilt 'lyre ornament' said to show to fine effect against a blue silk or satin, was 'constructed upon an entire new plan, it being designed to turn upon a swivel' – a device which obviated the necessity of moving the stand.

Figure 83 – A 'Horse Fire Screen'; from the *Drawing Book*

Pole screens (Fig. 84), made of mahogany, painted in white and gold or japanned, were provided with a sliding panel of smaller dimensions, frequently of oval or shield shape. 'Such screens as have very fine prints, or worked satin,' it was stated, 'commonly have a glass before them.' The somewhat studied elegance of the design of these articles, particularly noticeable in the form of the tripod bases, is characteristic of Sheraton's style.

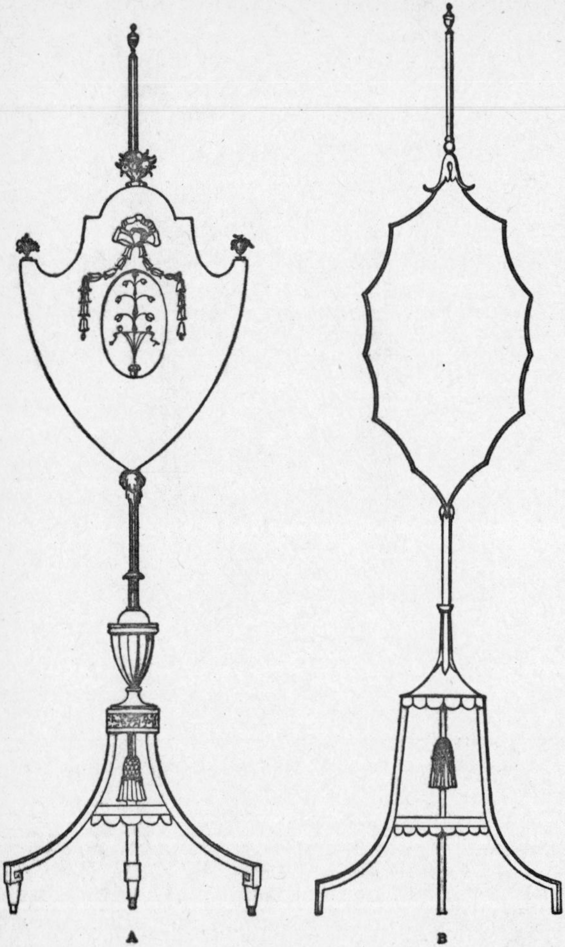

Figure 84 – Two 'Tripod Fire Screens'; from the *Drawing Book*

Tripod candle stands 'used in drawing-rooms, for the convenience of affording additional light to such parts of the room where it would be neither ornamental nor easy to introduce any other kind' were similar in character, and of stilted proportions. The four lights, 'one at the centre, and one at each angle', were constructed 'of strong wire, and the ornaments cemented to them', a fact which is illustrative of the decline in craftsmanship.

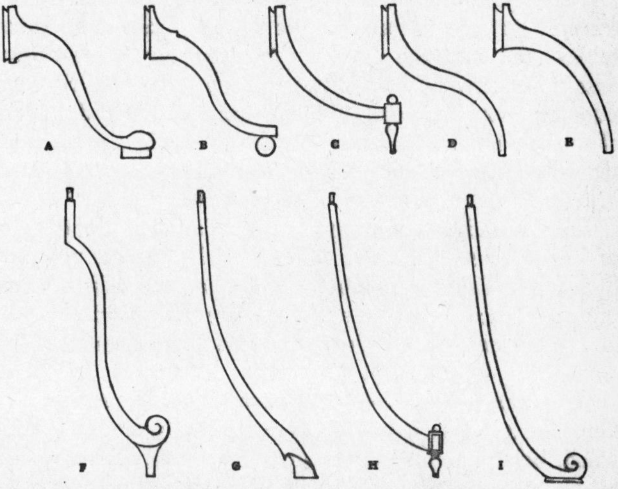

Figure 85 – Details of 'claws' (five) and 'standards' (four); from the 2nd edition of the *Cabinet-Makers' London Book of Prices*, 1793

The tripod form of support is seen to advantage in many of the small occasional and tea-tables of the last decade of the century. They were on the whole of lighter construction; in some cases the stand, which is their most distinctive feature, followed the long-established type with legs of round section (Fig. 85A); and the central shaft was still very frequently decorated with vase turning. It was, as Sheraton confessed in connexion with the equipment of the drawing-room (*Cabinet Dictionary*, 1803), 'extremely difficult to attain to any thing really novel'. Yet many pleasing varieties of tripod stand were produced by the cabinet-makers (Fig. 85C, D, E). The inward turning leg finishing in a peg foot became very generally adopted after about 1790, and was indeed graceful (Fig. 85C). The tops of these tables (round, oval, and polygonal) were usually made to tilt up so that they might be placed against the wall when not required for use.

These 'pillar and claw' supports were used for cheval fire screens, for pole screens, music stands, dining and other tables, and for such curious pieces as the 'lady's screen desk'. The inward and outward curving legs which were adopted about this time (Fig. 85C and Fig. 85D and E) were of square section; the faces were often 'panelled', ornamented with stringing lines or with a small beading. In many articles an extra (a fourth) claw was used.

An alternative type support or standard for tripod 'face' or fire screens, which was thin and delicate, was popular. Standards of similar character, but taller and more spidery in appearance, were also used for flower and candle stands, and represent the development of a type introduced by Adam (Fig. 85F, G, H, I).

Work tables, described as French and of the serviceable kind illustrated in figure 86, were popularly made of satinwood, being intended for use in the boudoir. The tray was hinged on one side, with the flap closing by thumb springs in the manner of a secretary drawer, while a brass moulding was mitred on the edge of the rim. The boat-shaped shelf below, bellying out to a width of 6 inches in the middle and purposed to hold the sewing materials, was to be 'made of inch stuff, and double tenoned into the standards'. Cross bars were screwed to the underside of the tray, and to these the standard supports were secured, also by double mortice and tenon. The article was to be strongly and simply made and was essentially of a practical nature; the form of the inward curving legs and peg feet is nevertheless characteristic of the Sheraton style.

Most specimens of this variety of furniture, introduced

about 1760, were designed with more regard to delicacy of appearance and ingenuity than to usefulness, and were constructed with hinged top, fitted well or bag, and sometimes a superstructure of small drawers. They were commonly called 'pouch' tables; the firm of 'M'Lean & Son' which was recommended by Sheraton (*Cabinet Dictionary*, 1803) as specializing in these small tables may be identified with that of 'John McClean and Sons, 58 Upper Mary le

Figure 86 – A 'French' work table; from the *Drawing Book*

Bone Street' whose trade label has been found on Regency furniture in the Egyptian taste.

The 'Harlequin Pembroke Table' (Fig. 87), 'with a nest of drawers to rise out of the top, and with a falling flap to write on', a composite piece intended to serve both as breakfast table and as lady's writing desk, was not the invention of Sheraton. Tables of this ingenious kind had already been made in the London workshops and Sheraton gave the credit for this particular example to a friend, from whom he received his 'first ideas of it'. The top was divided into four parts, the whole surrounded by an ornamental border, and measured, when opened, 4 feet by 2 feet 7 inches long. The ends were supported, in the usual way, by fly brackets. The 'till', a concealed desk, which comprised a series of small drawers with pigeon holes above, and which could be slowly raised or lowered at will, occupied half the

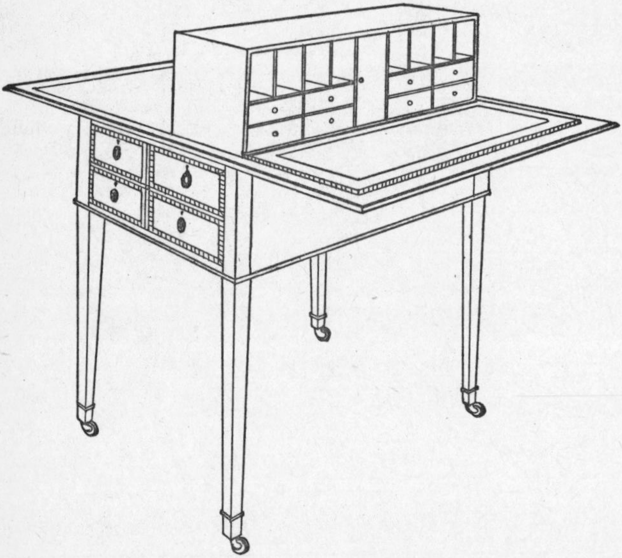

Figure 87 – A 'Harlequin Pembroke Table'; from the *Drawing Book*

accommodation provided below the fixed top, the other half being given up to two long drawers. The internal mechanism was necessarily complex, and was described in the *Drawing Book* precisely and at length. One particular advantage 'arising from the machinery' was as follows: '... although the till be raised and lowered by turning the fly bracket which supports the flap, yet the bracket is made to lose this effect or power by the turn of a key, and the bracket may then be drawn out to support the flap without raising the till, and the table can then be used, as is common, to breakfast upon.' The table was termed 'harlequin,' said the author, 'for no other reason but because, in exhibitions of that sort, there is generally a great deal of machinery introduced in the scenery.'

Another and less elaborate variety of Pembroke table in use at the end of the eighteenth century, which also served for writing, was fitted with a sliding top. Pembroke tables

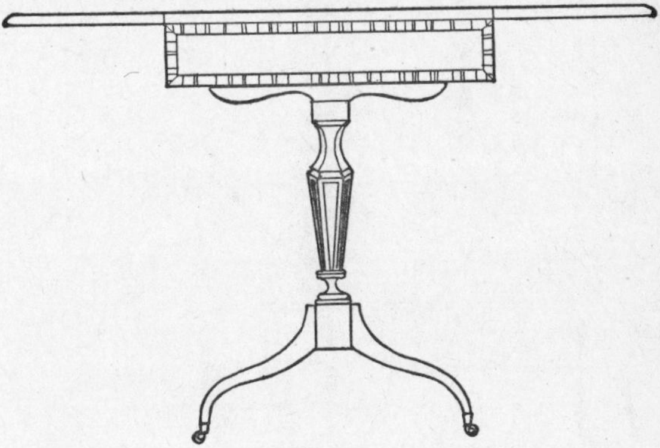

Figure 88 – An oval Pembroke table; from the *Drawing Book*

were made of mahogany or frequently were veneered with satinwood with 'japanned' (painted) ornament, being on the whole finished 'very neat, sometimes bordering upon elegance'. An oval table, supported on a central pillar and four outward-curving claws (Fig. 88), was an alternative type, one being shown in the *Drawing Book*. Preferably, the top was shaped as an irregular oval, with full, rounded ends; the ends, when down, then served to screen the joint rail.

A number of bookcases made at this period were of tall proportions, particularly as regards the height of the lower stage, which in general exceeded 3 feet 6 inches. The

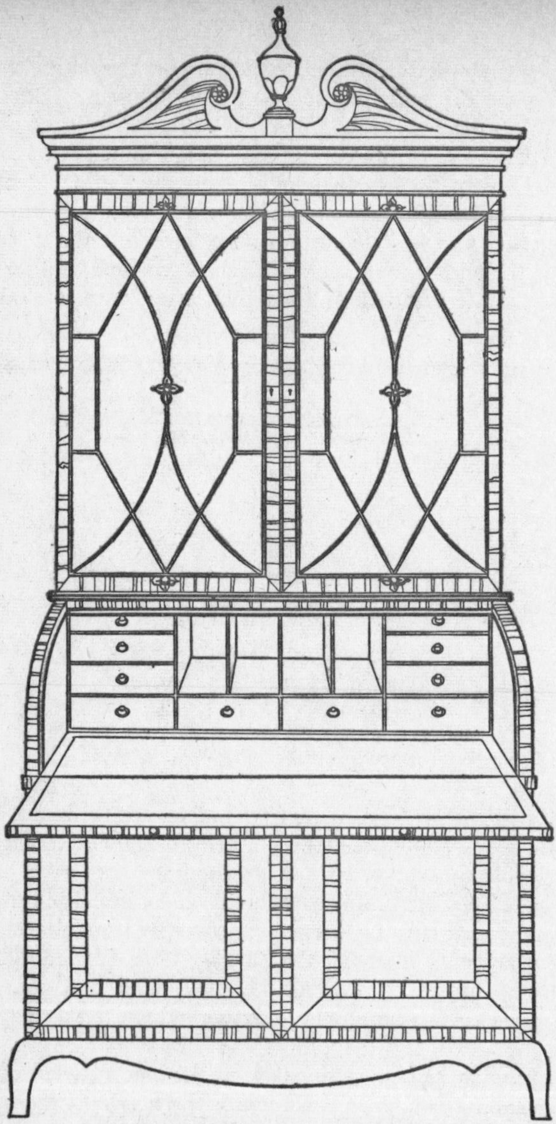

Figure 89 – A 'Cylinder Desk and Bookcase'; from the *Drawing Book*

development is exemplified in the 'Cylinder Desk and Bookcase', a design by Sheraton which is characteristic of his style and also of the general run of production (Fig. 89). The base portion of this piece contains both the desk, enclosed by a tambour front and furnished with writing-slide, and cupboards below which are fitted with press shelves, enclosed by solid doors. The recessed upper stage

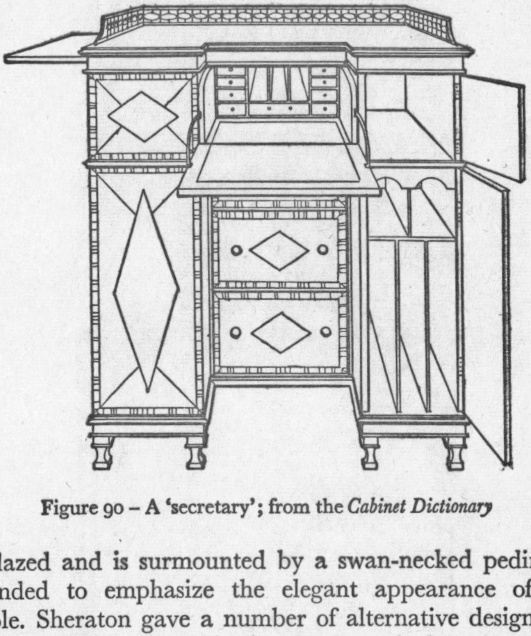

Figure 90 – A 'secretary'; from the *Cabinet Dictionary*

is glazed and is surmounted by a swan-necked pediment intended to emphasize the elegant appearance of the whole. Sheraton gave a number of alternative designs for pediments. This type of bureau bookcase is, however, more usually found with a straight cornice. The doors and drawer fronts, veneered in mahogany of chosen figure, were often edged with a decorative satinwood banding.

The secretary illustrated as plate 69 of the *Cabinet Dictionary* (Fig. 90) purposed to minister to the owner's convenience. 'The door,' to one side, explained Sheraton, 'incloses a cupboard for a pot and slippers ...' The piece is interesting in that it is designed for writing in a standing position, being 3 feet 7 inches to the writing-flap.

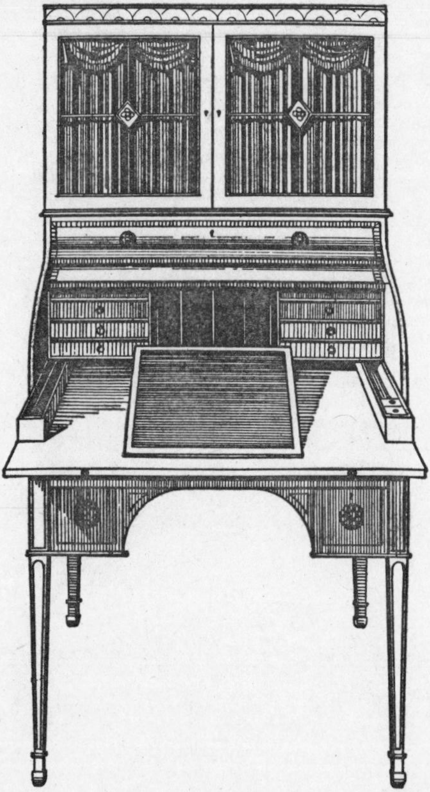

Figure 91 – A 'Lady's Cylinder Desk and Bookcase'; from the *Drawing Book*

A deep secretaire drawer falling on a quadrant was a common alternative to the 'cylinder front'. A 'Secretary and Bookcase', intended to be executed in satinwood, 'and the ornaments japanned', was of this form. The upper part was framed by Ionic pilasters, 'planted on the frame' and the doors 'hinged as usual', and was surmounted by a segmental pediment, bearing a central and two smaller outer vases. With some reduction of ornament it was recommended for execution in mahogany also.

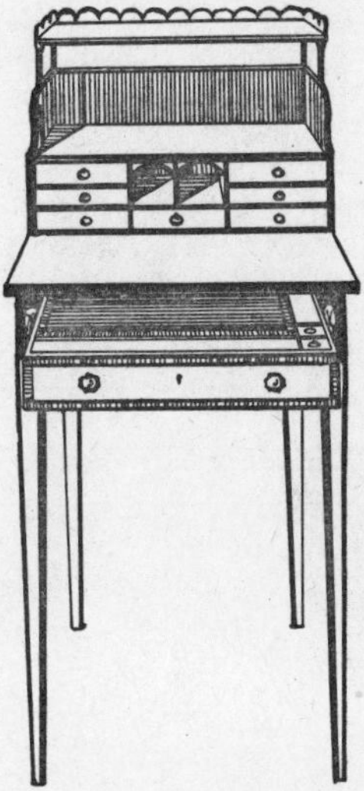

Figure 92 – A dwarf cabinet or writing table; end of the eighteenth century

These pieces resemble only in name the 'Cylinder Desk and Bookcase' which is illustrated in figure 91. Designed for a lady, and small (2 feet 6 inches), it was to be made of satin-wood, 'cross-banded and varnished', with a 'green silk fluting behind the glass and drapery put on at top', which would have a 'good look' if properly managed. The square figure of the doors was said to be much in fashion. The rim around the top was to be of brass.

A variety of dwarf cabinets and writing-tables, dainty in

appearance and finely executed in mahogany, satinwood, amboyna or harewood, was being made at this time. They were most ingeniously formed, often with a low superstructure fitted with shelves, small drawers, and pigeon

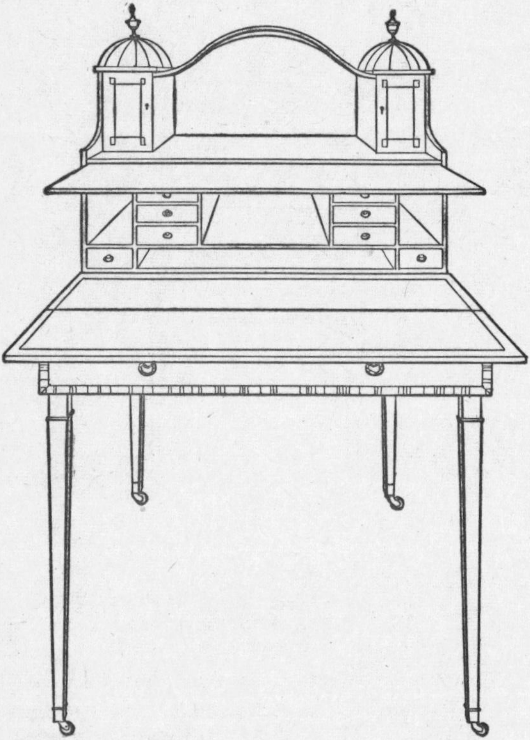

Figure 93 – A 'Lady's Cabinet'; from the *Drawing Book*

holes, and an open stand or table base which frequently contained a long drawer in the frieze (Fig. 92). In the *Cabinet Dictionary*, 1803, Sheraton stated the type with a base of drawers to be 'nearly obsolete in London; at least, ...

amongst fashionable people'. He was referring to the bureau. The term *bureaux* was 'generally applied to common desks with drawers under them ... made very frequently in country towns ... from 3 to 4 feet long and ... three heights of common drawers under them, the upper one divided into two in length'.

The 'Lady's Cabinet' (Fig. 93) is designed with some elaboration. The top of the writing-table is hinged; when opened for use, it folds over in the manner of a card table and is supported on the long drawer in the frame of the table. The cabinet drawers and letter holes are enclosed by a falling front which, as required, may be pushed home into a groove situated immediately beneath the uppermost section of the piece or may be locked into the table when both are closed. A shelf on top, as was usual in these small ladies' pieces, serves for the display of a few books and is flanked by nests of drawers concealed by the small doors.

Pier tables, being made 'merely for ornament under a glass', followed a light construction and were richly finished. The tops were 'most commonly veneered in rich satin, or other valuable wood, with a cross-band on the outside, a border about two inches richly japanned, and a narrow cross-band beyond it, to go all round'. Alternatively, marble tops were thought appropriate. Sheraton recommended that the frames of these tables be of 'gold, or [painted] white and burnished gold' and showed a preference for legs of cylindrical form, with carved and gilt enrichments (Fig. 94). In distinction, those legs for card tables, illustrated in figure 95, were square, tapered, and intended to be ornamented with stringing and inlaid panels. The pier table was often of an elaborated semi-elliptical or shallow D-shape and supported on two end and two centre legs (Fig. 96). It was mirrored in the tall surmounting glass, which sometimes extended towards the floor. A smaller, separate piece of glass was then fixed 'either in the dado of the room, or in the frame of the table', and appeared to be a continuation of the pier glass. Stretcher rails, which made 'the under part appear more furnished', had lately been reintroduced. They had the effect of minimizing 'the long appearance of the legs', and served also to carry a carved vase or basket of flowers. Some tables, with marble tops, were fitted with a thin marble shelf in place of the stretchers.

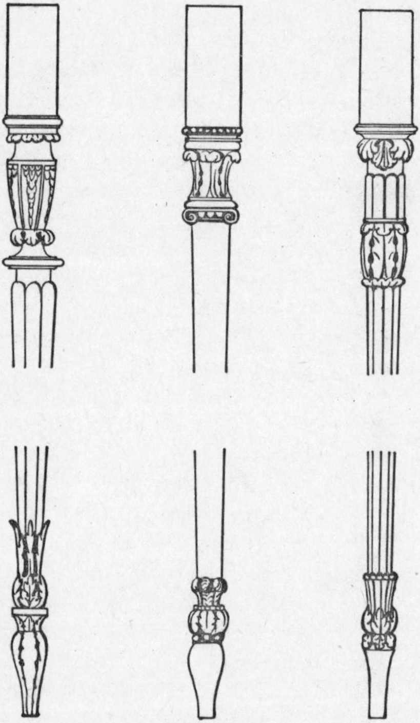

Figure 94 – Three 'Legs for Pier Tables'; from the *Drawing Book*

The oval library table illustrated in Fig. 97, which possessed the merit of having 'already been executed for the Duke of York, excepting the desk-drawers ... added as an improvement', was to be made of mahogany, with the decorative parts either carved or inlaid. Other wood, or japanned ornament, was not considered appropriate; library tables often met with hard usage. Brass mouldings were recommended as an alternative embellishment; they were solid, strong, and produced an effect well suited to

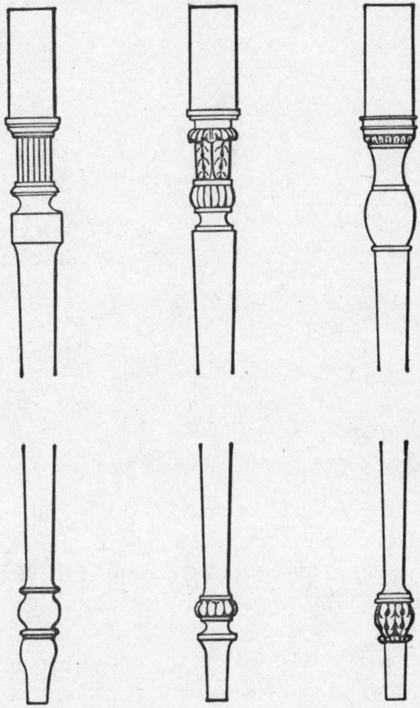

Figure 95 – Three 'Legs for Card Tables'; from the *Drawing Book*

such a design. A taste for metal enrichments, prevalent during the Regency period, was here foreshadowed. The reading-stands contained in the drawers at the ends of the table were provided to enable the user to read while standing, while one or more of the four cupboards, which

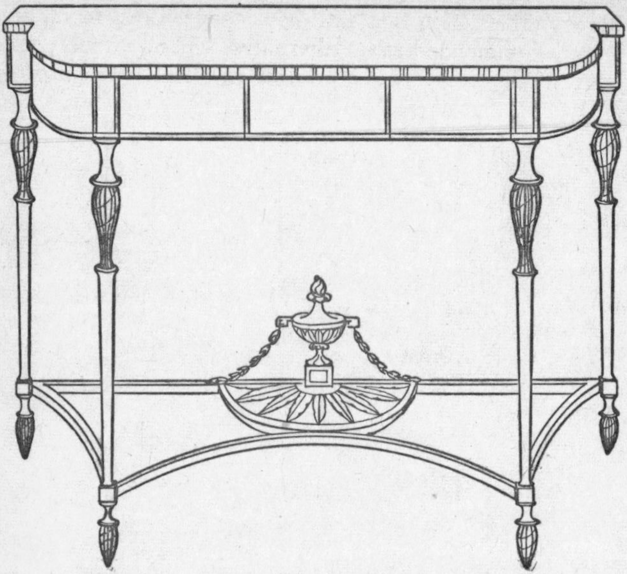

Figure 96 – A 'Pier Table'; from the *Drawing Book*

were unavoidably of an awkward shape, might be fitted with a nest of small drawers and pigeon holes. The table rested on castors, concealed by the plinth. The oval table was somewhat impracticable. The misplaced ingenuity which unfortunately is characteristic of much of Sheraton's work was apparent also in the subject of the next plate, a 'Kidney Library Table', so termed 'on account of its resemblance to that intestine part of animals'. The tiers of drawers were situated in the end pedestals, which were of an irregular semi-circular shape ill adapted to receive them. The form of writing-table known to contemporaries as the 'Carlton House' table (Fig. 98) was extremely popular in the last decade of the century. Its origin is not established; there is no evidence that the design was approved by the Prince of Wales, but tables of this type were in production by many makers soon after about 1790. One such design figures in the second edition of the *Cabinet-Makers' London Book of Prices* of 1793.

In a plan for the drawing-room of a town house (illustrated in the *Drawing Book* as the combined elevations of each of the four walls of the room), the pier tables have marble tops, as also the commode which was the most prominent feature of the wall opposite the fireplace (Pl. 51). This latter piece was provided with a large glass above, fitted with candle branches, and flanked, with careful regard to symmetrical appearance, by 'panelling on the walls done in paper, with ornamented borders of various colours'.

The demand for imported Chinese papers, patterned with flowers and birds, and for Caffoy (flock) papers,

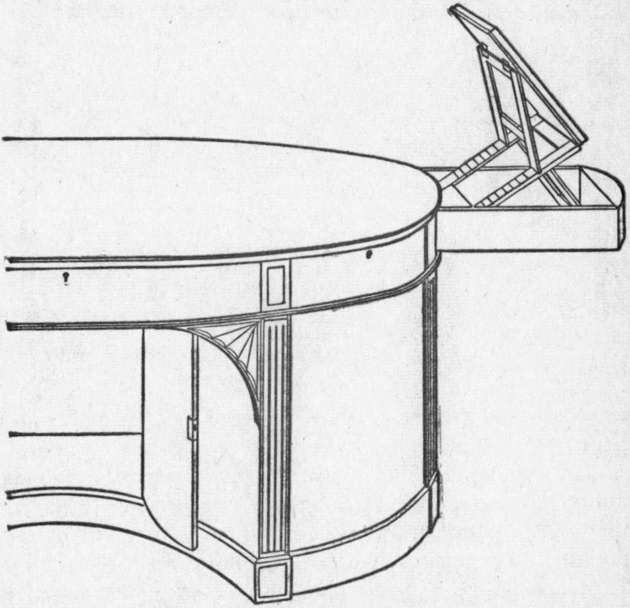

Figure 97 – A library table; from the *Drawing Book*

resembling damasks – prevalent about 1750 – had encouraged the native manufacture of wallpapers. The trade had developed considerably during the third quarter of the century with the effect that a papered treatment of wall, from being alternative to wainscot or to fabric hangings, was at this date general. From about 1700, throughout the

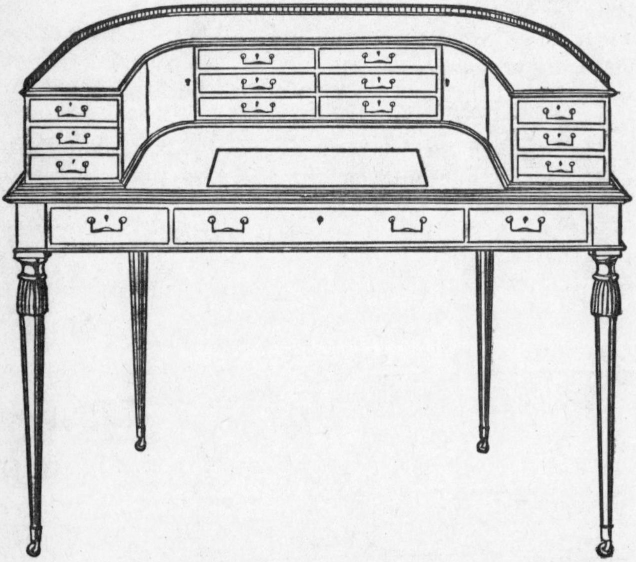

Figure 98 – A 'Carlton House' table; end of the eighteenth century

whole of the century, various flowered and figured wallpapers were made and sold at the 'Blew Paper Warehouse', Aldermanbury, London. For the most part the papers imitated fabrics, forming indeed a cheaper substitute for them. 'Abraham Price,' stated one early handbill of the manufactory, 'makes and sells the true sorts of Figur'd Paper Hangings, Wholesale and Retale, in pieces of twelve yards long, in imitation of Irish Stitch, Flower'd Sprigs and

Branches ... and a Curious Sort of Imboss'd Work resembling Caffaws (a rich silk). ...' Some 'stitch' papers were printed in black and white; others were the expensive flock papers.[3] The *Chinoiseries* were also a popular feature of this firm's production. Paper hanging was within the province of the cabinet-maker.

The commode was designed with four doors, the outer two being straight fronted and faced by pairs of free standing legs of columnar type. They were 'intended to stand a little clear of the wings'. The centre of the commode projected as a bow and contained in the frieze above the doors a tablet, 'made of an exquisite composition in imitation of statuary marble'. Tablets of this nature, 'of any figure, or on any subject', were to be had 'at Mr Wedgewood's [*sic*], near Soho Square', and were set in the wood, slightly raised above the surface. (The succeeding fashion, during the Regency period, was for tablets of bronze, chased in the antique taste.) The commode, pier tables, sofas, and chairs of the drawing-room were commonly painted and part gilded to match one another, with a neatness and propriety of effect which was enhanced by carved standing figures bearing lights in their hands, and by the sets of bronze lights which were placed on the chimney-piece, the commode or pier tables.

The character of the furnishing of rooms was fast changing. John Byng, later Fifth Viscount Torrington, during his tour in the north country in 1792 observed in the great houses 'a want of comfort, of habitation, of warmth, of proper furniture', and recorded his impressions of Raby Castle and Trentham House thus: 'In the drawing room, instead of large chairs, rolling upon casters there is nothing to be seen but little, light French chairs; and thick, welt-lined damask, or velvet curtains have given way to French linnen festoonings. I love large, firmly-fix'd writing tables in my library; and to have my breakfast, and dining tables substantial, and immoveable: and when I say immoveable, it is because my rooms, and every part of them, should be of an equal warmth; and there should be no need, as I see at present, of little skuttling tables being brought before a hearth. – In my house I repeat it, egoistically again, (and upon paper this may be allow'd) I should desire that no one would come within 6 feet of the fire place; nor would any-one wish it, because the grates would be ample, and the fire place high and extended; not a little, low dug hole, as at present, surrounded by a slip of marble, for people (genteel) to clap their elbows upon, whilst they, by turns, toasted their shins. – At Trentham House, there are no comforts; (here I did expect them) nor is the library fitted up as it should be! a library is the first of rooms? What stores of paper, pens, wax, ink standishes, albums, grand writing tables, should furnish a library? People spend fortunes, and waste great estates, without ever having passed one hour in a comfortable room, or in a good bed. A good bed is a great rarity.'[4]

Carpets, none the less, were in very general use by the end of the century and were no longer a luxury. 'Since the introduction of carpets, fitted all over the floor of a room,' stated Sheraton (*Cabinet Dictionary*, 1803), 'the nicety of flooring anciently practised in the best houses, is now laid aside.' Native manufactories existed at Kidderminster, Wilton, and Axbridge; not unnaturally, 'Persian and Turkey carpets' were more esteemed. The 'Parisian' imitation was said to be tolerable. The striped 'Venetian' carpet and the 'Scots' carpet were of inferior quality – the latter, in particular, being thought to be very poor.

Sideboards illustrated in the first edition of the *Drawing Book* resembled the designs of Hepplewhite and Shearer, but were all provided with drawers. Sheraton may have preferred this type to the sideboard table as permitting a more elaborate construction. One specimen, however, was shown with end pedestal cupboards, to be made separately and screwed to the main table. Sideboards were now frequently fitted at the back with a brass gallery, against which the large dishes were set; candle branches were attached to the rods and gave when lighted 'a very brilliant effect to the silver ware'. The sideboard was usually straight-, serpentine- or bow-fronted, although these forms were attended in common by certain disadvantages. 'If,' said Sheraton, 'a sideboard be required nine or ten feet long, as in some noblemen's houses, and if the breadth of it be in proportion to the length, it will not be easy for a butler to reach across it. . . . Besides, if the sideboard be near the entering door of the dining room, the hollow front will sometimes secure the butler from the jostles of the other servants.' He offered, therefore, a design for one with concave centre.

Some sideboards were supplied with a small cupboard purposed to contain a chamber pot. Louis Simond, a French-American who passed the years 1810–11 in Great Britain, remarked this custom: 'Drinking much and long leads to unavoidable consequences. Will it be credited, that, in a corner of the very dining-room, there is a certain convenient piece of furniture, to be used by anybody who wants it. The operation is performed very deliberately and undisguisedly, as a matter of course, and occasions no interruption of the conversation. I once took the liberty to ask why this convenient article was not placed out of the room, in some adjoining closet; and was answered, that, in former times, when good fellowship was more strictly enforced than in these degenerate days, it had been found that men of weak heads or stomachs took advantage of the opportunity to make their escape shamefully, before they were quite drunk; and that it was to guard against such an enormity that this nice expedient had been invented.' [5]

Knife cases, of the type resembling those illustrated in figure 99, are usually found to be of excellent quality and execution, and have survived in large numbers. The example with convex front was intended to be ornamented with corner pilasters inlaid with 'small flutes of white holly or other coloured wood'; the inner pilasters were painted with a decoration of small flowers, framed by a very delicate cross-banding. In general, the ornament of the lid of the case was in the form of an inlay of various woods. The statement that these cases were not made in 'regular cabinet

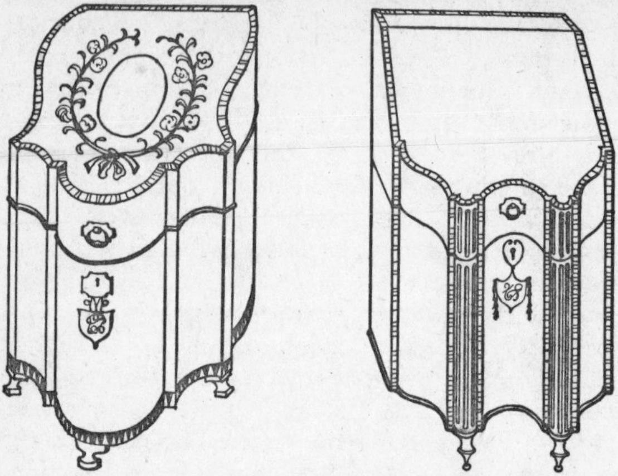

Figure 99 – Two knife cases; from the *Drawing Book*

shops' is somewhat surprising, but we are informed by Sheraton that specimens 'in the best taste' were to be obtained from John Lane, of 44 St Martin's-le-Grand, London, whose main business lay in their manufacture.

Those bedsteads given in the *Drawing Book* were for the most part of an exceptional nature and by no means provided a reliable indication of any type in popular use; allowing his fancy free rein, Sheraton exhibited such articles as an 'Alcove Bed', a 'Sofa Bed', an 'Eliptic Bed for a Single Lady', and a 'French State Bed'. A large and novel 'Summer Bed in Two Compartments', which supplied 'a nobleman or gentleman and his lady' with the means to 'sleep separately in hot weather', consisted of two single adjoining couches, united under one roof but separated by a narrow space of about 22 inches. The middle passage way, fronted by a miniature round-headed Ionic arch, conferred an additional benefit in that it gave an easy access to the servants.

Sheraton apparently admired the type of bedstead constructed with domed ceiling or surmounting cupola, usually choosing this form, as in the graceful specimen of elliptic shape proposed for the 'Single Lady'. In all his designs the disposition of draperies was most elaborate; vallances were festooned, braided and tasselled, and ornament excessive.

The simpler, traditional four-post bedstead, however, remained very popular. It was the type commonly required by well-to-do clients. Posts were cylindrical and frequently reeded, tapering upwards from a slender vase form, sometimes carved with wheat-ear or with acanthus, to a height of 8 or 9 feet, and usually supported on plain bases of square section.

Among the variety of small articles of bedroom, or 'lodging room', furniture produced during the late Georgian period, the 'Corner Basin Stand' of the type designated 'plain and common' (Fig. 100A) has survived in large numbers. Stands were useful and, if only by reason of their neat triangular form, convenient. The more elaborate of the two specimens illustrated (Fig. 100B) is provided with a folding top, serving when let down to enclose and conceal the wash basin, when raised to preserve the wall from water splashes. It contains a cupboard and drawer below; while the upper drawer is dummy. The shape of the top tallies of necessity with that of the bow of the front. Sheraton illustrated also a larger stand, with reeded decoration, to be made in the likeness of a cabinet, that it might be placed 'in a genteel room without giving offence to the eye'. This was designed with serpentine front, the upper part being enclosed by a sliding tambour frame. The cupboard base, fitted with hinged doors, provided a repository for the 'foul water'.

A tambour door was again introduced in the design for a square 'Pot Cupboard', raised on low legs of tapering cylindrical form above two long drawers. This piece was shown with a low superstructure at the back which consisted of a shallow cupboard with shelves 'intended to keep medicines to be taken in the night, or to hold other little articles which servants are not permitted to overlook'. A decorative cross-banding to the drawer fronts was recommended; pot cupboards, it was remarked, 'are used in genteel bedrooms, and are sometimes finished in satin wood, and in a style a little elevated above their use.'

A mahogany 'Cylinder Wash-hand Table,' so contrived as to resemble when closed a narrow roll-top bureau, was constructed with five long drawers (2 feet) and quadrantal

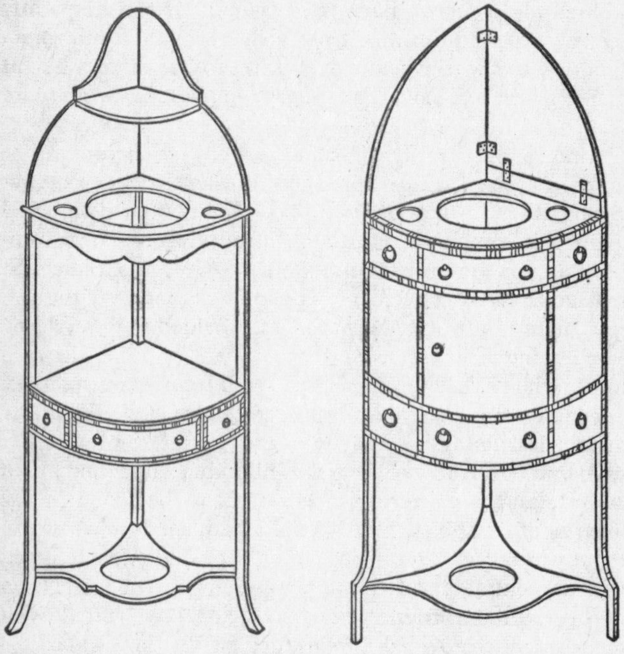

A B

Figure 100 – Two corner basin stands; from the *Drawing Book*

top above, and supported on shaped bracket feet. The drawers were sham; and 'the washing apparatus' (basin, water cistern, and tap) and an attached mirror glass were concealed by the cylinder front. The deception was similar to that which had been practised in the case of the 'cabinet' type tripod basin stand. These essentially useful pieces were desired to 'look neat'.

The relatively undistinguished plate in the *Drawing Book* for a break front wardrobe (8 feet) is now mainly of interest in as much as the accompanying description is informative in detail. It was to be made 'in four separate carcasses' – i.e. the wings in one piece. The base plinth and also the entablature (the only purely decorative feature of the wardrobe, excepting the figured door fronts) were made, in conformity with the usual practice, 'all in one frame' and attached by screws. The upper portion of the centre compartment was to contain six or seven clothes-press shelves, disposed at 6-inch intervals, each provided with a green baize cover, tacked at the front edge of the shelf. The wings (2 feet long by 16 or 17 inches deep) were recessed from the centre by some 6 inches, and were fitted with iron rods having 'arms, to hang clothes on, made of beech, with a swivel in their centre'.

Two 'Dressing Chests' (chests of drawers) shown by Sheraton were stated to be designed 'on a new plan', with the writing slide, found in numerous specimens of earlier date, elaborated to form a shallow drawer containing a rising writing flap, receptacles for ink, sand, and pens, as well as a number of small covered toilet boxes, but appearing, when shut, 'like a common slider, with a partition [banding] above and below'; and by the close of the century, chests of drawers were often constructed with a comparatively deep frieze beneath the top. A breadth of 22 or 23 inches was recommended; the height was 'governed by the slider', which was situated 'thirty-two or thirty-three inches from the floor'. These chests were designed with shaped fronts (in the one case concave, the other convex) and with square corners, faced either by reeded pilasters or by reeded, engaged columns finishing in short feet. Neither chest bore an apron piece. The user sat to dress at these pieces, as also at the kneehole type of chest or dressing commode which, it may be noticed, was made, for the sake of convenience, 3 or 4 inches lower than the standard article, with a total height of about 32 inches.

Fine furniture made in the last two decades of the

eighteenth century was technically at its most accomplished; the Sheraton style is one of elegant sophistication, and is to-day valued to the full; it lacks, nevertheless, the richness and vigour of earlier periods.

NOTES TO CHAPTER 10

1. Thomas Sheraton, *Cabinet Dictionary*, 1803, p. 118. The designs of the *Cabinet Dictionary* are of unequal merit – a fact which would seem to indicate that Sheraton's powers of invention were strained by 1803.
2. *Memoirs of Adam Black*, ed. by Alexander Nicolson, 1885, p. 32.
3. See article by E. A. Entwisle, 'The Blew Paper Warehouse in Aldermanbury, London', *Connoisseur*, May 1950.
4. *The Torrington Diaries*, ed. by C. Bruyn Andrews, 1934–8, vol. III, pp. 156–7.
5. L. Simond, *Journal of a Tour and Residence in Great Britain by 'A French Traveller'*, 1815, vol. I, p. 49.

CHAPTER ELEVEN

THE REGENCY PERIOD

'REGENCY' is a term used to describe a style in English decoration and furniture of which successive phases extended over rather more than the first quarter of the nineteenth century. The term is loosely applied: the period to which it refers does not, in fact, coincide with that of the Regency of George, Prince of Wales (1811–20); nor does the style itself reflect the personal taste of the Prince Regent during those years.

Reaction against Adam's refined adaptation of the antique was inevitable, and set in soon after 1790; its beginning roughly corresponded in date with the opening of the French Wars (1793). About the year 1800 an effective new style was to be seen in Henry Holland's designs for furniture at Southill, Bedfordshire (rebuilt and redecorated by him for Samuel Whitbread from 1795), and at Carlton House. Holland admired the revived classicism of French and continental taste and was inspired by French furniture of the *Directoire* years. 'Cabinet work' manufactured in Paris was then reputed to be of high quality, particularly as regards execution. (It was, in fact, inferior to that made during the pre-Revolutionary period, and also to contemporary English furniture.) Holland's architectural work was distinguished by restraint and good taste. In 1785, Horace Walpole, 'charmed' by the alteration and enlargement of Carlton House, had written: 'There is an august simplicity that astonished me. You cannot call it magnificent; it is the taste and propriety that strike. Every ornament is at a proper distance, and not one too large, but all delicate and new, with more freedom and variety than Greek ornaments; and, though probably borrowed from the Hôtel de Conde and other new palaces, not one that is not rather classic than French. . . . How sick one shall be after this chaste palace, of Mr Adam's gingerbread and sippets of embroidery.' [1] Such words might have been written with equal truth of Holland's furniture. His style was disciplined. He employed French craftsmen, and made use of applied ormolu mounts; and through acquaintance with the architect Charles Heathcote Tatham, was associated with the firm of Marsh and Tatham, principal cabinet-makers to the Prince of Wales.

Much of the furniture of the Regency period was plainly formed; shaped and curved *surfaces* were by preference avoided in its construction. It was made at less expense. Money had greatly depreciated in value as a result of the French war while the costs of materials and labour had risen. Various woodworking machines were adopted, with some deterioration in craftsmanship. Marquetry decoration, which had been favoured in finer work of the last quarter of the eighteenth century, was now unfashionable. Sheraton, in the *Cabinet Dictionary*, 1803, referred to an inlay of wood as being an 'expensive mode of decorating furniture used in the Cabinet-making of twenty and thirty years back'. Carved ornamentation was less in evidence. There were comparatively few skilled carvers in London, and their number was diminishing yearly. Some fine furniture was made, however, and furniture of fair quality was plentiful, and was also cheaper. Cabinet-makers tended to rely for effect on the striking figure and colour of certain new veneers, especially when combined with a decorative inlay of brass. Thus, rosewood and zebra wood were widely used, to a great extent replacing satinwood, at least during the first two decades of the century. After about 1815, zebra wood, which was obtained from Brazil, came into short supply and was procured only with difficulty. There was also a vogue for the golden-brown 'bird's eye' veneers of amboyna and for maple wood. Yet mahogany retained general popularity, particularly for library, bedroom, and dining-room furniture. The popularity of brass inlay and applied ornament was remarked by contemporary writers: 'There is another very important part in designing furniture in which the cabinet-maker ought to be skilful, that is harmonising metals with woods, so as not to overload the articles with bronze, or ormolu, which is so frequently seen.' [2] Metal enrichment, which, in English work, suggests a London origin, was valued both on account of its quality of permanence and for the finished appearance which it gave to furniture. Sheraton, decrying the French trade, had said: 'it is in this article [brass] they excel us, and by which they set off cabinet work; which, without it, would not bear a comparison with ours, neither in design, nor neatness of execution.' [3] Inlaid borders, composed of scrolled, floral or classical detail, and raised ornament in brass, such as small galleries, colonnettes, or bead moulding strips, are commonly found on Regency cabinet furniture. The fashion extended also to wire lattice-work, to cast metal feet, lion-mask handles, and other features.

Chased ormolu mounts are rare on English furniture and their presence suggests the hand of French immigrant craftsmen. A 'Monsieur Boileau [J. J. Boileau, working at Sloane Square] who was formerly employed in the decoration of Carlton Palace' (1783–9) was said to have possessed 'a light, an airy, and classic style of design for household articles of comfort' and to have been unsurpassed 'in his designs for ornamental plate or articles for casting in *Or molu*'. [4]

Boulle furniture was favoured in some quarters, a notable maker being Louis le Gaigneur of Queen Street, Edgware Road. In her journal for 14 November, 1820, Mrs Arbuthnot wrote: 'The King had talked of going to Hanover, but the Duke [of Wellington] says there is not much chance of that unless we allow him to take his eating & drinking money, his money for buhl furniture & for buying horses, which we could not think of doing.' [5]

A taste for contrasts of colour or material extended to the decoration of rooms. Draperies, upholsterers' fabrics, and wallpapers were prepared in bold, simple patterns. People showed a liking for the 'primitive tints'. Columns, entablatures, and carved architectural enrichment enjoyed by other generations were excluded from interiors.

About 1815 the original process of French polishing was adopted in England. The polish consisted of shellac dissolved in spirit, and, applied to a carefully prepared surface, it imparted a brilliant, durable finish to the wood – one greatly superior to that obtained by the more hasty methods of polishing or staining prevalent at the present day which go by the same name. French polishing was economical and its use was encouraged by demand. Much old walnut and mahogany furniture was stripped during the nineteenth century and 'French polished'. Comparatively few pieces survive in an untouched state.*

The main phase of Regency taste was known formerly as English Empire. In 1807, a book of designs entitled *Household Furniture and Decoration* was published by the scholar and architect, Thomas Hope (Pls. 54, 55, 56, and 58). The designs provide a record of the furniture made specially for his own use. Hope was a friend of the French architect and designer Percier with whose severe style he would seem to have had natural sympathy. 'I scarcely was

* At earlier periods, woods had been polished under friction, generally by the application of linseed or nut oil, or with the use of beeswax and turpentine. Processes were often laborious, but the wood received a smooth, permanent, and glossy surface, with an enhanced figure and colour. According to Evelyn, who was writing in the late seventeenth century, joiners put walnut wood 'into an oven ... or ... in a warm stable; and when they work it, polish it over with its own oil, very hot, which makes it look black and sleek'.[6] In the seventeenth and eighteenth centuries, the finer walnut, mahogany, and satinwood pieces were *varnished* (a lengthy proceeding) and afterwards were rubbed with Tripoly powder (rotten stone) and oil; less costly furniture was treated with oils or waxed. Country-made mahogany furniture of the eighteenth century was given a comparatively 'raw' finish. The wood was unvarnished, often having been treated only with soft wax, with perhaps 'a little red oil to help the colour'. It showed, therefore, in a more or less natural condition.

Sheraton stated that the 'plain cabinet work' of his day was generally

able to hold a pencil,' he wrote, 'when instead of flowers, landscapes, and all other familiar objects, I already began dealing in those straight lines which seem so little attractive to the greatest number.' Hope had studied architecture in Greece, Egypt, Turkey, and Syria, and was the owner of a large collection of antiquities. His interests were predominantly archaeological. He desired to exhibit the collection in surroundings which conformed to his doctrinaire ideals. He attempted to adapt (sometimes with success) in wood and bronze the forms of objects of ancient civilizations – Egyptian, Greek, and Roman. The lion monopodium, the griffin, the winged Sphinx and winged lion, the hocked animal leg, the Egyptian head, the Indian or bearded Bacchus, and the lyre were freely introduced in his designs. His approach, although disciplined and accurate, was theoretical. Precedents existed for chairs, couches, and tripods, but most of the pieces of domestic furniture in use in late Georgian England had no antique counterparts. Farington, in the company of George Dance, Doctor Burney, and the Charles Offleys, visited his London house in Duchess Street one afternoon in March 1804. They stayed about two hours. Farington wrote that Dance 'thought it

polished with linseed oil and brick dust, a mixture which produced 'a kind of putty' under the rubbing cloth, by which means, eventually, a fine polish was 'infallibly' secured; chairs on the other hand were treated with a hardish composition of wax and turpentine, coloured with Oxford ochre, to which was added a little red lead and copal varnish.[7] A red oil, composed of linseed oil, with alkanet root and a small quantity of dragon's blood, was, as a preliminary, often applied to the hard, close-grained mahogany, which was then left for some days before polishing commenced; open-grained Honduras wood was, in general, treated with wax and turpentine only. Domestic waxing provided wood with a fine surface or skin, and oiling, when continually applied as a preservative, tended to darken it. The practice of oiling furniture would appear to have been quite usual. The journal of Lady Eleanor Butler (who in company with her friend Miss Sarah Ponsonby had retired from society to Llangollen in North Wales) contains the following entry for Monday, 28 April, 1788: '... Oiled the Parlour eating table with the Spinhamland receipt. Dined in the kitchen to let the oil soak in it. ...'[8]

better than He expected, & that by the singularity of it good might be done as it might contribute to emancipate the public taste from that rigid adherence to a certain style of architecture & of finishing & unshacle the Artists. . . . He sd however much there might be [of] amusement in seeing the House we had gone through, it certainly excited no feelings of comfort as a dwelling.' [9] Within a few years, indeed, a noticeable change of temper was apparent in 'the public taste'. Hope himself observed in the preface to his book that, prior to its publication, imitations of his furniture had 'started up in every corner of the capital'; by 1807 the public were prepared to approve the somewhat massive forms and heavy applied bronze ornament of the style.

In the next year the cabinet-maker and upholsterer, George Smith, published *A Collection of Designs for Household Furniture and Interior Decoration.* The work contained 158 plates in colour, some showing designs for approved schemes of decoration for whole rooms (Pls. 57, 60, and 63). The author was advertised as being 'Upholder Extraordinary to His Royal Highness The Prince of Wales', and the latter was complimented on the good taste 'exhibited in his palaces in Pall Mall and at Brighton'. Smith claimed in this book to interpret the spirit of antiquity as found in the best examples of the Egyptian, Greek, and Roman styles. He added designs for furniture 'after the Gothic, or old English fashion and according to the costume of China'. His claims as to correctness of taste were unjustified, but the volume engaged the curiosity of the public and contributed to a popularization and consequent debasement of the new style. (Thomas Hope had attempted to render the letter of antiquity.)

Smith's knowledge of the Egyptian style, for instance, was often misapplied. Much of his information was culled from Baron Denon's *Voyage dans la Basse et Haute Egypte.* 'In the year 1804,' as Smith later explained (1826), 'Monsieur Denon's grand publication, detailing the antiquities of Egypt, became public. The novelty displayed throughout these fine specimens of art, calling to recollection so distant a portion of ancient history, gave rise and life to a taste for this description of embellishment.' Interest in Egypt had been sufficiently strong at the close of the eighteenth century to affect the work of isolated European artists and craftsmen, and the publication in 1802 of a reliable account of the country by Dominique-Vivant Denon, the Director-General of the Museums of France under the First Empire, subsequently exerted a brief but quite considerable influence on furniture design in France and in England. Denon accompanied Bonaparte on his Egyptian campaign of 1798–1801, leading the official archaeological expedition to that country. On his return Egyptian *motifs* were at once intro-

Figure 101 – Detail of frieze – anthemion *motif*

duced in furniture made for Napoleon's private apartments at the Tuileries, while Denon himself enjoyed a bedchamber which was furnished in the Egyptian taste.

The Egyptian vogue was at its height in England for a few years before about 1810. The younger Thomas Chippendale supplied 'Egyptian' furniture to Stourhead, Wiltshire, in 1804–5; and the fashion was generally established by the next year. Archaistic lion supports and, very frequently, Egyptian heads (forming the terminations of pilasters or the headings of table legs) were incorporated in the design of chairs, tables, cupboards, or dwarf bookcases of the period. Such features were customarily applied and were executed in brass. The metal was also used for inlaid detail, as the lotus and anthemion (see Fig. 101). Among the *motifs* which composed the borders of otherwise plain wall papers were mummies and sphinxes.

The Chinese taste was again revived during the Regency period. Japanned furniture of a bizarre and ornate character, embodying pagoda and dragon *motifs*, was produced concurrently with that in the new, dry archaeological manner of the early nineteenth century. In part, the Prince of Wales had been responsible for a revived interest in *chinoiseries*. The Chinese drawing-room at Carlton House, illustrated by Sheraton in the *Drawing Book* (1793), contained lavishly gilded furniture of rich effect; among the furniture designed to the Prince's order by Henry Holland were two pier tables of ebony, with elaborate ormolu mounts; the supports of the tables were headed by naturalistic figures of Chinamen in bronze, and ornamental dragons formed a central feature of the detail of the friezes. The work was not typical of Holland's style, which was normally restrained and severe. Black and gold lacquered furniture in mock Oriental taste was supplied to the Prince of Wales at a later date for Brighton Pavilion. (The Royal Pavilion was completed about 1820, at the time of the Regent's accession to the throne, when the character of the furnishing became more stately.) Much cheaper furniture, japanned or painted in colours, was subsequently made for the general public. The framework, especially of caned chairs, was frequently constructed in imitation bamboo.

At the close of the eighteenth century the form of the chair was remarkable for its lightness – a quality which was retained during the immediately succeeding period. The painted decoration of numerous beech wood specimens, which continued to be made, was severely classical, noticeably in the oblong panel incorporated in the back; and ringed front legs of circular section were frequently made with outward curving feet. The chair back was low and square with some horizontal emphasis to its design. The arms were placed high and often merged with the uprights at the level of the top rail (Pl. 53). Reeded ornament was commonly employed.

The type of chair fashionable during the Empire phase of design possessed in-curving, 'scimitar' shaped front legs; the back uprights and rear legs formed wide arcs, bisected approximately at their junction with the seat rail (Pl. 54, right). These members (uprights, front and rear legs) were disposed in opposed curves in a manner determined by classical prototypes. An outward and backward roll to the top rail was, at this time, also usual. Arms were often scrolled and supported on scrolled rests.

Many specimens survive of a heavier and more severe type of chair, constructed usually of mahogany or satinwood and inlaid with an ornament of straight ebonized lines; the deep, solid top rail formed a prominent feature and legs were sometimes straight, and of square or tapered form (Pl. 54, left). The mahogany *bergère*, with back, seat, and sides composed of canework, enjoyed a deserved and continued favour from before 1800. Most examples were designed simply, in graceful lines, with the appearance of being both comfortable and serviceable.

George Smith, in *Household Furniture*, 1808, illustrated chairs of a more elaborate nature, incorporating lion monopodia, Egyptian heads, and other exotic ornamental devices, with bronzing, gilding, and carved ornament. Chairs executed from these designs comprised a small part only of the production of the time.

The substantial proportions of the furniture to be made during the Victorian age were to be seen in fashions current at the end of the first quarter of the century.

Sir Walter Scott, contributing to the *Quarterly Review* for March 1828, remarked the alteration in styles which had occurred within a generation. 'Our national taste indeed,' he wrote, 'has been changed, in almost every particular, from that which was meagre, formal, and poor, and has attained, comparatively speaking, a character of richness, variety, and solidity. An ordinary chair, in the most ordinary parlour, has now something of an antique cast – something of Grecian massiveness, at once, and elegance in its forms. That of twenty or thirty years since was mounted on four tapering and tottering legs, resembling four tobacco-pipes; the present supporters of our stools have a curule air, curve outwards behind, and give a comfortable idea of stability to the weighty aristocrat or ponderous burgess who is about to occupy one of them.' He yet felt constrained to add that 'the age may ... be nothing the worse for being reminded that ... profusion of ornament is not good taste'. By then the ideal Grecian simplicity was debased. 'Grecian' taste had become commonplace before 1828.

Soon after about 1800, the settee became less fashionable; and its place in the drawing-room was taken by the sofa. The mahogany settee, dating from the early years of the nineteenth century, of which examples have survived, was intended usually to furnish the hall. The sofa and settee show a quite considerable divergence of style and construction. The form of the latter piece was clearly derived from the contemporary armchair of plain design: outward curving legs, scrolled arms, and reeded decoration were characteristic features at this date. The sofa, by comparison, was extravagantly shaped. Bold S-scrolled end pieces continued the line of the seat rail, and the legs were set in opposed curves. The vigour of the design often was enhanced by a repetitive scrolling of the framing of the back. Round bolster cushions were a usual accompaniment to the upholstered sofa which was, in most instances, painted. A number of sofas were of couch form, being made with ends of unequal dimensions and with a short arm rest in place of the upholstered back.

The stool, either as an ornamental and occasional seat for the drawing-room or as a piece appropriate to the furnishing of hall and corridor (Pl. 56), was adequately illustrated in several contemporary trade catalogues, but it was not an article to which prominence was given. Smith's *Household Furniture* showed various examples in the Egyptian taste, which was considered eminently suitable; the author gave also a number of designs for the small footstool. The latter would appear to have been particularly popular, and many Regency specimens survive. There was a demand also for a comfortably upholstered gout stool. In the *Guide*, Hepplewhite had exhibited one example: 'being so easily raised or lowered at either end' it was, he explained, 'particularly useful to the afflicted'. Much ingenuity was expended on novel furniture of this nature – library steps were designed to look like a stool, to rise from a library table or indeed from a Pembroke table. The chair-step and other combination pieces were also made.

Stools, both of mahogany and of painted wood with bronzed enrichments, were frequently provided with legs of animal form. An X-frame construction was quite usual; and the seat was placed either at the crossing of the members which were then continued upwards and outwards so as to form arm rests, or was laid across the upper arms of curved, X-shaped supports (Pl. 56). This form, which was associated with classical antiquity, was adapted also to some types of chairs.

The sofa table, perhaps by reason of a convenient size and form, was in general demand from the first years of the nineteenth century, being regarded as a proper part of the furniture of parlour, drawing-room, or library. As the name implies, it was purposed to stand immediately before a sofa and was intended primarily for the use of ladies engaged in reading, writing, or other sedentary employment. It proved also a practical substitute for the dining-table, especially in small households. These tables, when extended, were normally 5 feet or more in length and about 2 feet in breadth. Often, two drawers were contained below the centre portion. The article was directly evolved from the Pembroke table, and in many instances small rectangular end flaps, usually with rounded corners, were upheld, as in the latter, by fly brackets. The rather shorter Pembroke was in habitual use for the serving of refreshments. Jane Austen, writing about 1804 of 'a circle of smart people ... arranged with all the honours of visiting round the fire', described 'Miss Watson seated at the best Pembroke Table, with the best tea things before her'.[10] The sofa table, however, was constructed with two ornamental end supports which were united by a horizontal stretcher rail or was supported on a central pedestal, mounted on a platform with splayed feet.

The placing of various small occasional tables about the living-rooms was considered a genteel practice, and now general in the houses of well-to-do people. Rectangular tables with end supports; little work tables; sets or nests of three or four tables which were called respectively 'trio' or 'quartetto' tables (Pl. 59); Pembroke and occasional tables – these were made in increasingly large numbers early in the nineteenth century. A desire for ingenious constructions and for novelty of form perhaps signified the approaching break-up of good design. One author observed that it now evaded 'the most skilful artists to produce any new forms'.[11]

In September 1801, Fanny Burney, who was attempting to furnish her small cottage (Camilla Cottage) at trifling expense, wrote to Dr Burney thus: '... Charles brought us the *tapis* – so that, in fact, we have yet bought nothing for our best room – and meant – for our own share – to buy a table ... and if my dearest father will be so good – and so naughty at once, as to crown our *salle d'Audience* with a gift we shall prize beyond all others, we can think only of a table. Not a dining one, but a sort of table for a little work and a few books, *en gala* – without which, a room looks always forlorn.' In the event, Dr Burney supplied two card tables which, it was said, would 'do a thousand times better than any Tavolina', and which were to be placed on the two sides of the room. 'I think,' wrote his daughter, 'no room looks really comfortable, or even quite furnished, without two tables – one to keep the wall and take upon itself the dignity of a little tidyness, the other to stand here, there, and everywhere, and hold letters and *make the agreeable*.'[12]

Interiors had lost the quality of formal grace which had belonged to the eighteenth century and were more variously and completely furnished.*

* An account of the London 'rout' of the period (held at a late hour of the evening) would suggest that this form of entertainment necessitated an extensive preparation – although guests stayed but a short while before leaving to visit other houses. Louis Simond has phrased his account of this aspect of fashionable town life thus: 'For two hours [after dinner], or nearly, there is a pause; at ten a *redoublement* comes on. This is the great

Fewer card tables were made and these were of comparatively simple construction. About 1810 rosewood and zebra wood were in favour, and decoration consisted often of an inlay of brass, holly or ebony. A straight-fronted table on tapered legs with outward curving feet (both back legs pivoting on the frame) vied in popularity with a D-shaped table, opening to a roughly circular form, supported on pedestal and claws. The combination games and work table would appear to have received more attention from makers, and a number of complex examples were produced. 'This ornamental piece of furniture,' wrote George Smith, 'will admit of every variety in execution and where expense is not an object, the whole frame may be gold, and the ornament in bronze.' [14] One variety of rectangular work table was fitted with flaps which folded back to disclose a chess board. The table had a shallow drawer and workbag below and was designed with lyre-shaped end supports.

Most large pedestal library tables followed of necessity a traditional form which offered the workshops little scope for novelty, save in such details of ornament as engaged columns with lotus leaf headings, ebonized inlaid stringing lines or metal mounts and lion-paw feet in the Empire taste. A library writing-table made for Stourhead, Wilts., in 1805, by Thomas Chippendale the younger, is, however, designed with supplementary, rounded D-shaped ends which are supported by four free-standing 'therms with Egyptian heads'.[15] As a consequence the table is unusually large,

crisis of dress, of noise, and of rapidity – a universal hubbub. ... Great assemblies are called routs or parties; but the people who give them, in their invitations only say, that they will be *at home* such a day, and this some weeks beforehand. The house in which this takes place is frequently stripped from top to bottom; beds, drawers, and all but ornamental furniture is carried out of sight, to make room for a crowd of well-dressed people, received at the door of the principal apartment by the mistress of the house standing, who smiles at every new comer with a look of acquaintance. Nobody sits; there is no conversation, no cards, no music; only elbowing, turning, and winding from room to room ... every curtain, and every shutter of every window wide open, shewing apartments all in a blaze of light, with heads innumerable, black and white (powdered or not), in continual motion.' [13]

being more than 8 feet in length. George Smith presented in his *Household Furniture* (1808) a table of similar character, observing that 'the chimeras may be carved in wood or bronzed'. His design for a writing-table (Pl. 60A) in the same taste was less complex: the rectangular top was supported at each of the four corners by a stylized, full-length Egyptian figure; shallow drawers were contained in the frieze, decorated with applied masks and a formalized pattern executed in an inlay of ebony. A large number of plainer writing-tables following this construction were made. The main alternative type, designed with a central turned column and inward-curving, reeded legs, usually four in number, came into general use as the century advanced. The writing-table with a tambour front was, according to Sheraton, writing in 1803, 'almost out of use'.[16] Many specimens of the circular drum top table survive. Usually a series of drawers was fitted in the frieze, but in some instances the area was divided into partitions for books. This arrangement was rather more convenient in use when applied to tables of rectangular or polygonal form. In later years the central support took the form of a massive pedestal, resting on a solid base with animal feet.

Long, sectional dining-tables were produced in considerable variety. The supports were frequently in the form of central, turned columns with curved legs. The separate sections of the table were bolted together as required for use. Sheraton, writing in 1803, stated: '... there are various sorts now in use, and some under the protection of his Majesty's patent. The common useful dining tables are upon pillar and claws, generally four claws to each pillar, with brass castors. A dining table of this kind may be made to any size, by having a sufficient quantity of pillar and claw parts, for between each of them is a loose flap, fixed by means of iron straps and buttons, so that they are easily taken off and put aside.'[17] A fine rectangular dining-table of similar construction at the Town Hall, Liverpool, dates from about 1820.[18] It is supported on four short thick columns designed with spreading bases, heavily carved with acanthus and horizontal lion-paw feet. An allowance of 2 feet to each person sitting at table was regarded as giving ample room to diners, and a number of attempts had been made to invent a new, satisfactory form of enlargement; several patents were taken out, those by Richard Gillow (1800) and by George Remington (1807) being notable. The type with telescopic, diamond-shaped underframing was so constructed as to be provided with straight turned legs at each corner and at the edges.

The large circular table was again in use (Pl. 58). Louis Simond, on his visit here, observed that 'among people of fashion the master and mistress generally abandon the ends of the table, – which indeed has often no end, being round'.[19]

A table of this variety, with heavy circular base or plinth, is illustrated by George Smith (1808), and was 'intended to do away the necessity' and the 'inconvenience' of 'large projecting claws'.[20]

A number of smaller circular or octagonal tables, designed with carved and gilt lion monopodia supports (Pl. 55, left), and with brass ornamentation, were provided with a platform at knee level or rested on a shaped plinth. They were in use as occasional tables, mostly dating from the first decade of the century.

During the earlier Regency period the side-table continued to be made as dining-room furniture. This type resembled that in use in the middle eighteenth century which was referred to as the 'side-board table'. Specimens with carved lion monopodia supports, and sometimes provided at their base with a low platform or plinth, survive in mahogany and occasionally in other woods such as rosewood. The sideboard proper, a large article, with carved decoration of similar character, was fitted usually with an elaborate brass gallery and contained shallow drawers in the frieze. In one variety, pairs of animal supports, grouped at each end of the piece and resting on separate square plinths, flanked a standing cellaret, which was sometimes of sarcophagus form (established soon after 1800) and was customarily placed below the sideboard in a central position.

The more commodious pedestal type sideboard returned to favour during the early nineteenth century. Sheraton had stated 'the most fashionable sideboards' to be 'those without cellerets, or any kind of drawer, having massy ornamented legs, and moulded frames'. But George Smith, a few years later, showed in *Household Furniture* (1808) a preponderance of plates illustrating examples which were designed with a centre table and flanking pedestals. There would seem to have been a revived taste for these pieces. The pedestal cupboards, fitted as cellaret and plate warmer, were characterized by a slight taper. Surmounting knife boxes were also of tapered rectangular shape. It was still customary for the glasses and cutlery to be washed by servants in the dining-room. Sideboards were later made with a superstructure or with a solid back-piece and attained ungainly, massive proportions.

A variety of the dumb waiter, still at this date considered a very useful piece of furniture, is found with tiers of rectangular shape, the upper sometimes having hinged flaps. A tripod base gave way to a four-legged pillar-and-claw support, resembling that employed for some dining-tables.

The 'supper Canterbury' introduced as an accessory piece in the dining-room and also intended for use when servants were not present, held 'knives, forks, and plates at that end, which is made circular on purpose'.[21] It was, in effect, a deep, partitioned tray with one semi-circular end and was supported on four turned legs. (The term 'Canterbury' was also descriptive of a small music stand.)

The mahogany four-post bed, very heavily curtained, retained general popularity throughout the earlier nineteenth century. A silk, chintz, a printed calico or 'Merino damask' was recommended for the drapery, and was trimmed with tassels and fringes. 'In a climate so variable as that of Britain,' wrote George Smith in 1826, 'where the transitions are so sudden from cold to heat, and from wet to dry, &c. one uniform system, both as regards dress as well as the fitting up of our apartments, has been found the most beneficial and conducive to health; and in point of comfort the old English four post bedstead with its curtains and drapery, will always be found to claim a preference before any other, although it does not follow from hence, that it is necessary to close the curtains so effectually as to exclude the free ingress and egress of fresh air. . . .' [22] The proportions of the bed became progressively heavier as the century advanced; and curtains and festooned valance were disposed with little elegance. The nature of Victorian taste was already foreshadowed in the cumbersome designs for foot posts (Pl. 57) recommended by George Smith, 1826, which were described as being rather more than 9 feet in height, and as requiring a scantling of mahogany of $5\frac{1}{2}$ or $6\frac{1}{2}$ inches square.

The lighter 'tent' or 'field' bed was suitable for a single person and for smaller rooms and was commonly to be found in villas and superior cottages (Pl. 62). The posts which were lower, sometimes about 5 feet high, were masked by gathered curtains. 'Formerly,' explained Smith, 'the curtains adapted to this kind of bedstead became in themselves too close a covering,' but now 'can be partially drawn aside to the head and foot.' A shaped and rising roof or 'tent' was supported on curved rods uniting the tops of head and foot posts. According to Sheraton, field beds had been so called from 'being similar in size and shape to those really used in camps', which were usually rather less than 6 feet high, to the crown of the tester, and were made with 'folding tester laths, either hexagonal or elliptical shaped and hinged so as to fold close together'.[23] Beds of this nature were in general use in the eighteenth century. Horace Walpole mentions a tent bed in a letter to Sir Horace Mann of 1752: 'Our beauties,' he wrote, 'are travelling Paris-ward: Lady Caroline Petersham and Lady Coventry are just gone thither. . . . [Lady Coventry] has taken a turn of vast fondness for her lord: Lord Downe met them at Calais, and offered her a tent-bed, for fear of bugs in the inns. "Oh!" said she, "I had rather be bit to death, than lie one night from my dear Cov!" '[24] Servants and children often slept in field beds.

The 'French bedstead' consisted in its simplest form of a kind of couch, placed against the wall and again intended for the use of a single person. (French beds were imported, and were adapted to English designs. They were often boat-shaped, with scrolled ends, in mahogany or painted wood, and with applied brass enrichments in the classical taste.) The drapery was suspended over a pole, which projected from the wall and was centred over the bed at a height of perhaps 10 feet. The stuff hung in loose folds over lower subsidiary poles which were placed immediately over each end of the bed, and was by this means kept free of the sleeper. A more elaborate type of bed was surmounted by a high, domed canopy at the head, with drapery hanging down to the floor, and resembled in form the half-tester bed which had enjoyed occasional favour as early as the late seventeenth century.

A greater diversity is apparent in Regency bedroom furniture; mahogany, satinwood, rosewood, and painted or grained soft woods were variously employed. The fitted dressing-table gave place to a plainer and more commodious piece purposed to be used in conjunction with a detached dressing-glass. An example illustrated in George Smith's *Household Furniture*, 1808, was intended to be made in mahogany or satinwood with an inlaid decoration of ebony, and was of ample proportions (Pl. 60B). The table, supported on solid end pedestals, terminating back and front in scrolled feet, was provided with three shallow and two deep drawers and a wide shelf beneath. The drawers, shown without handles, were to be governed by a spring release. A practical and popular design for this type of table in which short turned legs were united immediately above the base by a low platform, was derived from an earlier pedestal form. The table was straight-fronted and devoid of constructional refinements.

Small modifications only were made to the design of the

chest of drawers. Most examples were bow- or straight-fronted. Reeding was a popular ornamental device, and many chest fronts were framed by reeded columns attached at the angles. After about 1810, the columns were often spirally reeded and are found used in conjunction with lion mask and ring handles which are characteristic of the period. The deep, plain frieze above the two top drawers was a development of the last years of the eighteenth century. The bracket foot was replaced by a slender, turned foot of taller proportions.

The dressing-glass was most often of oblong shape and swung between turned balusters fixed to a box stand of small drawers. Alternatively, the standards terminated in trestle feet which were tied by a turned stretcher, and the stand was dispensed with – a construction similar to that employed for the large, upright, full-length cheval glass, appropriately termed a 'Psyche' (Pl. 55, right). For some glasses a lyre-shaped support took the place of a simple baluster form. The mirror frame was of flat or convex section and was cross-banded. Most of these articles were plainly constructed and, apart from those with a slight bow to the box stand, were unshaped. The keyhole surround, knob handles, and small ball feet were sometimes of ivory or bone.

The long, oblong overmantel glass, intended to be placed immediately above the chimney shelf and to extend over the greater part of its length, continued in fashion during the Regency period. Larger and more elaborate glasses, which were usually gilded and of an undistinguished architectural character, were composed of three sections: the central, bevelled mirror plate was flanked by two smaller ones of upright rectangular shape, divided by narrow moulding strips. These pieces were designed with a straight cornice and with pilasters or colonnettes at each side. Sometimes the frieze was deep and decorated with classical figure subjects in relief.

The circular mirror frame, familiarly surmounted by an eagle with outstretched wings, or with carved foliage, sometimes with candle branches at the sides and a base of pendant acanthus, was fitted with a convex plate which had the effect of strengthening the colour and taking off 'the coarseness of objects by contracting them'. This type of mirror frame, an innovation of the late eighteenth century, was extremely popular and was made in varying sizes, the smallest being rather less than 12 inches in diameter. The gilt frame, in many instances enclosing an ebonized reeded fillet, was of cavetto section and sometimes ornamented with small and regularly spaced gilt balls. An alternative enrichment was the twisted rope form. The outer edge of the frame was commonly moulded with reeding and banded at intervals with crossing ribbons.

A plainer and graceful type of upright frame, in the austere taste prevailing at the end of the first decade of the century, was surmounted by a pediment in the Greek style; square bosses faced with paterae, were placed at the corners of the framing.

Various kinds of shelved dwarf cabinets and low bookcases were supplied at this period to supplement the larger pieces constructed in two stages. The low cabinet or cupboard, enclosed by doors fitted with a decorative wire trellis backed by silk curtains, was designed both with and without a shelved superstructure. Light bookcases were now used in sitting-rooms and sometimes were of a movable nature, being made to house books on either side. The circular revolving bookstand had been introduced by about 1810.

A secretaire cabinet in two stages, in the Victoria and Albert Museum, is of the smaller dimensions then fashionable (Pl. 61). It is little more than 5 feet in height, and is made of mahogany with a veneer of zebra wood and with satinwood bandings. Two water-colour drawings, signed by J. Baynes and dated 1808, which are framed behind the glazed astragal doors of the low upper stage, provide an indication as to the year of origin. The projecting lower stage is flanked by pilasters mounted with Egyptian heads in metal. The secretaire drawer which lets down on a quadrant is fitted with small drawers and pigeon holes of satinwood and surmounts a shelved cupboard. The flat mouldings and straight severe lines of the cabinet, the use of zebra wood, and a concession to the Egyptian taste apparent in the mounts suggest a period of manufacture of about 1810.

Pieces of this nature were not on the whole greatly affected by the excesses of later Regency styles. But from the closing years of the reign of George IV, deterioration in design and a poverty of invention became as obvious in case furniture as elsewhere. The bureau bookcase, while sometimes of pleasing proportions, exemplifies the decline. The pattern of the glazing bars was comparatively coarse; the form and the detail of the carved columns which often framed the lower portion were heavy and meaningless. Pediments reminiscent of Grecian models were to be found without any supporting architectural members.

The Cabinet-maker and Upholsterer's Guide was published by George Smith in 1826. The work was somewhat pretentious in character and contained lengthy treatises on geometry and perspective, as well as the large number of engravings for furniture and interior decoration, of which many were coloured, and which are more interesting. The designs possessed little original merit, however, and reflected the impending bankruptcy of taste in England. Smith's tone was unctuous, but his attempt to find pleasing and original forms for furniture was unsuccessful; his incongruous employment of debased Grecian and Gothic ornament, invariably of coarse conception, was most unhappy. He deplored 'the necessity for economy urged by many at the present day'. But such furniture of the reign of George IV is not without attraction, in so far as the style of the Regency is retained.

'The Octangular Tent Room' (Pl. 63), reproduced in colour as frontispiece to the 1826 *Guide*, provided a suggestion for the boudoir of a lady of rank and fortune. It was to answer 'as a morning room for the receiving of visitors', and, in the evening, 'thrown open for the reception of a numerous assembly', to make one of a suite of apartments. The rather gaudy splendour of the trappings, although at variance with furniture of archaeological cast, is in the tradition of the Regency and imparts a consistent style to the room. A 'loo table', here of octagonal form, is set down in the centre of the room beneath large, ornamental tassels dependent from a rosette in the roof. The table is supported on a massive central pillar rising from a base with three feet, and is intended to be constructed of rosewood, with gilt enrichments. Mahogany at this period was thought appropriate to the library and dining-room, as rosewood to the drawing-room and boudoir.

Seating accommodation is provided by three varieties of chair, a pair of ottomans placed in the window recesses, and a *chaise longue* with scrolled end and stumpy, top-shaped legs. The design of both elbow and single chairs is uncertain. In each case the front legs are substantial and clumsy, approximating in form to an elongated, inverted cone; the backs finish 'with a broad and hollow yoke', the marked concavity of this ungainly top rail being purposed to ease the body of the chair's occupant. The cabinet is also of quasi-Grecian description. The pediment takes the form of two horizontal, opposed S-scrolls, and both the upper and lower stage comprising the body of the piece are faced with a pair of round-headed glazed windows, backed by curtains but without glazing bars.[25]

The Regency style was long-lived, and indeed survived until the early years of the reign of Victoria. Competent, if uninspired, designs of Regency character were published in such works as *The Practical Cabinet Maker, Upholsterer and Complete Decorator*, by Peter and Michael Angelo Nicholson, 1826 (it is significant in this connexion that the plates were re-issued in an edition of 1835), and Ackermann's *Repository of Arts*, published in monthly parts from 1809–28. Yet Smith, in *The Cabinet-maker and Upholsterer's Guide* of 1826, seems to have looked forward to a new style. He dismissed his own *Household Furniture*, of 1808, as having 'become wholly obsolete and inapplicable to its intended purpose, by the change of taste and rapid improvements' of the last twenty years. In his pages, Victorian taste of the period of the Great Exhibition was anticipated, despite complacent mention of the current Etruscan, Roman, Gothic, and French styles, and obligatory tribute to the Greek. He was constrained to admit that 'the spirit for design' was at length checked and weakened; he knew the cabinet trade to be commercialized.

NOTES TO CHAPTER II

1. *Letters of Horace Walpole*, ed. by Peter Cunningham, 1861–6, vol. IX, p. 14. To the Countess of Ossory, from Strawberry Hill, Sept. 17th, 1785.
2. Richard Brown, *Rudiments of Drawing Cabinet and Upholstery Furniture*, 1820.
3. Thomas Sheraton, *Cabinet Dictionary*, 1803, p. 117.
4. George Smith, *Cabinet-maker and Upholsterer's Guide*, 1826, p. 194.
5. *The Journal of Mrs Arbuthnot, 1820–1832*, ed. by Francis Bamford and the Duke of Wellington, 1950, vol. I, p. 53.
6. John Evelyn, *Sylva: or a Discourse of Forest Trees*, 5th edit., 1825, vol. I, p. 172.
7. Sheraton, *op. cit.*, pp. 289–90.
8. *The Hamwood Papers*, ed. by Mrs G. H. Bell, 1930, p. 91.
9. *Farington Diary*, ed. by James Greig, 1922–8, vol. II, pp. 218–9. March 31st, 1804.
10. Jane Austen, *The Watsons*, written *c.* 1804.
11. Brown, *op. cit.*
12. Letter of Sept. 6th, 1801, quoted by Constance Hill, *Juniper Hall*, 1904, pp. 258–9.
13. L. Simond, *Journal of a Tour and Residence in Great Britain by 'A French Traveller'*, 1815, vol. I, pp. 27–8.
14. In 1808.
15. Illustrated by M. Jourdain, *Regency Furniture*, 1948 edit., Fig. 127.
16. Sheraton, *op. cit.*, p. 316.
17. Sheraton, *op. cit.*, p. 195.
18. Illustrated by Percy Macquoid and Ralph Edwards, *The Dictionary of English Furniture*, 1924–7, vol. III, Tables – Dining, Fig. 30; revised edit. by Ralph Edwards, 1954, vol. III, Tables – Dining and Hall, Fig. 36.
19. Simond, *op. cit.*, vol. I, p. 45.
20. The type is to be found also in Smith's work of 1826.
21. Sheraton, *op. cit.*, p. 127.

22. Smith, *op. cit.*, p. 181.
23. Sheraton, *op. cit.*, pp. 123–4.
24. Cunningham, *op. cit.*, vol. II, pp. 293–4. To Sir Horace Mann, from Arlington Street, July 27th, 1752.
25. See *Regency Furniture*, by the late Margaret Jourdain (reprinted 1948), 'Country Life' Ltd, for a full and authoritative account of the furniture of the period 1795–1820.

GLOSSARY OF TERMS

ACANTHUS. A conventionalized leaf exemplified as classical ornament in the capitals of the Corinthian and Composite orders; frequently found in mahogany furniture, 1725–60; less frequently in that of the seventeenth century (Fig. 52).

ALPACA. A silken fabric, made from the hair of the Peruvian sheep.

AMORINI. Cupids; a *motif* much in favour during the latter half of the seventeenth century, and again after 1750 (Fig. 29).

ANTHEMION ORNAMENT. Of Greek derivation; related in form to the flower of the honeysuckle. Popularized in England during the second half of the eighteenth century, in particular by Adam and later during the Regency period (Figs. 79B and 101).

APRON PIECE. The ornamental member situated below the seat rail of a chair or settee, sometimes uniting the legs at their junction with the rail; also found below the frieze of cabinet stands and side tables (Pl. 31).

ARABESQUE (ARABIAN) ORNAMENT. An inlaid, painted or carved enrichment of flat surfaces, consisting of a fanciful intertwining of leaves, scrolls or animal forms; featured in the floral and 'seaweed' marquetry decoration of *c.* 1700, and the gesso decoration of table tops, 1690–1725, and later in work of the Adam period.

ARCADED DECORATION. Frontal representation of a series of arches on colonnettes or pillars. In use *c.* 1610–70 (Pl. 6).

ASTRAGAL. A small moulding, of plain, semi-circular section; loosely descriptive also of the glazing bars of case furniture made from *c.* 1750 (Pl. 61).

ATLASS. An imported Eastern fabric with a rich surface; a silk-satin in popular demand during the walnut period for use as a bed hanging.

BACK STOOL. A term current in the seventeenth and eighteenth centuries for an upholstered single chair.

BAIZE. A coarse lining cloth introduced from the Low Countries before 1600.

BALUSTER. A turned member of columnar form, variously twisted, straight, tapered, and vase-shaped (Figs. 13 and 25).

BALL FOOT. Mainly employed during the late seventeenth century as a terminal to cabinets or to the turned legs of tables, etc. *See* BUN FOOT.

BAMBOO TURNING. Executed in a soft wood, usually painted or japanned and simulating the natural appearance of the bamboo; normally met with in furniture in the Chinese taste, dating from the later eighteenth century or from the Regency.

BANDING. A decorative, inlaid border or broad edging of contrasting wood or woods. In the later eighteenth century, broad bandings in various exotic woods were used; satinwood in particular was laid against mahogany. *Straight banding* is one which has been cut along the length of the grain; *cross-banding*, across the grain; and *feather banding*, at an angle between the two former. A herringbone inlay and a plain cross-banding were frequently employed in walnut furniture (Fig. 28).

BEAD. (1) A moulding resembling a string of beads, and (2) a small, plain moulding of semi-circular section.

BEAD AND REEL. A decorative border found in the form of inlay in the sixteenth and seventeenth centuries, particularly on 'Nonesuch' chests; also, a smaller variety of bead moulding was used in the eighteenth century and consisted of alternating round and oblong forms.

BERGERE (BARJAIR, BURJAIR). An armchair with upholstered sides; during the eighteenth century the term was descriptive also of a variety of couch.

BOLECTION MOULDING. A projecting moulding of ogee shape, raised round a panel.

BRACKET FOOT. Introduced *c.* 1690 and used on chests of drawers, cabinets, etc. (Pls. 22, 34, and 42).

BRANCHES. A term used for chandeliers, seventeenth to eighteenth century.

BROCADE. A rich silk, figured or striped, and worked originally in gold or silver thread.

BULB. The bulb-like part of the turned supports of furniture (dining tables, court cupboards, etc.), of the Elizabethan and Jacobean periods; often carved with an Ionic capital above a turned neck, and attaining extravagant proportions; of Flemish origin, this member was usually divided by a moulding into the 'cup and cover' form (Figs. 10A and B, and 14).

BUN FOOT. A flattened ball foot, introduced in the last half of the seventeenth century (Pl. 12).

CABOCHON. As in the form of a gem, one which is oval, polished, and usually convex, but not cut into facets; this *motif*, bordered by ornamental carving, is found, in particular, on the knees of chair legs of *c.* 1740 (Fig. 39).

CABRIOLE LEG. Curved outwards at the knee, which is rounded, and reversing and tapering into an inward (concave) curve below; variously terminated by club, hoof, bun, paw, claw-and-ball or scroll feet; in general use during the first half of the eighteenth century (Figs. 43, 48, 49, and 60C and D).

CALAMANCO. A glossy, woollen material, plain or patterned, manufactured in England and Flanders. It is chequered in the warp, thus the checks are visible on one side only.

CAMLET. Originally a costly Eastern fabric made from the hair of the Angora goat; later European substitutes of wool, silk, and hair (Brussels camlets were reputed to be of fine quality) were variously figured or stamped, watered, and waved.

CANTED. A surface which is bevelled, chamfered, or obliquely faced (Fig. 42).

CAP. The heading of a pilaster (Pl. 22).

CAQUETEUSE. A (conversational) chair, adopted in Scotland from France in the late sixteenth century, with triangular seat, narrow back, and spreading arms; a woman's chair. English examples are known.

CARCASE. The 'body' of a piece of furniture, to which the veneers are applied.

CARD-CUT ORNAMENT. Chinese latticing, carved in low relief; a feature of 'Chinese Chippendale' (Pl. 38).

CARPET. Formerly (until the late Georgian period), any thick fabric covering for table, cupboard, floor, etc.

CARTOUCHE. A tablet in the form of a scroll, or sheet of paper with rolled-up ends, sometimes bearing arms, an ornamental monogram, or an inscription. A variant of the *escutcheon*, it is often found on the centre of apron pieces or as the centre of cabinet pediments (Pl. 38).

CARYATID. A female sculptured figure employed (as a column) as a support to an entablature or mouldings. In the early seventeenth century found on chest and cupboard fronts; again, popular from the close of the eighteenth century (Pl. 6).

CAVETTO. A hollowed moulding forming in profile the quadrant of a circle; a prominent and comparatively large feature of the cornice on some case furniture (Fig. 42).

CEILER. The head of the medieval 'hangyd' bed, and made of fabric. Soon after the introduction of the posted bed (by 1500), the ceiler was replaced by a wooden headboard; and later, the tester or roof, also, was made of wood.

CHAMFERED. A surface or edge which has been smoothed off, bevelled, or cut away from the square.

CHANNELLING. Parallel grooving, often found in furniture of the oak period (Fig. 2).

CHEQUER ORNAMENT. An inlay of light and dark woods forming a pattern of squares like that of a chess board; decorative border much used during the sixteenth and seventeenth centuries (Pl. 3).

CHEVRON. A moulding or inlay of zig-zag pattern.

CHINTZ. A glazed calico, printed in colours on a light ground.

CHIP CARVING. Rough, shallow ornament obtained by chisel and gouge; the roundel decoration of early chests; persisted throughout the oak period (Fig. 1).

CLAW AND BALL FOOT. Of Oriental derivation; terminal to the cabriole leg representing an animal's paw, or dragon's or bird's claw, clutching a ball; fashionable 1710–60 (Fig. 40A).

CLUB FOOT. The commonest terminal to the cabriole leg, in use from *c.* 1705 to late in the eighteenth century. *See* PAD FOOT.

CLUSTERED COLUMNS. A *motif*, found in medieval architecture, adopted in the Gothic taste of the mid eighteenth century; having the form of pillars clustered together.

COCK BEADING. Astragal moulding; small and applied to the edges of drawer fronts, 1730–1800 (Pls. 34 and 46).

CONSOLE TABLE. A wall table supported by two brackets; the term is applied also to the side table, customarily surmounted by a long mirror or pier glass.

COQUILLAGE. Carved ornament in the form of a shell (Fr. *coquille*, a shellfish); of common occurrence on mid eighteenth century furniture in the French style, especially on the centre of the seat rail of a chair or settee (Pl. 37).

CORBEL. A bracket (architectural).

CUP AND COVER. *See* BULB.

CUPID'S BOW CRESTING. Introduced *c.* 1730 and frequently found forming the top rail of a chair or chair-back settee of the Chippendale period (Pl. 40).

CUSHION FRIEZE. The section of the frieze which is of convex or cushion shape.

CUSPS. The apexes between small arcs in Gothic tracery. The *motif* was revived in the 'Gothic' furniture of the mid eighteenth century (Fig. 3).

CYMA RECTA. Ogee moulding, concave in the upper part and convex below; opposed to the '*cyma reversa*'.

DAMASK. (1) A silk fabric (originally from Damascus) woven with a rich, raised pattern, usually floral; and substitutes of wool or cotton. (2) A twilled table linen, of which the pattern is made apparent by opposite reflections of lights from its surface.

DENTIL. The under moulding of a cornice consisting of a series of small rectangular blocks or 'teeth' (Pl. 42).

DIAPER. Geometrical pattern formed by lines crossing diamond-wise and enclosing dots or some other diversification; used mostly for border decoration.

DOLPHIN MASK. A *motif* which was introduced into England in the late seventeenth century, popularized by William Kent and subsequently by Chippendale and his contemporaries.

DOWEL PIN. Round, headless wooden peg used to fasten together two pieces of timber.

EAGLE'S HEAD. A popular termination to the arms of chairs and settees of the early Georgian period. The round convex mirror, which enjoyed a great vogue *c.* 1800, was commonly crowned by the full eagle (Fig. 38).

EBONIZED WOOD. Stained black so as to simulate ebony.

EGG AND TONGUE, EGG AND DART, EGG AND ANCHOR. Enrichments carved usually on ovolo mouldings; the forms are repetitive and represented alternately (Fig. 45).

EGYPTIAN DETAIL. Introduced before 1800, and extending in vogue for the first decade or two of the nineteenth century; prominent *motifs* included the sphinx, the lion head, the Egyptian terminal figure, and the lotus-headed capital (Pl. 60A).

ESCUTCHEON. In the eighteenth century a popular central *motif* of the pediment of cabinets and mirror frames (Pl. 38).

FAUTEUIL. A French arm-chair, to be distinguished from the *bergère* in that it is not upholstered beneath the arms.

FIELDED PANEL. A panel with bevelled edges, enclosing a flat central field (Fig. 41).

FINIAL. Knob or crowning ornament, sometimes in the form of

a carved vase with drapery; found at the intersection of stretchers to tables, chairs and stools, on cabinets, and at the top of pole screens, etc. (Figs. 30 and 84).

FLUTING. Grooves, concave and semi-circular in shape; characteristic of the last quarter of the eighteenth century (although in use from the sixteenth century) and succeeded by reeding (Figs. 61 and 99, right).

FRETS. Open, fretted galleries (pierced) were usually laminated, the designs being often in the 'Chinese' taste; fretted ornament to friezes and to legs was sometimes cut 'in the solid', sometimes applied (Pls. 36 and 38).

GADROONING, NULLING, AND LOBING. Carved ornamental edging, of repetitive forms, concave or convex, upright or twisted. A popular ornament during the early Oak period and again in the mid eighteenth century, when gadrooned metal strips were employed on some pieces (Fig. 53B).

GALON. A braid, woven of silk, gold or silver thread.

GESSO. A composition of chalk and parchment size, carved in low relief and gilded. Applied to pieces of furniture, particularly side tables, mirror frames, and chairs, *c.* 1690–1725.

GREEK FRET. *See* KEY PATTERN.

GUERIDON. A small pedestal stand for a candlestick.

GUILLOCHE. Carved ornament found on oak furniture of the sixteenth and seventeenth centuries and throughout the eighteenth century, taking the form of braided, twisted, or symmetrically interlaced bands or ribbons which make a continuous series of interlaced circles.

HERRING-BONE, OR FEATHER BANDING. A decorative border of inlay characteristic of furniture of the walnut period and distinct from cross-banding in that two strips of veneer compose the banding and are laid together at an angle of approximately 90° one with the other, and so as to form a herring-bone or feather pattern against the ground veneer (Fig. 28). *See* BANDING.

HIPPING. An extension of the cabriole leg above the seat rail, usually found in fine chairs and settees of the first half of the eighteenth century (Pl. 28B).

HOOF FOOT. An early terminal to the cabriole leg, fashionable 1695–1720 (Pl. 19).

HORSEHAIR. Hair cloth. Covering introduced in late eighteenth century; at a later date sometimes patterned and dyed; recommended by Chippendale for use on chairs.

HUSK. With 'honeysuckle' and 'wheat-ear' a favourite ornament on furniture of the Adam and Hepplewhite periods. Festoons of husks (in a repeating or diminishing pattern) popularly incorporated in the design of chair backs (Fig. 60B).

INDIAN MASK. The Indian mask with plumed head-dress was a *motif*, rare at the end of the seventeenth century, popular in the first two decades of the eighteenth century, particularly in mirror frames (Fig. 32).

INLAY. Let into the solid (1550–1650); to be distinguished from marquetry, introduced *c.* 1680.

KEY PATTERN. Frieze, border or strip ornament; a repetitive pattern, composed of lines set at right angles to one another (Pl. 35).

KNURL FOOT. A reversed whorl or French scroll foot; the scrolling is inward turning, *i.e.* on the inner side of the foot. Mid eighteenth century.

LAMBREQUIN. Ornamental drapery, with the lower edge of jagged outline, hanging at the top of a window, a bed, or from a mantelshelf.

LINENFOLD OR PARCHMENT PATTERN. Of Flemish origin, fashionable in England *c.* 1480–1550 and used as a panel decoration – at first in the form of a linen pattern without folds; subsequently with few folds (ogee shaped at top and bottom) and plain; later *fleur-de-luced* or carved with grapes, tassels, or other emblems; and finally with incised lines representing the embroidery of napkins (Fig. 4).

LION MASK. Carved ornamental feature, most often found on the knee of the cabriole leg, 1720–40, and sometimes used in conjunction with the lion's-paw foot. The *motif* was revived during the Regency.

LOBING. *See* GADROONING.

LOTUS. *Motif* popular during the period of Egyptian taste, *c.* 1810.

LUNETTE. Fan-shaped *motif*, with carved decoration, frequently found on oak furniture; revived in painted or inlaid form in the late eighteenth century (Fig. 16).

MIRROR. About 1800 was more particularly descriptive of the convex glass then fashionable.

MITRE JOINT. Employed on mouldings framing a panel, each of the two edges being cut at an angle of 45° (Fig. 14).

MODILLION. In furniture of architectural character, a series of projecting brackets which are found in the pediment and below the cornice.

MOHAIR. A fabric made from the hair of the Angora goat; used in furnishing in the early eighteenth century.

MOIRÉ. A 'watered' silk, closely woven with a lustrous surface.

MONEY PATTERN. An ornamental enrichment which has the appearance of a line of regularly disposed, overlapping discs or coins. *See* GUILLOCHE.

MOREEN. A coarse woollen fabric, sometimes used for upholstery in the late seventeenth and eighteenth centuries.

NANKEEN. A plain cotton fabric, named after its place of manufacture (Nanking).

NULLING. *See* GADROONING.

OGEE. In the shape of a double curve, concave below and convex above. *See* CYMA RECTA.

OVOLO MOULDING. A wide convex moulding, in section a quarter circle or quarter ellipse.

OYSTERSHELL. The small branches of walnut, laburnum, and some other trees were cut transversely and laid together as a decorative veneer. This oystershell veneering, used for cabinet doors and drawer fronts, was introduced from Holland in the late seventeenth century and remained fashionable for some years (Fig. 21).

PAD FOOT. Resembling the club foot but set on a disk (Fig. 43).

PALMETTE. Conventionalized palm leaf ornament, resembling a spread fan.

PARQUETRY. Used contemporaneously with marquetry, sometimes in association with it, and consisting of a geometric mosaic of woods, often in the form of an inlay (Fig. 21).

PATERA. A flat, round or oval disk, applied or carved as ornament, or painted on satinwood in low relief (Pl. 56, above).

PAW FOOT. A terminal to the cabriole leg, carved in the form of a lion's paw; mid eighteenth century (Fig. 40c).

PEDIMENT. Member surmounting the cornice of bookcases, cupboards, cabinets, etc.; the unbroken form was popular 1675–1760, the broken 1715–1800 (Pls. 37 and 43).

PIECRUST DECORATION. A raised edging, commonly employed in the decoration of mahogany tea and china tables during the third quarter of the eighteenth century; scalloped and resembling the outer edge of a piecrust.

PLINTH. The low square base of a column; a foundation supporting the body of a piece of furniture.

POPLIN. A silk and worsted fabric, with corded surface, introduced from France in the early eighteenth century.

QUATREFOIL. Gothic decorative *motif* in the form of four leaves – similarly 'trefoil' three leaves, 'cinquefoil' five leaves.

RAM'S HEAD. A mask; a favourite *motif* of Adam, found in wood (carved, gilded, inlaid, and painted) and as a metal enrichment.

REEDING. The reverse of fluting; convex, raised ornamentation in the form of a series of pipes or reeds, frequently found on chair and table legs, etc., at the end of the eighteenth century (Fig. 94, left and right).

RIBAND AND ROSETTES. An ornamental moulding strip, very popular in the third quarter of the eighteenth century, which consists of a series of rosettes alternated by ribands.

ROMAYNE CARVING. Decorative *motifs* taking the form of small profile heads in medallions, introduced in the early sixteenth century.

SCAGLIOLA. A substitute for marble (at first imported from Italy) composed of plaster of Paris and glue, to which small pieces of marble and other ingredients were added, and coloured in imitation of marbles or other ornamental stone. It takes a high polish, and was in much demand in England in the eighteenth century.

SCROLL FOOT. The 'French' scroll foot became fashionable in the mid eighteenth century. The leg terminates in an outward upturned scroll (Fig. 40B).

SCRUTOIR. A secretary or writing cabinet. The term was almost obsolete by *c.* 1800 (Fig. 36).

SHELL (SCALLOP). One of the most popular ornamental *motifs* of the first three quarters of the eighteenth century, although in use at an earlier date. In the Walnut period, treatment was comparatively formal: in what was a very usual form the exterior of the shell was represented, arranged in a simple fan pattern, often with dependent husk(s); at a later date the design was elaborated, the interior shell more often being selected for representation (Pls. 28A and 30).

SPADE FOOT. Tapered rectangular foot in use in the later eighteenth century.

SPANISH FOOT. A popular terminal in the late seventeenth century.

SPINDLE GALLERY. In the second half of the eighteenth century a popular alternative to the ornamental fretted gallery (Fig. 53A).

SPLAT. The vertical member, generally shaped or pierced, contained between the uprights of the chair back (Pl. 19).

SPLIT BALUSTER. Introduced as applied ornament to most varieties of furniture before the mid-seventeenth century (Fig. 20).

STANDISH. An archaic term for inkstand.

STILE. The vertical or upright section of a framing (of panelled chest, wainscot, door, etc.); *cf.* 'rail' – a horizontal or cross section (Fig. 16).

STRAPWORK. Carved decoration, employed *c.* 1570–*c.* 1650, and later in the Chippendale period (Fig. 8A and B).

STRETCHER. A horizontal bar uniting and strengthening the legs of a chair, table, etc.

STRINGING. A decorative inlay in the form of fine lines.

SWAG. Festoon; a chain of flowers, fruit, leaves, drapery, etc., curved as if hung between two points (Pl. 31).

TABBY. A rich, waved silk, with variegated surface, first manufactured in England after the Restoration by Huguenot immigrants.

TAFFETY. A fine, glossy silk, plain, striped and patterned, and used for hangings.

TAMBOUR FRONT. A roll front, of narrow strips of wood laid side by side on canvas backing, often used for desk tops (Fig. 91).

TAMMY. A worsted cloth, sometimes glazed.

TEAPOY. A small tripod table, or stand, supported on a central pillar; 'used in drawing rooms ... when taking refreshment'. (Smith's *Household Furniture*, 1808.)

TENON (AND MORTISE). A joint. That part or end of one timber, shaped so as to fit into a corresponding cavity (mortise) in another. Introduced in sixteenth century 'joyned' furniture.

TESTER. A wooden canopy, particularly that over the bed.

TURKEY WORK. Wools drawn through a canvas foundation, knotted and trimmed to form an even, deep pile. Made in imitation of a Turkey carpet.

VITRUVIAN SCROLL OR WAVE PATTERN. A frieze ornament; a band of convoluted scrolling which resembles waves. Basically the pattern consists of a series of connected 'C's, but is often elaborated with carved foliage (Pl. 35).

VOLUTE. A spiral scroll.

WHORL FOOT. *See* SCROLL FOOT.

GLOSSARY OF WOODS

ACACIA. Yellow with brown markings; hard and durable; in eighteenth century used as a substitute for tulip wood, and for inlay and bandings.

ALDER. Flesh-colour, often with curled figure; in eighteenth century used for country furniture, in particular the rails of some types of 'Windsor' chair.

AMBOYNA. From West Indies; rich, light brown with a close 'bird's eye' figure; resembles and often confused with thuya wood; in eighteenth century used both to cover whole surfaces and as a decorative banding.

APPLEWOOD. Light reddish-brown; hard, heavy, and close-grained; resembles pear wood; in seventeenth century used as a veneer and for inlay.

ASH. Greyish-white, with light brown veining; tough, hard, and heavy (Evelyn, in *Sylva*, mentioned a variety then called 'Green Ebony'), but readily attacked by worm; after 1700 much used for cheaper varieties of country furniture, in particular for chairs and the seats of 'Windsor' chairs, and for drawer linings; a decorative veneer of ash obtained from the polled trees is sometimes found in late Georgian pieces.

BEECH. Light brown with speckled grain; soft, very subject to worm, and therefore most perishable; continuously in use from mid seventeenth century; a common substitute for walnut, in particular for the caned chairs of Restoration period; late Georgian painted chairs were frequently of beech (it was then one of the cheapest woods available); employed also for carcase work, as the seat rails of chairs, couches or bedframes.

BIRCH. In eighteenth century employed in chair-making and for cheaper country furniture; some figured cuts closely resemble satinwood, and were used as a substitute for it from about 1780.

BOXWOOD. Yellow, without figure; hard and very heavy, with fine grain; from sixteenth century used for inlay on oak and walnut, and in late eighteenth century for border lines on satinwood.

BRAZILWOOD. Red and strongly marked, resembling mahogany; hard, heavy; in seventeenth century used as inlay, and (rarely) later in fine work.

CALAMANDER. From Ceylon; brown, mottled and streaked, with black; hard, with fine grain; from about 1780, for some fifty years, popularly used as a veneer and for bandings.

CEDAR. A comparatively inexpensive, light reddish-brown wood, resembling mahogany; soft; variously used for drawer linings, boxes, the insides of cupboards and wardrobes, especially after about 1750.

CHERRY. Reddish; hard, with close grain; used for smaller articles and, in seventeenth century, as an inlay; ages to resemble mahogany.

CHESTNUT. Horse chestnut: white; used for small drawer linings. Sweet chestnut: ageing to reddish-brown; durable; numerous late seventeenth century carved chairs in chestnut resemble walnut specimens. Both varieties, when figured, used as a veneer, and both, in some cuts, resemble satinwood, being (as birch) used as a substitute for it at end of eighteenth century.

COROMANDEL. 'Streaked ebony'; from the Coromandel coast; a decorative, striped wood, resembling calamander, zebra, and black rosewood; Sheraton (*Cabinet Dictionary*) stated it to be 'lately introduced into England [from India] and much used ... for banding'; a popular veneer at that time.

CYPRESS. From Persia and the Levant; reddish; hard, durable, with close grain; employed at a very early date, particularly for chests or articles of furniture intended for the storing of clothes – as 'resisting the worm and moth' (Evelyn, *Sylva*).

DEAL. Scots pine; large quantities imported from N. Europe as red and yellow deal; straight grained and easily worked; yellow deal (and after about 1750, red deal) much used for carcase work, for plainer furniture, and for wainscoting.

EBONY. Many varieties; black; hard, very heavy, with close grain; used as an inlay from sixteenth century, and for turning. By 1800, pear and other close-grained woods were stained black in imitation of ebony, which was then little used.

ELM. Brownish; hard, tough, but liable to warp; subject to worm – although in general use from medieval times, few early pieces survive; in eighteenth century employed for seats of 'Windsor' chairs, for other country furniture, and as a veneer (burr elm).

HAREWOOD. Sycamore veneer stained a greenish-grey colour; in late eighteenth century popularly used for bandings and as a decorative veneer; sometimes called 'silverwood'.

HICKORY. From North America; akin to walnut tree; hard, heavy, tough.

HOLLY. White; hard, with fine grain; from sixteenth century used as an inlay and in marquetry furniture; frequently stained.

KINGWOOD. From Brazil; similar to rosewood, but lighter in colour and with more contrasted markings; some late seventeenth century cabinet-work wholly veneered with kingwood, then known as 'princes wood'; in late eighteenth century veneered furniture, frequently employed in cross-banded borders.

LABURNUM. Yellow, with brown streaking; used in parquetry furniture of late seventeenth century and as an 'oyster piece' veneer.

LIGNUM VITAE. From West Indies; dark brown streaked with black; extremely hard and heavy; in seventeenth century used as veneer and for turned work.

LIME. Whitish-yellow; soft, with close grain; much used by Grinling Gibbons, and by carvers in general.

MAHOGANY. (1) 'Spanish' mahogany was introduced into general use in England early in the eighteenth century; varieties were obtained from Cuba, Jamaica, Puerto Rico, and San Domingo; (2) Honduras mahogany or 'baywood', softer and lighter both in colour and weight; popularly used from late eighteenth century; (3) 'Canary wood', a light, yellowish brown mahogany, was obtained from Madeira.

MAPLE. White; from seventeenth century, sometimes stained and used as a veneer and in marquetry furniture; the 'bird's eye' variety (cut from the American sugar maple) found employed in nineteenth century furniture and particularly for picture frames.

OAK. Both native and imported largely from Scandinavia; after late seventeenth century mainly restricted to carcase portions of fine and veneered furniture, although still very generally employed in the country, in both cases being usually 'plain sawn' (*i.e.* sawn parallel with diameter of the trunk) and *not* quarter cut. Bog oak, which is wood preserved in peat bogs and thereby turned nearly black, was used as an inlay with holly and other woods during the 'oak period'. 'Clapboard', the imported wood, was whiter, softer, and with finer grain than the native variety. Oak was generally seasoned in water for a period.

OLIVE. Greenish-yellow, with black veining and spots; hard, with close grain, taking an excellent polish; somewhat like walnut or yew; in late seventeenth century used in parquetry, and later, to a small extent, as a veneer.

PADOUK. From Burma; red, and, in texture, resembling rosewood; hard and heavy; used in the solid (but rarely) for some years after about 1730, when it was first imported.

PARTRIDGE WOOD. From Brazil; streaked red and brown in a manner resembling a partridge's feather; heavy, with close, straight grain; in seventeenth century used as an inlay, in the eighteenth as an occasional veneer.

PEAR. Yellow or pale brown, and without figure; not unlike cedar in appearance; tough and durable; works well and sometimes used by carvers; used in country furniture and as an inlay. *See* EBONY.

PINE. *See* DEAL.

PLANE. White; close-grained and rather tough; in latter part of eighteenth century used as a veneer and an inlay, and in the country districts as a substitute for beech, for painted chairs, rails of card tables, etc.

PLUM. Yellow to reddish brown; hard and heavy; used in turning and as inlay in seventeenth century.

POPLAR. Greyish; hard, with fine grain; used as an inlay from an early date.

'PRINCES WOOD'. Distinct from present day 'princewood'. *See* KINGWOOD.

PURPLE-WOOD. From Brazil; purple turning to brown on exposure to the air, when it is not unlike rosewood; hard and heavy; in later eighteenth century used as a veneer and a banding, sometimes on satinwood.

ROSEWOOD. Varieties from Brazil and India; light hazel to a rich brown, marked with dark streaks; hard and heavy, with even grain; used from sixteenth century as inlay and veneer, and frequently during the Regency in the solid.

SABICU. From Cuba; used to some slight extent in early eighteenth century, and later, as a substitute for mahogany, which it greatly resembles; extremely tough and hard wearing.

SATINWOOD. (1) The West Indian, or Guiana (introduced about 1760), and (2) the East Indian (introduced about 1780) are distinct varieties and differ appreciably; both are yellow (with fine, plain grain and also richly figured), but the latter is more cloudy under polish; from late eighteenth century, used both as a veneer and inlay and in the solid. Supplanted in fashion by rosewood from about 1800–20, but regained popularity subsequently. *See* BIRCH and CHESTNUT.

SNAKEWOOD. Red, with dark brown spots and markings; occasionally used as an inlay in seventeenth century and as a veneer in the late Georgian period.

SYCAMORE. White, resembling plane wood; fine-grained, taking a good polish; used in the floral marquetry furniture of late seventeenth century, and as a veneer in the late eighteenth century. *See* HAREWOOD.

TEAK. Deep reddish brown; tough, oily, and heavy; occasionally used in eighteenth century work.

THUYA WOOD. From Africa; golden brown, with 'bird's eye' pattern; in early eighteenth century used as a veneer.

TULIP WOOD. From Brazil; yellowish brown with reddish stripes; in eighteenth century and during the Regency largely used for cross-banding.

WALNUT. In use from the Tudor period. *Juglans regia*, the ordinary English variety, and *Juglans nigra*, the black walnut, were both being grown in England by second half of seventeenth century, when the latter was more prized: 'This black bears the worst nut, but the timber is much to be preferred; and we might propagate more of them if we were careful to procure them out of Virginia, where they abound, or from Grenoble ...' (Evelyn, *Sylva*). This harder, denser variety (greyish-brown with considerable dark veining) was not liable to attack from worm and might be got in larger planks. Till about 1740, and the general introduction of mahogany, walnut was variously used as a veneer (and plain wood for construction in the solid); the burrs of English walnut (*Juglans regia*) were finely figured, and 'oyster pieces', cut transversely from saplings, were used with decorative effect. French and Italian walnuts were lighter in colour, mainly without figure.

WILLOW. Dyed black and used as a substitute for ebony in seventeenth and eighteenth centuries.

YEW. Reddish-brown; hard and close, taking a good polish with friction; in use for small work from an early period; often found in backs of 'Windsor' chairs; burr veneers from polled trees employed as a substitute for amboyna.

ZEBRA-WOOD. From Guiana; brown, with vivid stripes of very dark brown; in late eighteenth century employed as a veneer.

SHERATON'S RECEIPT FOR A POLISHING WAX

'. . . take bees wax and a small quantity of turpentine in a clean earthen pan, and set it over a fire till the wax unites with the turpentine, which it will do by constant stirring about; add to this a little red lead finely ground upon a stone, together with a small portion of fine Oxford ochre, to bring the whole to the colour of brisk mahogany. Lastly, when you take it off the fire, add a little copal varnish to it, and mix it well together, then turn the whole into a bason of water, and while it is yet warm, work it into a ball, with which the brush is to be rubbed as before observed. And observe, with a ball of wax and brush kept for this purpose entirely, furniture in general may be kept in good order.' (*Cabinet Dictionary*, 1803.)

A LIST OF CABINET-MAKERS* AND DESIGNERS

ADAM, ROBERT (1728–92). Architect and a designer of household furnishings in the neo-classical style. In Italy and Dalmatia, 1754–8. Published (with his brother, James): *Works in Architecture*, from 1773. The furniture designed by Adam for Harewood House and Kenwood was executed by Chippendale.

BELCHIER, JOHN (d. 1753). Cabinet-maker at *Ye Sun*, St Paul's Churchyard; working in second quarter eighteenth century, and succeeded by Thomas Atkinson.

BELL, PHILIP. Cabinet-maker at *The White Swan*, St Paul's Churchyard, where before *c.* 1770, he succeeded his mother, Elizabeth, widow of Henry Bell (working *c.* 1740).

BENNETT, SAMUEL. Cabinet-maker working in London in the late seventeenth and early eighteenth century, died by 1741. A finely executed bureau in two stages, veneered with burr walnut and inlaid with seaweed marquetry, is in the Victoria and Albert Museum; the frieze is treated with marked individuality; the piece is signed (inlaid inscription on the inside of the door of the upper stage), as is at least one other known example of his work.

BLAND, CHARLES. Cabinet-maker to Charles II.

BOROUGHS, JOHN. Cabinet-maker to Charles II; partner of William Farnborough at *Ye Looking Glass*, on Cornhill. Continued to supply the Court at the time of William and Mary.

BOULTON, MATTHEW (b. 1728). Manufacturer at Birmingham of ormolu, silver plate, and metal mounts, the best work being from 1762 to *c.* 1775.

* *The London Furniture Makers*, by Sir Ambrose Heal, 1953, records the names, addresses, and working dates of some 2,500 cabinet-makers, upholsterers, etc., with many reproductions of their trade cards. '... Of the great majority of these craftsmen, little is known, either of their lives or works. Their names occur in old newspapers, directories, registers, or in diaries and memoirs. Our present knowledge of them, even of their working dates, is most incomplete.'

BRADBURN, JOHN. Carver and cabinet-maker of Long Acre; supplied furniture to the Royal household during the decade from *c.* 1765. Formerly employed by the firm of Vile and Cobb.

BRETTINGHAM, MATTHEW (1699–1769). Architect and furniture designer. A pupil of William Kent.

BROOKSHAW, GEORGE. Cabinet-maker of Great Marlborough Street. Supplied furniture to the Prince of Wales *c.* 1783.

BROWN, JOHN. Cabinet-maker of St Paul's Churchyard, at the sign of *The Three Cover'd Chairs and Walnut-tree* (time of George II).

CAMPBELL, ROBERT. Cabinet-maker and upholsterer of Marylebone Street, Golden Square; supplied furniture to the Prince of Wales at Carlton House, 1789.

CASBERT, JOHN. Cabinet-maker and upholsterer to Charles II.

CASEMENT, WILLIAM. Supplied a few of the designs to the *Cabinet-Makers' London Book of Prices*, 1788. (The main contributors to this work were, however, Thomas Shearer and Hepplewhite.)

CHAMBERS, SIR WILLIAM (1726–96). Architect to George III; and designer of furniture for his own buildings, employing Benoni Thacker, cabinet-maker, and Samuel Alker, carver. Somerset House and the Pagoda at Kew were his work. In his youth (before 1755) stayed in China and passed some years in Italy. Published: *Designs for Chinese Buildings, Furniture, Dresses, etc.*, 1757; *Treatise on Civil Architecture*, 1759, and re-issued 1791; and *Dissertation on Oriental Gardening*, 1772.

CHIPPENDALE, THOMAS (1718–79). Cabinet-maker of St Martin's Lane (from 1753); senior partner of the firm of Chippendale, Haig & Co., from about 1771. The designs of *The Gentleman and Cabinet-Maker's Director*, 1754 (Third Ed., 1762), the first comprehensive pattern book for furniture, were largely the inventions of Matthias Lock and H. Copland. The posthumous fame of Chippendale's name rests on the *Director* and is by no means merited in full; his reputation among contemporaries was not unduly high. Significantly, he supplied furniture to the nobility but not to the Crown; and his workshop with 'chests of 22 workmen' was comparatively small. Probably his best work (marquetry and inlaid pieces) was in the neo-classic style of Robert Adam and executed during the closing years of his life, perhaps from the latter's designs.

CHIPPENDALE, THOMAS, THE YOUNGER (1749–1822). Cabinet-maker of St Martin's Lane; the son of Thomas Chippendale, and from 1779–96 partner in the firm of Chippendale and Haig; made bankrupt 1804; employed at Harewood House, Yorkshire, 1796–7, and at Stourhead, 1795–1820.

CIPRIANI, GIOVANNI BATTISTA (1727–85). In England from 1755; a fashionable painter and decorator, exerting a considerable influence on late eighteenth century style in furniture. Horace Walpole, in a letter of 1782, referred to him as 'that flimsy scene-painter'.

COBB, JOHN (d. 1778). Partner of the firm of William Vile and John Cobb of 72 St Martin's Lane, cabinet-makers and upholsterers to George III, and the foremost makers of the period 1755–65. A number of articles made by the firm remain in the Royal Collection, Buckingham Palace. Cobb, who was purse-proud, directed in his will that of his fortune, the principal £20,000 Stock had 'never to be broke into ... that there should always be the interest aforesaid to support ye name of Cobb as a private gentleman'.

COPLAND, H. Furniture designer. *See* MATTHIAS LOCK.

COXED, G., and WOSTER, T. Prominent cabinet-makers at *The White Swan*, St Paul's Churchyard (*fl. c.* 1710–36). Woster d. 1736, and soon afterwards the premises were occupied by Henry Bell.

CRUNDEN, JOHN. Architect and author of *The Joyner and Cabinet-maker's Darling*, 1765, which contains various ornamental 'Chinese' fret patterns, probably much used by the trade.

ELLIOTT, CHARLES. Cabinet-maker of New Bond Street; upholsterer to George III. Active at end of eighteenth and beginning of nineteenth century.

FARNBOROUGH, WILLIAM. Cabinet-maker to Charles II and William III. Partner of John Boroughs.

FRANCE and BECKWITH. Cabinet-makers and upholsterers of 101 St Martin's Lane, supplied furniture to the Crown during the last quarter of the eighteenth century. *C.* 1770, France, with Thomas Chippendale the younger, supplied furniture to first Lord Mansfield at Kenwood, some of which has been identified.

GALE, CORNELIUS. Cabinet-maker to William III, supplying the Royal Palaces, 1690–6.

GATES, WILLIAM. Cabinet-maker to the Crown, of Long Acre, supplying inlaid pieces, 1777–83.

GIBBONS, GRINLING (1648–1720). 'Monumental Carver and Master Carpenter to George I'. Employed at Windsor, Kensington, and Hampton Court Palaces; by Wren at St Paul's and the City Churches; at Petworth, Cassiobury Park (destroyed), and elsewhere.

GILLOW, RICHARD (d. 1811). Son of Robert Gillow and from 1757, his partner.

GILLOW, ROBERT (1703–73). Cabinet-maker, of Lancaster, where furniture for the Oxford Street, London, branch of the firm was made. The branch was opened about 1770. Exported freely to the W. Indies and elsewhere. Occasionally in late eighteenth century, and, after 1820, always, the work of the firm was stamped 'Gillow's' or 'Gillow's, Lancaster'. The firm's cost books survive from a late eighteenth century date.

GOODISON, BENJAMIN (d. 1767). Cabinet-maker of Long Acre, at *The Golden Spread Eagle* (1727); one of the leading makers of the reign of George II; supplied furniture to the Royal Palaces, to Holkham, Longford Castle. Died worth approximately £20,000.

GRENDEY, GILES (1693–1780). Joiner and chair-maker of St John's Square, Clerkenwell. His workshop in part of old Aylesbury House was destroyed by fire in August 1731. From the contemporary accounts given in newspapers, it would seem that he was in a good way of business and that he exported furniture (perhaps to Spain and Portugal) on a considerable scale. Elected, 1766, Master of the Worshipful Company of Joiners of the City of London. His trade label has been found affixed to furniture of his making. He died, in retirement at Palmers Green, a wealthy man.

GRENE, WILLIAM, and successively his sons JOHN and THOMAS, were Coffer-makers to the Crown in the sixteenth century. In addition to leather covered travelling coffers, etc., they supplied richly upholstered seating furniture (X-framed chairs, stools, and footstools), screens, close-stools, and jewel cases to the Royal Palaces – articles which at this date did not fall within the province of the upholsterer. (*Connoisseur*, March 1941, R. W. Symonds, '*The Craft of the Coffer-maker*'.)

GRIFFITHS, EDWARD. Cabinet-maker of Dean Street, Soho; one-time assistant to Benjamin Goodison; supplied furniture to the Earl of Cardigan shortly before 1750.

GUMLEY, JOHN (d. 1729). Cabinet-maker to George I and, from 1705, looking-glass manufacturer at Lambeth; a prominent and successful man, whose daughter, Anna Maria, was married to William Pulteney, Earl of Bath. In partnership with James Moore, until the latter's death in 1726. The firm of 'Mrs Elizabeth Gumley & Co.', cabinet-makers to George II, incurred the Royal disfavour in 1729. (Mrs Elizabeth Gumley was his mother and partner.)

HAIG, THOMAS. Partner of both the elder and younger Thomas Chippendale (1771–79–96), and concerned with the furnishing of Harewood House, of Garrick's house in the Adelphi, and of Corsham Court, *c.* 1785–7. He may have been formerly James Rennie's book-keeper.

HALFPENNY, WILLIAM and JOHN (father and son). Architects and authors of books of designs, including *New Designs for Chinese Temples*, 1750. This volume contained a few designs for chairs.

HALLETT, WILLIAM (1707–81). Of Great Newport Street, and, from 1753, St Martin's Lane and Long Acre. Perhaps the foremost cabinet-maker of his time. In middle life, re-built Canons, Middlesex (formerly the property of the Duke of Chandos) for his own use. His grandson, William Hallett, and his wife, are the subjects of Gainsborough's *The Morning Walk*, 1786.

HEPPLEWHITE, GEORGE (d. 1786). Cabinet-maker of Cripplegate. Apprentice of Gillow of Lancaster. *The Cabinet-maker and Upholsterer's Guide*, 1788, was issued posthumously. The designs, many of which are for inlaid furniture, are in the classical style of *c.* 1780–5 and of a conservative character. Hepplewhite did not, apparently, supply furniture to the Crown and his contemporary reputation as a maker was in no way exceptional.

HERVE, FRANCIS. 'French chair-maker' of John Street, Tottenham Court Road. Supplied furniture to Carlton House, 1783–6, and to Althorp.

INCE, WILLIAM. Partner of the firm of Ince and Mayhew, cabinet-makers and upholsterers of Broad Street, Soho, and later of Marshall Street, Carnaby Market. The activities of the firm, which had a high contemporary reputation, extended into the first decade of the nineteenth century. Published the *Universal System of Household Furniture*, 1759–63; the work was issued in rivalry with Chippendale's *Director*.

JENNENS AND BETTRIDGE. Manufacturers of papier-mâché articles and furniture during the nineteenth century. (The technique had been introduced by Henry Clay, a japanner at Birmingham, soon after 1770.)

JENSEN, GERREIT (or JOHNSON, GARRETT). 'Glasse-seller' and cabinet-maker to the Crown, *c.* 1680–1714. (He had 'left off trade' by 1715.) Maker of arabesque marquetry, japanned and 'Boulle' furniture; much influenced by French designs. ('Boulle work' enjoyed a certain popularity in England in the first half of the eighteenth century; in 1738, for instance, one Frederick Hintz, cabinet-maker of Newport Street, near Leicester Fields, at the sign of the Porcupine, was advertising for sale furniture inlaid with brass and mother of pearl. This was probably of a comparable nature.) Employed at Chatsworth: Celia Fiennes, on her Northern tour during 1697, noted there his wainscoting of 'the Duchess's Closett ... with the hollow burnt japan and at each corner peers [pier glasses] of Looking-glass ...'.

JOHNSON, THOMAS. Carver and drawing master; author of *Twelve Girandoles*, 1755, and *One Hundred and Fifty New Designs*, 1756–8. His designs are in the French taste, eccentric and unusual but often weak and impracticable.

JONES, WILLIAM. Author of *The Gentleman's and Builders' Companion*, 1739, with designs in the Palladian style.

KAUFFMANN, ANGELICA (1741–1807). Painter, employed by the Adam brothers. In London after 1766–82. Married Antonio Zucchi in 1781.

KENT, WILLIAM (1685–1748). Designer, architect, and landscape gardener. In early years, a portrait and 'history' painter; became acquainted with Lord Burlington when in Italy, 1710–19, and thenceforward maintained close association with him. Designed furniture for Holkham, Houghton, and Devonshire House, where he was employed in his capacity as architect.

LANGLEY, BATTY and THOMAS. Architects and authors of *The City and Country Builder's and Workman's Treasury of Designs*, 1740. Batty, the elder brother, was an early protagonist of the Gothic revival of the mid eighteenth century.

LANGLOIS, PETER (b. Paris, 1738). Cabinet-maker of Tottenham Court Road. Much of his work was in an inlay of metal and tortoiseshell after the manner of Boulle. Supplied furniture to Horace Walpole at Strawberry Hill and to Syon House, *c.* 1760–70.

LINNELL, JOHN (d. before 1800). Perhaps the son of William Linnell. Designer, carver, cabinet-maker, and upholsterer, of Berkeley Square. He may have specialized in mirrors and wall-lights. The Victoria and Albert Museum has a number of his original drawings for furniture for the period 1773–81; from notes on these drawings it is to be inferred that he possessed a good clientele.

LINNELL, WILLIAM (d. 1763). Carver of Berkeley Square. Member of the Cheron and Vanderbank Academy in St Martin's Lane (1720).

LOCK, MATTHIAS. Carver and designer. Largely responsible for the introduction of the rococo style to favour in England. Between 1752–68, with his collaborator Copland (who probably was not a practising craftsman), was presumably employed and 'used' by Thomas Chippendale. His published works include: *A New Drawing Book of Ornaments, Shields, Compartments, Masks, etc., c.* 1740; *Six Sconces*, 1744; *Six Tables*, 1746; *A Book of Ornaments; A New Book of Ornaments – Chimneys, Sconces, Tables, etc.* (with H. Copland), 1752. The earliest surviving published designs in the classic style (soon afterwards adopted by Robert Adam) occur in his later works which include: *A New Book of Ornaments, etc.* (with H. Copland), 1768; *A New Book of Pier Frames*, 1769.

MANWARING, ROBERT. Cabinet- and chair-maker, in the Haymarket. Published: *Carpenters' Complete Guide to the Whole System of Gothic Railing; The Cabinet and Chair-Makers' Real Friend and Companion*, 1765; *The Chair-Maker's Guide*, 1766.

MAROT, DANIEL. Designer of decorations and furniture. Probably concerned with the decoration of the State Rooms at Hampton Court for William III, and exerted considerable influence on contemporary taste in England, which he visited in 1694; he returned perhaps to Amsterdam in 1697 and revisited England in 1698.

MARSH, WILLIAM. Cabinet-maker and upholsterer of Mount Street. At the close of the eighteenth century 'Wm. Marsh & Co., upholders' were principal cabinet-makers to the Prince of Wales.

MAYHEW, THOMAS. *See* INCE, WILLIAM.

MOORE, JAMES (d. 1726). Cabinet-maker to the Crown; partner of John Gumley. Employed by the second Duke of Montagu (Master of the Great Wardrobe); supplied furniture to Stowe House, Bucks; associated with William Kent in respect of work at Kensington Palace. Occasionally, his incised signature is found on gilt gesso pieces of high quality and individual character.

MOORE, JAMES, THE YOUNGER (d. 1734). Cabinet- and chair-maker to Frederick, Prince of Wales.

NEWMAN, EDWARD. Master of the Joiners' Company, 1749.

NORMAN, SAMUEL. Cabinet-maker, employed by the Adam brothers. Presumably 'the eminent cabinet-maker, carver and gilder' whose premises in King Street, Covent Garden, were destroyed by fire in 1759.

PARRAN, BENJAMIN. Cabinet-maker; nephew and partner of Benjamin Goodison, and succeeded him in supplying furniture to the Royal Palaces, 1767–83.

PAUDEVINE, JOHN. Crown upholsterer in the Restoration period.

PELLETIER, JOHN. Carver and gilder. Gilt furniture, of a type showing French influence, was supplied by him to the Crown from *c.* 1690.

PERGOLESI, MICHELE ANGELO. Decorator employed by the Adam brothers. In England from *c.* 1758. His series of *Original Designs*, 1777–1801, had a considerable influence on the style of painted furniture.

PHILL, THOMAS (d. 1728). Upholsterer to the Crown during the reigns of Anne and George I.

PRICE, RICHARD (d. before 1686). Joiner and chair-maker to Charles II, for whose Household he supplied some fine caned furniture, etc., as well as articles of a more expensive nature.

RENNIE, JAMES (d. 1766). Partner of Thomas Chippendale.

ROBERTS, RICHARD. 'Chairmaker to His Majesty'. (*London Journal*, 1728.)

ROBERTS, THOMAS. Joiner and chair-maker. During the reigns of William and Mary, and Anne, provided the Crown with seating furniture and fire screens; supplied Chatsworth, 1702.

RODWELL, JAMES. Cabinet-maker of Moorfields, at *The Royal Bed and Star* (reign of George II).

SEDDON, GEORGE (1727–1801). Cabinet-maker of Aldersgate Street. Master of the Joiners' Company, 1795. The unusually large, fashionable, and comprehensive firm of Seddon employed (1786) about 400 journeymen – carvers, joiners, gilders, metal-workers, upholsterers, etc., and carried enormous stocks of furniture of varying quality and types. The firm flourished in the nineteenth century and was actively employed at the renovation of Windsor Castle.

SHACKLETON, THOMAS. Partner of George Seddon, whose son-in-law he was; later (after 1800), a partner of Oakley, Shackleton and Evans, of Old Bond Street.

SHEARER, THOMAS. Cabinet-maker and designer. Author of: *Designs for Household Furniture*, 1788, wherein were reissued his designs for *The Cabinet-Makers' London Book of Prices*, 1788.

SHERATON, THOMAS (1751–1806). Designer. Although Sheraton was 'bred to the cabinet business', it is unlikely that he was ever master of a workshop, and no furniture can be assigned to his hand. Published: *Cabinet-Maker and Upholsterer's Drawing Book*, 1791–4; *Cabinet Dictionary*, 1803.

SMITH, GEORGE. Cabinet-maker and designer. Published: *A Collection of Designs for Household Furniture and Interior Decoration*, 1808, and other works. Patronized by George IV.

TATHAM, THOMAS (1763–1818). Partner of William Marsh. After 1809, senior partner of the firm of Tatham and Bailey. Died worth £60,000.

TURING, WILLIAM. Looking-glass maker at *The Eagle and Child*, Bedford Street (early eighteenth century). A partner of John Gumley in the 1720's.

VILE, WILLIAM (d. 1767). Senior partner of the firm of William Vile and John Cobb. *See* COBB, JOHN.

ZUCCHI, ANTONIO PIETRO (1726–95). Painter; and second husband of Angelica Kauffmann. With Robert Adam in Italy, and later much employed by him.

A SHORT LIST OF CABINET-MAKERS ESTABLISHED IN BUSINESS AT LONDON IN THE YEAR 1803

SHERATON, in *The Cabinet Dictionary*, 1803, publicized the names of some 250 and more master cabinet-makers, upholsterers, and chair-makers, who were working in and about London in that year – and, not unnaturally, his list was incomplete.

The well-known firm of *Mayhew and Ince* was recorded as being at 47 Marshall Street, Carnaby Market; another *Ince* at 23 Holles Street, Cavendish Square; *Gillow and Co.* at 176 Oxford Street; *Seddon's* at 150 Aldersgate Street; and *Seddon and Co.* (probably an offshoot of the foregoing) at 24 Dover Street.

St Paul's Churchyard was still a popular place of business, with the firms of *Oakley, Shackleton and Evans* (No. 22), *G. Beauchamp* (No. 18), *William Yateman* (No. 12), *Simson* (No. 19), *Morris* (No. 26), and *Graham* (No. 7).

Thomas Chippendale, Jnr, was at St Martin's Lane (No. 60), with *France and Beckwith* (No. 101), *Graham and Lichfield* (No. 72), and *John Bolton* (No. 109) as neighbours.

The trade favoured also Oxford Street, 'the Oxford Road', Soho, and the side streets of the area, in particular Wardour Street, with *Barrett and Wicksteed* (Nos. 53–4), *Samuel Deacon* (No. 22), *Fawley and Ward* (No. 43), *Turner and Gee* (No. 49), *Newton* (No. 63), *Potts and Son* (No. 90), *Watson* (No. 21), *Pringle*, and *Smith*, and also Broad Street, Charlotte Street, Rathbone Place, Mortimer Street, Dean Street, and Greek Street.

Cabinet-makers were housed at various addresses in the City, at Finsbury, Westminster, and Southwark.

The comparatively new thoroughfare of Piccadilly contained the shops of *James Bagster* (No. 20), *Blades and Palmer* (No. 177), *T. Glover* (No. 201), *C. Glover* (at the corner of Albemarle Street), *Randall* (No. 171), *Stephens* (No. 217), *Swift, Grant and Hurley* (No. 226), and *G. Woolley* (No. 196). *Elliott and Co.*, 'Upholsterers to His Majesty', were at 97 New Bond Street.

As reflecting the fashion for painted furniture, it is of interest that the following were listed as 'Japan Chair' manufacturers:

Adams, 403 Oxford Street; *H. Buckingham*, Old Street, Mint; *Wyburd and Terry*, City Road; *A. Bounfall*, Middle Row; *J. Cockerill*, Curtain Road and 203 Oxford Street; and *Fawley and Ward*, 43 Wardour Street. One, *B. R. Thompson*, of 62 Red Lion Street, Clerkenwell, was described as a 'Dyed Chair-maker'.

AGES OF OAK (TO 1660) AND

	Periods	*Styles*	*Individuals*	*Publications*
1540	EARLY TUDOR			
1550				
1560	ELIZABETHAN or LATE TUDOR (1558–1603)			
1570				
1580		'Italianate' with strong Flemish influence		
1590				
1600				
1610	EARLY STUART or JACOBEAN (1603–49)			
1620			Inigo Jones (1573–1652)	
1630				
1640				
1650	COMMONWEALTH (1649–60)			
1660	RESTORATION (1660)			
1670				Evelyn, *Sylva*, 1664
1680		Dutch and Flemish influence	Grinling Gibbons (1648–1720)	
1690	WILLIAM AND MARY (1689)		Daniel Marot (*c.* 1660–1720)	Stalker & Parker, *Treatise*, 1688
1700	QUEEN ANNE (1702) and EARLY GEORGIAN			
1710				
1720				
1730			William Kent (1685–1748)	

WALNUT (1660 TO ABOUT 1730)

Introduction of Pieces	*Materials*	*(and Remarks on)*	*Characterized by*
Trestle table with fixed top			
Press and ct. cupboard, long table with 6 or 8 legs, and draw table. Small glass mirrors (imported). Joined stools			
		Walnut used for some fine pieces, particularly ct. cupboards	
			Bulbous supports
Chest of drawers (evolving from mule chest)			
Gate-leg table with turned legs	Introduction of caning		
	Veneering	and the beginnings of the craft of the 'Cabinet Maker'	Twist turning
Day bed Large mirror glass 'Scrutoir' and cabinet	Marquetry, lacquer; upholstery becomes general. Gesso		
		Much beech furniture, painted black, as substitute for walnut	Early form of cabriole leg
Upholstered wing chair Pier glass, bureau			Oriental taste henceforward enjoys varying popularity
Card table			
Archit. bookcase			
			Greatly increased influence of architects on furniture design
Console table, pedestal writing-table. Wine cooler			

AGE OF

	Periods	*Styles*	*Individuals*	*Publications*
1730	GEORGIAN	Palladian		
1735			William Kent (1685–1748)	
1740				
1745		Rococo		
1750		'Gothic' and 'Chinese' tastes (intermittent popularity for nearly three-quarters century)	Thomas Chippendale (1718–79)	
1755				Chippendale, *Director*, first edition, 1754. Ince and Mayhew, *Universal System*, 1759–63
1760				
1765		Classical revival	Robert Adam (1728–92)	
1770			George Hepplewhite (d. 1786)	
1775				
1780				
1785				
1790			Thomas Sheraton (1751–1806)	Hepplewhite, *Guide*, 1788; Sheraton, *Drawing Book*, 1791–4
1795		Greek revival		
1800				
1805		English Empire	Thomas Hope (1770–1831)	Hope, *Household Furniture and Interior Decoration*, 1807
1810	REGENCY (1811–20)	Egyptian taste		
1815				
1820				
1825	PRE-VICTORIAN	Gothic revival		

MAHOGANY

Introduction of Pieces	*Materials*	*(and Remarks on)*	*Characterized by*
Tea table	Mahogany begins to supplant walnut as fashionable wood; solid construction in place of veneers (of walnut)	Oak and other native woods used for much plain furniture, particularly in country districts throughout the eighteenth century	Cabriole leg
Pembroke table Basin or washing stand	Veneers (of mahogany) again become general	Use of walnut almost discontinued	Straight leg, for furniture in Gothic and Chinese tastes, which, within 20 years, almost completely displaces the cabriole
	Popularity of satinwood (1760–1800)		
Fitted work table	Marquetry revival		
	Painted furniture	Beech	
			Straight taper leg and slender turned leg
	Popularity of rosewood (1800–20)	Spring upholstery introduced	
Ottoman			
	Renewed popularity of satinwood (1820)		
	Cast iron introduced	Beginnings of machine-made furniture	After more than a century the architects' influence on furniture design declines

INDEX

Numbers in italics refer to plates

C

S. H. Steinberg

FIVE HUNDRED YEARS OF PRINTING

Since this book first appeared in 1955 it has established itself as a standard work, been published in a hardback edition, and been translated into German and Italian. For this fully revised edition there are many new illustrations, which have now been worked into the body of the text for greater ease of reference.

Five Hundred Years of Printing traces the close inter-relation between printing and culture. The author's erudite but highly readable survey takes in not only a long time-span, but also particular topics like censorship, best-sellers, popular series, and the connexion between printing and education, language and literature. Here indeed, as Beatrice Warde writes in her foreword, 'are the five hundred years of printing as a creator of changes in human lives'.

'A concise and scholarly but entertaining account of the story of the relation between printing and civilization' – *The British Printer*

Gerald Taylor

SILVER

British Plate from the Middle Ages to the Present Day

This is a thoroughly revised edition of the well-known work on British plate. Several recent exhibitions and the growing public collections of plate in Britain and North America have stimulated many people who are not themselves collectors to take an interest in the history of the British goldsmiths' and silversmiths' craft. Most catalogues describing and illustrating such plate presuppose that a reader already knows something of the technical and historical background. This is in some measure true of the more general expositions. Besides, many of the most useful works are expensive and difficult to obtain. This book is intended to provide an introductory explanation of the potentials of the two precious metals, silver and gold, and of their domestic use in England from the Middle Ages until the present day. It contains 64 pages of plates and many drawings. The abbreviated tables of hall-marks of the London and main provincial assay offices provide a convenient means of dating plate from the sixteenth century onwards.

'An outstanding contribution to the literature of gold and silver plate'—*The Times Literary Supplement*

George Savage

PORCELAIN THROUGH THE AGES

The art of pottery is older than history, but 'porcelain' is a comparatively recent development. In this volume George Savage traces it from its beginnings in China more than twelve hundred years ago, through its European apotheosis in the eighteenth century, to its emergence as a factory-made product in the nineteenth and twentieth centuries. He discusses a number of aspects which are related to the subject, such as the numerous existing forgeries and reproductions of valuable porcelain, and the better-known methods of identifying the factory origin and the artist responsible. A list of the more common marks is appended as an aid to identification, and there is a comprehensive bibliography of the European literature of the subject.

The book is illustrated with 64 plates of important specimens in well-known public and private collections in England and the United States.

Edited by Anthony Baines

MUSICAL INSTRUMENTS THROUGH THE AGES

What is (or was) a crumhorn? Which comes first, the composer or the instrument he writes for? How is a drum-roll played? The answers to these and many other questions about the performance of music are to be found in this book.

Today music, via the record-player, TV, and radio, is becoming more and more of a technical business. Consequently the musical instruments themselves are receiving much more attention; the acoustics of the studio and the modern concert hall demand a higher standard of instrumental perfection than was dreamt of fifty years ago.

One of the ways in which this improvement in manufacturing techniques has come about has been through the historical study of old instruments—a Stradivarius violin, for example, or a primitive African drum-head. Much pioneer work here has been done by the Galpin Society, to which all the contributors to this book belong. From them we learn that the modern development of music is based on a close study of the past.

'This is a uniquely valuable book, packed with information, curious learning and a wide knowledge of classical and modern music'–*The Times Literary Supplement*